Brain Plasticity
and Behavior

Brain Plasticity
and Behavior

Bryan Kolb
University of Lethbridge

LAWRENCE ERLBAUM ASSOCIATES, PUBLISHERS

1995   Mahwah, New Jersey

Lawrence Erlbaum Associates, Inc., Publishers
10 Industrial Ave
Mahwah, NJ 07430

Library of Congress Cataloging-in-Publication Data
Kolb, Bryan, 1947–
      Brain plasticity and behavior / Bryan Kolb.
          p.   cm.
      Includes bibliographical references and indexes.
      ISBN 0-8058-1520-1
      1. Brain—Growth.   2. Neuroplasticity.   3. Nervous system—
   Regeneration.   4. Brain damage.   I. Title.
   QP356.25.K65   1995
   612.8'2—dc20   94-45561
                                                        CIP

Books published by Lawrence Erlbaum Associates are printed
on acid-free paper, and their bindings are chosen for strength
and durability.
Printed in the United States of America
10   9   8   7   6   5   4   3   2   1

Contents

John M. MacEachran
Memorial Lecture Series

The Department of Psychology at the University of Alberta inaugurated the MacEachran Memorial Lecture Series in 1975 in honor of the late John M. MacEachran. Professor MacEachran was born in Ontario in 1877 and received a PhD in Philosophy from Queen's University in 1905. In 1906 he left for Germany to begin more formal study in psychology, first spending just less than a year in Berlin with Stumpf, and then moving to Leipzig, where he completed a second PhD in 1908 with Wundt as his supervisor. During this period he also spent time in Paris studying under Durkheim and Henri Bergson. With these impressive qualifications the University of Alberta was particularly fortunate in attracting him to its faculty in 1909.

Professor MacEachran's impact has been significant at the university, provincial, and national levels. At the University of Alberta he offered the first courses in psychology and subsequently served as Head of the Department of Philosophy and Psychology and Provost of the University until his retirement in 1945. It was largely owing to his activities and example that several areas of academic study were established on a firm and enduring basis. In addition to playing a major role in establishing the Faculties of Medicine, Education, and Law in the Province, Professor MacEachran was also instrumental in the formative stages of the Mental Health Movement in Alberta. At a national level, he was one of the founders of the Canadian Psychological Association and also became its first Honorary President in 1939. John M. MacEachran was indeed one of the pioneers in the development of psychology in Canada.

Perhaps the most significant aspect of the MacEachran memorial Lecture Series has been the continuing agreement that the Department of Psychology at the University of Alberta has with Lawrence Erlbaum Associates, Publishers, Inc., for the publication of each lecture series. The following is a list of the Invited Speakers and the titles of their published lectures:

1975   Frank A. Geldard (Princeton University)
Sensory Saltation: Metastability in the Perceptual World

1976   Benton J. Underwood (Northwestern University)
Temporal Codes for Memories: Issues and Problems

1977   David Elkind (Rochester University)
The Child's Reality: Three Developmental Themes

1978   Harold Kelley (University of California, Los Angeles)
Personal Relationships: Their Structures and Processes

1979   Robert Rescorla (Yale University)
Pavlovian Second-Order Conditioning: Studies in Associative Learning

1980   Mortimer Mishkin (NIMH-Bethesda)
Cognitive Circuits (unpublished)

1981   James Greeno (University of Pittsburgh)
Current Cognitive Theory in Problem Solving (unpublished)

1982   William Uttal (University of Michigan)
Visual Form Detection in 3-Dimensional Space

1983   Jean Mandler (University of California, San Diego)
Stories, Scripts, and Scenes: Aspects of Schema Theory

1984   George Collier and Carolyn Rovee-Collier (Rutgers University)
Learning and Motivation: Function and Mechanism (unpublished)

1985   Alice Eagly (Purdue University)
Sex Differences in Social Behavior: A Social-Role Interpretation

1986   Karl Pribram (Stanford University)
Brain and Perception: Holonomy and Structure in Figural Processing

1987   Abram Amsel (University of Texas at Austin)
Behaviorism, Neobehaviorism, and Cognitivism in Learning Theory: Historical and Contemporary Perspectives

1988   Robert S. Siegler and Eric Jenkins (Carnegie Mellon University)
How Children Discover New Strategies

1989   Robert Efron (University of California, Martinez)
The Decline and Fall of Hemispheric Specialization

1990   Philip N. Johnson-Laird (Princeton University)
Human and Machine Thinking

1991   Timothy A. Salthouse (Georgia Institute of Technology)
Mechanisms of Age-Cognition Relations in Adulthood

1992   Scott Paris (University of Michigan)
Authentic Assessment of Children's Literacy and Learning

1993   Bryan Kolb (University of Lethbridge)
Brain Plasticity and Behavior

Eugene C. Lechelt, Coordinator
MacEachran Memorial Lecture Series

Sponsored by The Department of Psychology, The University of Alberta with the support of The Alberta Heritage Foundation for Medical Research in memory of John M. MacEachran, pioneer in Canadian psychology.

Preface

This monograph evolved from a series of lectures given as the MacEachern Lectures at the University of Alberta in October 1993. Although this volume began as a summary of the lectures, it has expanded significantly to include more background literature that allows the reader to see my biases, assumptions, and hunches in a broader perspective.

My goal in writing this volume was twofold. First, I wanted to initiate the senior undergraduate or graduate psychology, biology, neuroscience, or other interested student to the issues and questions regarding the nature of brain plasticity. In particular, I wanted to focus on the issue of recovery of function after brain injury and the correlated changes in the brain. I was encouraged that there was a general interest in the question of brain plasticity and behavior by the positive response to an article that I wrote several years ago for *American Psychologist*. One advantage of a short article is that one can steer clear of complexities, and as I wrote this monograph I was aware of the pitfall of losing the simplicity of my original article. I have no doubt that parts of this volume may appear to some to be "overkill" on particular aspects of the topic, but it is my hope that the volume can be used as a starting point for senior undergraduate courses and graduate seminars on the topic of brain plasticity and recovery of function.

Second, I wanted to write this monograph in the form of an extended summary of the work that my colleagues and I have done on brain plasticity and recovery of function. It is seldom that one gets an opportunity to put together a lifetime's work on a single topic, as scientific articles are necessarily terse and textbooks must focus on the broader perspective. My interest in plasticity and behavior began in about 1972 and has taken numerous detours and followed many dead ends. My colleagues and I have come a long way toward understanding some of the mysteries regarding recovery from brain injury, and we have, in the course of things, dispatched many myths and misunderstandings about recovery from brain damage. In this regard I owe a large debt to Paul Cornwell, who remains the model of how to do behavioral neuroscience well.

I must apologize to many others working in this field for my selectivity in choosing citations. I have chosen to emphasize those ideas and experiments by others that are most relevant to my own line of thinking. I have scarcely considered the extensive work on plasticity in the spinal cord or work on nonmammals. My focus has been squarely on the cerebral cortex. As I wrote this volume I began to realize the difficulty in writing a comprehensive review of brain plasticity and behavior and quickly abandoned any pretense of writing the definitive volume on this subject. This would be a truly ambitious project that must await another time.

The reader will quickly discover that I have had many colleagues and helpers over the last two decades. I want especially to acknowledge the help, guidance, and friendship of Ian Whishaw, who was instrumental in convincing me to come to the University of Lethbridge in 1976. Moving from McGill University to a small liberal arts institution with virtually no laboratories or equipment and no graduate students was undoubtedly the most challenging experiment I have attempted in the last two decades! I owe Ian a great debt for putting up with my harebrained ideas. He has acted as a rein on my overly ambitious projects and has put his stamp indelibly on me and my research. Rob Sutherland was my first postdoctoral fellow and later became a colleague. He introduced me to the concept of the neuromodulators and has constantly challenged my fuzzy thinking. I was very sad to see him leave for New Mexico, but my research will bear his influence for a long time to come. I must also express my deepest gratitude to Robbin Gibb. She first worked in my laboratory in 1977, and after a stint in graduate school and time off for children, she has been my right and left hands for the last 10 years. Although her official title is "technician," she has acted as a colleague in every sense of the word, and many of our experiments, and the details of many others, are hers alone. The University of Lethbridge experiment has been successful in large part because she has been here. I must also acknowledge the contributions of Arthur Nonneman, who collaborated with me in the early years and provided me with the benefit of his pioneering work with rabbits and cats.

But there have been others, too. Grazyna Gorny has worked with us for the past 5 years, and she has brought the talented eyes of a plant cytologist to work on neurons, in both the light microscope and the electron microscope. She has shown us things that we never would have seen with our biased "neuroviews." She has put up with my naive cytological questions and my tendency to want to move to the next experiment before properly completing those in progress. Brigitte Byers has had the less glamorous job of preparing much of the histological material for others to study for the past decade. I thank her for her patience with someone who kept changing his mind on what stain to do or how many sections to keep. And there were several who helped me to study animals and to draw cells, especially including Marion Buday, Kristin Buhrmann, Jennifer Hewson, Debbie Muirhead, Allan Ouellette, and Christine Warren.

Next, there have been my colleagues in Montreal and Toronto. Brenda Milner and Laughlin Taylor at the Montreal Neurological Institute have provided me with a continuing opportunity to study cortical functions in the human. Jane Stewart at Concordia University introduced me to the study of hormones and encouraged me to do experiments that I would never have attempted without her. Derek van der Kooy invited me to spend several months in his laboratory at the University of Toronto. Derek's knowledge and enthusiasm for anatomy and behavior is infective, and he showed me that anatomy can be fun. He also showed me what a truly multidisciplinary approach to neuroscience is all about.

I must also thank my postdoctoral fellows (Hannie de Brabander, Bryan Fantie, and Margaret Forgie), graduate student (Sharon Rowntree), and dozens of undergraduates who contributed both intellectually and with sweat and the seat of the pants to the top of the chair. In the end it is the quality of these folks that determines much of the progress that we might make in science.

Finally, I must thank Gene Lechelt and his colleagues at the University of Alberta for inviting me to give the lectures and to attempt this monograph. I could not have imagined this project without the opportunity that they provided me. I must also deeply thank Jan Cioe and Ian Whishaw for reading the entire manuscript and providing helpful comments on the organization and ideas. They improved the manuscript, but the errors that remain are solely mine.

Bryan Kolb

To Debbie
Putting up with two books in one year was a lot to ask of anyone . . .

I
BRAIN PLASTICITY

In principle, it would seem easy to study brain function. Brain cells are relatively large and can be seen in a light microscope. Brain cells have electrical properties that tell us when they are and are not active. Brain cells are chemical so we can do various assays. There are several fields devoted to the study of behavior (comparative psychology, ethology, kinesthesiology). Thus, it would seem that by putting the information from these areas together one would be able to get a pretty good idea of how the brain works. One of the formidable problems, however, is that the organization of the brain can be fundamentally altered by experience. Experience includes not only external events, but also internal events such as the actions of hormones, the effects of injury, the relentless effects of development and aging, and even thoughts. An understanding of how the brain changes is therefore an important topic in neuroscience. Chapters 1 and 2 provide basic information on the nature of brain plasticity. Chapter 1 considers basic properties of the nervous system that contribute to plasticity and provides examples of brain plasticity. Chapter 2 gives more details on how plasticity is measured and the conditions under which it occurs.

1 Some Basic Concepts, Examples, and Biases

BRAIN PLASTICITY

Donna was born on June 14, 1933.[1] Her memory of her early life is sketchy, but those who saw her early on report that she did not seem to know anything for some time. She could neither talk, nor walk, nor even use a toilet. Indeed, she did not even seem to know who her father was, although her mother seemed more familiar to her. Like all children, Donna grew quickly, and in no time she was using and understanding simple language and could recognize lots of people by sight almost instantly. Donna began taking dancing lessons when she was 4 years old and was a "natural." By the time she finished high school she was ready for a career as a dancer with a major dance company. Her career as a dancer was interrupted in 1958 when she married and had two children. Donna never lost interest in dancing and kept fit in her years at home with the kids. In 1968 her children were in school so she began dancing again with a local company. To her amazement, she still could do most of the movements, although she was pretty rusty on the classic dances that she had once so meticulously memorized. Nonetheless, she quickly relearned. In retrospect she should not have been so surprised, as she had always been known as a person with a fabulous memory.

In 1990 Donna was struck by a drunk driver as she was out on an evening bicycle ride. Although she was wearing a helmet she suffered a closed head injury (among other injuries!) and was in a coma for several weeks. As she awakened from the coma she was confused and had difficulty in talking and in

---

[1]Donna is not a real person, but rather a fictitious case who is based on others that I have studied.

understanding others, she had very poor memory, she had spatial disorientation and often got lost, she had various motor disturbances, and she had difficulty recognizing anyone but her family and closest friends. Brain scans revealed diffuse cerebral injury with some focal injury on the ventral surface of the temporal and frontal lobes where the brain presumably was banged against the skull in her fall.

Over the ensuing 10 months she regained most of her motoric abilities and language skills, and her spatial abilities improved significantly. Nonetheless, she found herself to be short-tempered and easily frustrated with her slow recovery. She suffered periods of depression. Two years later she was once again dancing, but she now found it very difficult to learn new steps. Her emotions were still labile, which was a strain on her family, but her episodes of frustration and temper outbursts were becoming much less common. A year later they were gone and her life was not obviously different from that of other 55-year-old women. She did have some cognitive changes that persisted, however. She could not seem to be able to remember the names or faces of people that she met and was unable to concentrate if there were distractions such as a television or radio playing in the background. She did not seem able to dance as she had before her injury, and she retired from her life's first love.

Donna provides a pretty typical example of one of the most intriguing and important properties of the human brain: It has a capacity for continuously changing its structure, and ultimately its function, throughout a lifetime. This capacity to change, which is known as *brain plasticity,* allows the brain to respond to environmental changes or changes within the organism itself. Consider the plasticity in Donna's brain. When she was a newborn she was confronted with a world that nature could not possibly have prepared her for. She had to learn language, to distinguish different faces, to walk, to ride a bicycle, to read, to dance, and so on. Because her brain is solely responsible for her behavior, this means that her brain somehow had to change to reflect her experiences. When Donna reached puberty her body changed and so did her thoughts. Her dreams often had sexual content and, because her dreams are a product of her brain, there must have been some change in her brain activity to change her dreams so dramatically. This change was likely induced by the estrogen surge of adolescence. When Donna returned to dancing after a 10-year break, she had retained much of her skill, even though she had not practiced at all. In this case the brain somehow did not change and she could quickly relearn what she had lost. After her accident, Donna had to "relearn" how to talk and walk and so on. In actual fact she did not go through the same process that she had as a baby, but something in her brain had to change in order to allow her to regain her lost abilities. Whatever changed in her brain must have had some limits, however, because she never did fully recover her memory or her ability to learn new dances.

Thus, in the life of Donna we can see several different types of brain plasticity. First, during her early childhood the brain changed dramatically in its structure, organization, and behavior. These changes were not accomplished quickly: Her brain was fundamentally different from its adult form until at least at 12 or 14 years. Indeed, the plastic changes in the developing brain are so profound that a child is effectively a different creature at different stages of its own development! The brain's plasticity reflects more than mere maturational change, however, as it includes the ability to change with experience. Indeed, the capacity to alter brain structure and function in response to experience provides the nervous system with the ability to learn and to remember information. Some experiential changes are self-evident, such as the acquisition of specific bits of knowledge, whereas other changes are more subtle, such as perceptual learning or the development of different problem-solving strategies. Nonetheless, regardless of the nature of experiential change, the brain has altered its form and function. Finally, after a brain injury, processes are recruited to change the brain again. In this case the brain must reorganize, at least in part, in order to allow the production of behaviors that have been lost.

Although the property of brain plasticity is most obvious during development, the brain remains malleable throughout the life span. It is evident that we can learn and remember information long after maturation. Furthermore, although it is not as obvious, the adult brain retains its capacity to be influenced by "general" experience. For example, being exposed to fine wine or Pavorotti changes one's later appreciation of wine or music, even if encountered in late adulthood. The adult brain is plastic in other ways, too. For example, one of the characteristics of normal aging is that neurons die and are not replaced. This process begins in adolescence, yet most of us will not suffer any significant cognitive loss for decades because the brain compensates for the slow neuron loss by changing its structure. Similarly, although complete restitution of function is not possible, the brain has the capacity to change in response to injury in order to at least partly compensate for the damage.

The brain is plastic in another way, too. Imagine the problem of learning a completely new skill, such as juggling while perched on a unicycle. Initially one is totally inept, but with practice at least some people can master the task. Thus, a new behavior, or set of behaviors, has been acquired. From what we have just discussed, it should be obvious that the brain has changed. But what has changed it? One candidate is the behavior itself. That is, if we repeatedly engage in a particular behavior, the behavior itself can alter the brain, which in turn facilitates the behavior. The idea that activity might change the heart or muscles is seldom questioned. The possibility that behavior could change the structure and function of the brain is seldom considered! Nevertheless, it is an important aspect of brain plasticity. Indeed, there is little doubt that even thought can change the brain. Consider the now extensive research on the variables influencing eyewitness testimony. Different people's accounts of the same events are notoriously inconsistent, in part because they are altered significantly by questions or thoughts "planted" by others. That is, the "memory," and therefore by inference the brain, is altered by cognitive activity. In a general sense this is the process of perceptual learning where we learn about the world by observing and thinking about sensory experience.

The property of brain plasticity confronts us with a host of fundamental questions. First, as we assume that the brain produces behavior, then how is that a changing brain can produce the same behavior at different times? Shouldn't behavior change if the brain is changing? Indeed, how do we remember anything if the brain is changing every time we learn something? Second, it has been assumed since the time of Broca (i.e., the mid-1800s) that at least some functions are localized in the cortex. If the brain is plastic, what does this imply for the nature of cortical organization? Third, what are the constraints on plasticity? There must be factors such as hormones or other chemicals that can directly control processes fundamental to plasticity. Fourth, it seems likely that the brain has some type of limits in the extent to which it is plastic. What are the limits and what determines them? Fifth, there is the general question of establishing what the properties of the nervous system are that enable it to be plastic. And, more specifically, are all regions of the brain equally plastic? Sixth, there is a clinical, and even potential educational, question: Can we gain control of the plasticity and turn it on or off at opportune times? Finally, there is the interesting question of what factors influence plasticity and whether individual differences in different abilities may at least partly reflect differences in the brain's capacity for plasticity.

In sum, the study of brain plasticity provides a window on some of the fundamental questions in psychology and neuroscience. In particular, it allows a way of looking at the neurological bases of fundamental psychological processes such as learning and thought, and the manner in which these develop. It also leads to consideration of important clinical issues surrounding behavioral change, whether it be related to recovery from neurological injury or disease, or psychopathology related to other causes.

ASSUMPTIONS AND BIASES

As we consider the properties of the brain that make it plastic, we need to consider several biases and assumptions that underlie thinking about plasticity.

1. *Behavioral states, including mind states, correspond to brain states.* Although this proposition is not novel, and probably appears to be self-evident to most neuroscientists, it has been a central philosophical issue since the time of Descartes. In fact, modern-day philosophers still debate this issue seriously, in large part because mind (or "cognitive processes" in modern jargon) is the central problem of psychology. In this volume I assume that it is the brain that thinks and

controls behavior, and try to show that an understanding of plasticity will be enlightening with respect to how it does these tricks!

2. *The structural properties of the brain are important in understanding its function.* It follows from my first assertion that changes in the physical structure of the brain will be reflected in changes in its functioning. Although many behavioral scientists (e.g., Pylyshyn, 1980; Skinner, 1938) have seen the structure of the brain as virtually incidental to the study of its function, this is not my view. Rather, I assume not only that changes in structure underlie behavioral change but also that it is possible to identify and potentially influence those changes. This does not imply that a single structural change is responsible for all behavioral change, nor that a particular behavioral change is due solely to one morphological change, nor that an understanding of morphology means an understanding of the functional properties that emerge from the morphology. It does mean, however, that the cerebral organization places significant constraints on the computations of the brain and may provide important clues for understanding the nature of those computations.

3. *Plasticity is a property of the synapse.* The Spanish anatomist Ramon y Cajal postulated in the early part of this century (1928) that the process of learning might produce prolonged morphological changes in the efficiency of the connections between neurons (Fig. 1.1). However, it was not until 1948 that a Polish neuroscientist, Jerzy Konorski, formally proposed a mechanism. He suggested that appropriate combinations of sensory stimuli could produce two types of changes in neurons and their connections: (a) an invariant but transitory change in the excitability of neurons, and (b) an enduring plastic change in neurons. In other words, Konorski suggested that when neurons are active they change. This change might be transitory, much as when one looks up a phone number and then forgets it, or it might be enduring, such as the case in which a telephone number is memorized. The idea that neurons are somehow changed with use is important, for it means that one could look at the neuron and try to identify the changes. The question is, however, where do you look? A Canadian psychologist, Donald Hebb, proposed in 1949 that the logical place to look is at the synapse (Fig. 1.2). He suggested that when synapses are active, they change *if the conditions are right.* For Hebb, the most important condition was that two neurons had to be coincidentally active and if so, then the connection between them was strengthened.[2] Hebb's addition was important, for it (a) specified the conditions under which plasticity would occur and (b) pointed to a role of both the pre- and postsynaptic side of a connection in plasticity. This latter conclusion

---

[2]Neurons do not have to be active at the same time, even though they may be connected. Thus, if a given neuron has multiple connections, only a few are likely to satisfy the condition that the pre- and postsynaptic neurons are active concurrently. Indeed, if a synapse is inhibitory, they cannot be coincidentally active.

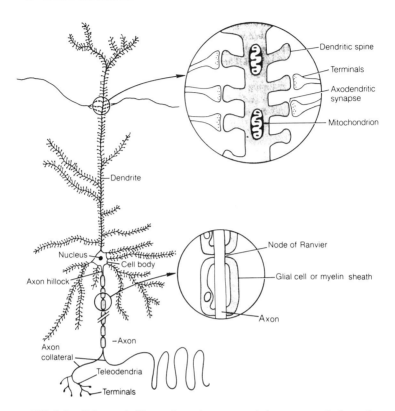

FIG. 1.1.   Schematic illustration of a neuron. It is composed of a cell body and neural processes, which include an axon and dendrites. At the end of the axon are multiple terminals, which are sometimes referred to as the terminal field of the axon. Each of these terminals synapses with another neural process, usually a dendrite. Axon terminals are therefore also known as the presynaptic part of the neuron. Many axons are surrounded by a myelin sheath, which is made up of a type of glial cell known as an oligodendrocyte. The dendrites are the receptor surface of the neuron. Many dendrites have small stubby protrusions, known as spines, on them. Synapses can occur on spines or on the cell body, which both form the postsynaptic surface. After Kolb and Whishaw (1990).

means that plasticity can be measured either pre- or postsynaptically. It also follows from Hebb's proposals that during development, learning, recovery from injury, and aging, there are changes at the synapse that allow the brain to be functionally plastic.

4. *Behavioral plasticity results from summation of plasticity of individual neurons.* It should be self-evident that no single neuron will have much influence on functional plasticity, but this needs to be stated explicitly. After all, in a brain

with 10^{10} neurons (or more!) it would be inconceivable to think that any one neuron would make much difference. Note, however, that in animals with very simple nervous systems, such as tiny worms that have only a few hundred neurons, changes of a single neuron may be very important. We might predict that such "brains" would be less plastic than the human brain, because it would make no sense to have it changing every time one of the neurons was especially active.

5. *Specific mechanisms of plasticity are likely to underlie more than one form of behavioral change.* The nervous system is likely to be conservative in its construction. Thus, general mechanisms that are used for one type of behavioral change, such as in learning and memory, may also form the basis of other types of behavioral change, such as in recovery from brain injury. This preconception does not exclude the possibility of specific mechanisms for different types of plasticity, but it has the advantage in that it allows studies of one form of plasticity to provide insights into mechanisms involved in others. Indeed, it has become clear in recent years that the structural changes underlying experientially induced plasticity such as in perceptual development are remarkably similar to those underlying recovery from some types of brain injury.

6. *The cortex is the most interesting candidate for neural plasticity.* Some neural structures are likely to be more plastic than others. It is reasonable to suppose that if one were designing a brain it would make little sense to make all synapses equally plastic. After all, one presumably needs some constancy in a

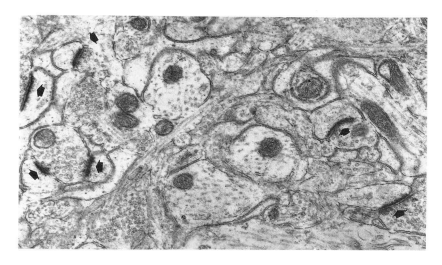

FIG. 1.2. Photomicrograph through a section of cortex. There are many synapses visible (arrows). The postsynaptic side is dark. Note that the synapses vary in size. (Magnified 45,000×.)

labile system if function is going to remain stable. For example, one could imagine that it might be advantageous for basic spinal reflexes to be less plastic than those processes involved in lexical memory (i.e., vocabulary). One difficulty, however, is that it is often difficult to predict a priori what features of neural organization are likely to be more or less labile. There are several reasons to suppose that the mammalian cortex might be a place to search for plasticity. First, it is the cortex of humans that has grown the most in brain evolution. Hence, when calculations are corrected for body size, it the cortex that has grown disproportionately in the human brain: The human cortex is three times larger than one would expect for a typical mammal (Stephen, Bauchot, & Andy, 1970).

One of the functional correlates of this increased cortical volume is an increase in behavioral flexibility, so it follows that the cortex might be the most interesting place to look for a relationship between plasticity and behavior. Cross-species comparisons of cortical structure are enlightening in this regard (see Fig. 1.3). For example, if one compares the thickness of cortex across mammalian species, one of the most obvious observations is that cortical thickness correlates with perceived intelligence. Monkeys have thicker cortex than carnivores, who in turn have thicker cortex than rodents. One striking similarity, however, is that the number of neurons in a "column" of cortex is the same across species (Rockel, Hiorns, & Powell, 1980). That is, mice and humans have the same number of neurons across a slab of cortex (Fig. 1.3). This means that the difference in cortical thickness is due to neural processes (dendrites and axons), blood vessels, and glial cells. This increase in neural processes, blood vessels, and glia is required in order to allow the tissue to have more synapses. We can see therefore that adding synapses has a significant tissue cost. At any rate, we see that increasing the processing capacity across species is associated with an increase in synapses. Similarly, within a species, there is a marked difference in cortical thickness during development, even though the number of neurons declines significantly during development. Again, it is the connectivity that accounts for the increase in thickness. In sum, the cortex is a particularly interesting candidate for studying plasticity–behavior relationships. Of course, a disadvantage is that the cortex is complex in structure and in function. Although this may be a compelling argument to consider "simpler" neural systems, such as the commonly studied sea slug, *Aplysia,* it is not a substantive argument for not studying the cortex. Indeed, the complexity has an advantage in that the cortex contains a wide variety of neuron types, transmitter types, and receptors for hormones and other growth factors. This would seem like fertile ground for study, in spite of the complexity.

7. *Behavior is not sexy but it is as difficult to study as molecules.* There is a temptation to assume that things we are familiar with, such as behavior, are easy to understand whereas things that we cannot actually observe, such as neurons, are difficult. This view is seductive and wrong. Behavior is at least as difficult to

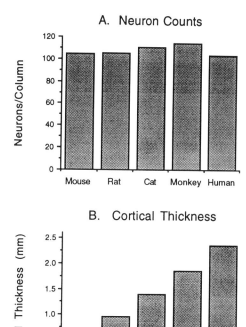

A. Neuron Counts

B. Cortical Thickness

FIG. 1.3. (A) Summary of the comparison of neuron counts in parietal cortex of different species of mammals. There are no significant differences across the different species. (B) Summary of the cortical thickness across the parietal cortex. Note that the cortex of the human is four times greater than that of the mouse. Because the number of neurons is the same, the difference in thickness must be due to other neural, glial, and vascular elements. (Data from Rockel, Hiorns, & Powell, 1980.)

study as the brain. Consider the following example. A rat is given a unilateral surgical injury to the motor cortex. Initially, the animal has difficulty walking normally, but over the ensuing days it improves and looks "normal." The animal still has difficulty using its affected forepaw, but this gradually seems to improve over time. We construct some type of rating scale or efficiency measure (e.g., number of times a small piece of food is dropped) and find that the behavior has improved. We now try to correlate the observed behavioral change with structural change in the brain. Although our behavioral analysis is reasonable, it is very naive. First, we failed to notice that when the animal had difficulty using its affected limbs, it relied on the nonaffected limbs. This change in behavior can potentially change the brain. In fact, in an interesting set of experiments Schallert and his colleagues have shown this to be the case (see Chapter 5). In this case brain plasticity reflects compensation by the normal limb, rather than the basis of recovery of the impaired limb. Second, when we concluded that the gait was normal, we were trying to observe behavior that occurs very quickly. When the behavior is filmed and analyzed very carefully using various scoring schemes, we find that it is far from normal. In fact, the animal is now walking in a very different manner. Does the brain control this in the same way as normal gait? Third, Whishaw and his colleagues have shown that although we saw an improvement in limb use for manipulating food, this improvement was misleading. When the behavior is analyzed in slow motion, they discover that the posture of the animal is abnormal, the speed and trajectory of limb movements are altered, and the manner in which the digits are used is different (Whishaw, Pellis, Gorny, & Pellis, 1991). We are now left with the problem of deciding if there really was functional "recovery" or whether the animal is simply using a different strategy to get around its problems. Now consider the problem of studying changes in "cognitive" behavior. We have an even more daunting task. The message is that the analysis of behavior is difficult and can be very misleading when done poorly. Unfortunately, it is not as sexy as studying neurons! It is just as important, however, and if we are to understand the relationship between brain plasticity and function, it must play an integral part in understanding cause and effect.

SOME EXAMPLES

The case of Donna provided a general background for the the questions we next address. Consider now two more specific examples of brain plasticity.

Building a Better Brain

An interesting story is unfolding at a nunnery in Mankato, Minnesota. A group of about 700 elderly sisters in a Catholic order has become an experiment in brain building. There are two unusual things about the sisters of Mankato. First, they are long-lived. Of the 150 retired nuns at Mankato, 25 are older than 90. Curiously, according to David Snowden, who has been studying them, those nuns who earn college degrees, who teach, and who are constantly challenging their minds live longer than less educated nuns who clean rooms or work in the kitchen.[3] Second, the nuns have agreed to donate their brains to neuroscientists to study. The idea is that there should be a fundamental difference between the brains of the long-lived, well-educated nuns and the shorter lived, less well-educated nuns. What might this difference be? Given the assumptions that we considered earlier, the likely difference is in the synapse.

At the same time that Hebb was proposing a synaptic explanation for learning, he did an interesting experiment. He brought several laboratory rats home from his laboratory at McGill University and released them in his home. The idea was that these animals would get a more stimulating environment in his home, especially as his wife chased them around the kitchen with a broom, and this

---

[3]We are assuming that the long-lived nuns did not self-select early in life so that those who were to be long-lived went to university and those who were to be short-lived did not.

might increase their "IQ." To test out his idea he compared the later maze-learning performance of his pet house rats to their littermates who lived in a drab and unstimulating laboratory cage. The results were unequivocal. The "enriched" experience improved maze performance. Subsequent studies by many groups have shown that the reason was that the brains changed. For example, my colleagues and I have found that living in a large rat condominium with lots of toys can increase overall brain weight by up to 10% in 2 months (see Chapter 7 for details of such experiments). What causes the increase? Again, based on Hebb's idea, we have looked at the synapse. The simplest way to do this is to examine the dendrite (Fig. 1.1). The dendrite is basically an extension of the cell body on which synapses can be made. Consider an arboreal metaphor. Suppose you want to increase the number of leaves on a tree in order to increase the total amount of photosynthesis. There would be three basic ways. First, one can increase the density of the leaves. Second, one can lengthen the branches and keep the density constant. Third, one could increase the amount of photosynthesis by simply increasing the size of the existing leaves. If one imagines the leaves as synapses, then there are three potential synaptic changes: increased density on the dendrites, increased dendritic length, and increased synapse size. In fact, all three types of changes are found. Thus, the enriched experience has built a brain with more synapses—in effect, a better brain. Thus, when the brains of the Sisters of Mankato are studied, it is likely that there will be a clear increase in the dendrites.

Rebuilding a Broken Brain

About 600,000 Americans and Canadians will suffer a stroke this year, and an equal number will suffer a closed head injury. Both stroke and closed head injury victims have "broken brains" and thus broken behavior. Until recently it was believed that because we cannot grow new brain cells after birth, there was no possible way to recover from brain damage. Any improvement that was seen after brain injury was considered to be a result of a reduction in swelling or shock. It is now becoming clear, however, that the brain has built-in mechanisms that can affect at least some repair. Thus, as the brain changes in response to experiences, it also changes in response to injury. That the brain has such a capacity may not be surprising when we consider that brain injury involves the loss of neurons. Because we lose neurons constantly during our lifetime, the brain must have a mechanism in place to accommodate this loss (e.g., Coleman & Buell, 1985). Imagine a region of the cortex about 1 mm wide and 3 mm thick with 500 neurons. Assume each neuron has 10,000 connections. Simple arithmetic tells us that the region has $500 \times 10,000 = 5,000,000$ connections. Now assume that 10% of the neurons die, leaving us with 450 neurons and a loss of 500,000 synapses. If the number of connections was important to maintaining function, then we ought to be able to increase the number of connections in the remaining neurons. Thus, increasing the connections of each remaining neuron by about 10% leaves us with the same number of connections. This is what happens to some parts of the brain during aging (e.g., Flood, 1993) . Thus, up until very old age, there is a continual increase in the number of connections on each of the remaining cortical neurons. As a result, most people suffer very little behavioral loss until well into old age. In the case of dementing diseases, such as Alzheimer's, this increase in synapses fails to occur and there is behavioral loss much sooner. The key here is that the loss of neurons is gradual and not in a concentrated location. In a sense, we spend most of our adult life rebuilding a breaking brain!

Let us now consider what happens when the brain is broken suddenly and in a localized area, such as in a stroke. In this case, millions of neurons and billions of connections are lost. As long as at least some of the original functional regions are intact, it ought to be possible to stimulate them to grow more connections, much as in aging, and this will allow some recovery of function. The complete loss of a given area would be impossible to recover from, however. For example, adding new connections to a region involved in vision does allow language to recover.

Studies in laboratory animals have shown that when there is significant recovery of behavior, there is often a growth in the dendritic trees, and thus in the number of connections, in the remaining regions involved in the damaged behaviors. Furthermore, it appears that various factors may play an important role in stimulating the growth of new connections. These are known as *trophic factors,* and they are chemicals that the brain normally produces during development in order to assist in generating connections in the first place. In addition, it should be apparent that because experience can influence connectivity, it ought to be possible to develop therapies that would stimulate the brain to produce more connections that might assist in recovery of function.

One of the implications of the plastic changes that underlie both recovery from the processes of aging and brain injury is that the brain may be more successful in recovering in younger animals than in older ones because there are more remaining neurons to change. This is unfortunately the case. Another implication is that people who have brain damage early in life may not be as successful in staving off the effects of age on the brain. When the brain changes to allow recovery from injury, it may exploit mechanisms to be used later for compensating for aging. When this change is needed, the brain is not able to respond.

CONCLUSIONS AND DIRECTIONS

One of the fundamental, and most interesting, properties of the brain is its plasticity. This feature of the brain allows us to learn and to benefit from experience. It also allows us to live a relatively long life during which we are able to continue to learn new things. Work on neuronal plasticity is elaborating the ways that the brain is plastic and discovering ways to control the mechanisms that underlie plasticity. This offers considerable hope that sometime in the not too distant future we will be able to build better brains and to repair broken ones.

The goals of the rest of this book are to: (a) identify the constraints on behavioral change, (b) describe the neuronal correlates of the behavioral changes, and (c) identify those factors that control or influence the brain and behavioral changes. The analysis of brain and behavioral change is necessarily correlational, which makes it difficult to make conclusions about causation. In addition, my focus must also be on experiments that have done both behavioral and anatomical investigations. The critical experiments must therefore be those in which one attempts to challenge the correlations between brain and behavioral changes. As we shall see, these are also some of the most difficult experiments to conduct.

2 Plasticity in the Normal Brain

Brain plasticity results from changes in the synapse. The formation of new synapses has a cost, however, as there are also increases in dendrites, axon terminals, glia, and blood capillaries. The mechanisms controlling plasticity therefore include more than just those things that directly change synapses or create new ones, but also include those mechanisms that change the supporting cast of the synapse. One thing that follows from the multiple changes in the brain accompanying plasticity is that plasticity can be inferred from the study of many things, including the direct measurement of synapses as well as the measurement of axon terminals, dendritic arborizations and spines, glia, and capillaries.

This chapter reviews the likely mechanisms of plasticity in the cortex. It begins by reviewing some important features of the neocortical organization that are central to understanding the constraints on cortical plasticity. It then considers the most likely candidates for making inferences about cortical plasticity and behavior. Finally, there is a review of the evidence for plasticity in the normal developing brain, mature brain, and aging brain.

SPECIAL FEATURES OF CORTICAL ORGANIZATION

Although the concept of localization of function has been controversial for more than 100 years, one of the principal tenets of modern neuropsychology is that functions are localized to relatively discrete neocortical locations. Evidence supporting the idea of localization of functions is based largely on functional studies, which include behavioral analyses of brain-damaged subjects as well as evidence of localized metabolic and vascular changes correlated with specific behaviors in normal subjects (e.g., Kolb & Whishaw, 1995). Because functional specificity is relatively constant across different people, it is reasonable to conclude that localization of function must be based on regional differences in neocortical morphology. In fact, when we examine different neocortical areas under the microscope, different areas are clearly dissimilar. They can be distinguished by differences in the architecture, which includes differences in cell sizes and cell density, and by differences in the distribution of receptors for transmitters, but the most important differences are in the connections; different cortical regions have distinctly different inputs and outputs, and these define the function. Thus, it has been suggested that there is a fundamental intrinsic neuronal circuit underlying all cortical function and that the principal functional differences between cortical areas result from differences in the afferent and efferent connections of the common cortical circuit (Douglas, Martin, & Witteridge, 1989; Peters & Sethares, 1991; Szentagothai, 1975).

There is, however, another feature of cortical organization that is as important as the connections, and this is the nature of the intrinsic cortical circuit. In fact, the intrinsic circuit of the cortex may be the key to plasticity of functional areas, because it accounts for the major proportion of cortical connectivity. This is a surprising property of cortical organization, because standard textbook drawings of cortical connectivity tend to emphasize long connections between cortical regions or to and from subcortical regions. A recent analysis by Nicoll and Blakemore (1993) is instructive. They examined the patterns of connections of pyramidal cells, which are the almost exclusive outputs of the neocortex. The axons of pyramidal cells make long-range connections to other cortical regions or subcortical structures, but they also have axon collaterals that form extensive arborizations with nearby cells. In fact, the most common target of pyramidal cells is other cortical pyramidal cells. Nicoll and Blakemore estimated that roughly 70% of the excitatory synapses on any layer II/III pyramidal cell are derived from pyramidal cells in the near vicinity. It is highly likely that most of these intrinsic cortical synapses are made with axons that travel horizontally from their cell body and synapse *en passant* with neighboring cells, as illustrated in Fig. 2.1. It is likely that local intrinsic connections of these pyramidal neurons are much more important than any distant connection in determining the output of a given layer II/III pyramidal cell.

The intrinsic wiring of the cortex has additional important properties that influence, and to some extent constrain, its plasticity. Szentagothai (e.g., 1975) and others have shown the cortex has an exquisite vertical organization that has several features (Fig. 2.2). There is a vertical distribution of neuron types: The cells that are located in the superficial layers (II and III) differ from those in layer IV, and they, in turn, differ from those in the output layers (V, VI). The inputs to this vertical organization are stratified. That is, there are different inputs going not only to different cortical layers, but also to different regions of the output neurons. For example, the major specific cortical afferents terminate in layer IV,

FIG. 2.1.   Illustration of the axonal arborization of a layer III pyramidal neuron. Note that most of the axonal arbor is confined to cortex around the neuron. This suggests that most cortical connections are local (or intrinsic) ones made within the cortex. The inset drawing illustrates the *en passant* synapses that are likely the most common type of plastic cortical connection. The black dots represent synaptic vesicles in the presynaptic, or axonal, side of the connection. After Gilbert, Hirsch, and Wiesel (1990) and Steward (1991).

whereas cortico-cortical projections are largely in more superficial layers. Furthermore, the output cells (i.e., pyramidal cells) have different inputs on different regions of their dendritic arborization (Fig. 2.3). This property is important for plasticity because it means that specific portions of the neurons could show plastic changes whereas other regions do not. In addition, in the event that one input is lost through injury, it is possible for existing inputs to other parts of the neuron to expand to fill the place of the lost ones.

Consider the example in the bottom part of Fig. 2.3. The two neurons have roughly the same amount of dendritic space but it is organized differently. The neuron on the left has more apical dendrites, which are the dendrites extending vertically from the cell body, whereas the neuron on the right has more basilar dendrites, which are the dendrites extending laterally from the cell body. The intrinsic organization of the cortex effectively forms functional "columns." These columns are thus the basic processing unit of the cortex and can be expected to exhibit significant plasticity. In other words, changes in cortical function will be reflected in changes in the organization of this circuit.

One way for the functioning of the intrinsic circuit to change is for the field of influence of a neuron to change (Fig. 2.4). For example, the diameter of a cell's dendritic field could expand, allowing the cell to interact with a larger number of neurons. Alternatively, the axon terminals could redistribute to enlarge the field of influence, too. The fact that neurons can expand their field of influence means that if neurons die, remaining ones could enlarge their field to make up for some of the lost processing power.

When we examine the developing brain there is a fundamental difference in the apparent organization that we see in the adult and infant brain. Early in

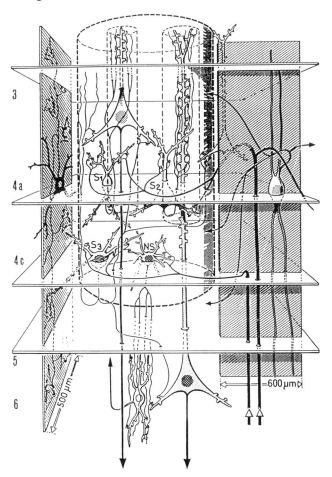

FIG. 2.2.   Highly schematic illustration of the organization of the cortex. The connections, inputs, and outputs of the neurons tend to run vertically, forming functional columns, which is illustrated by the white region. Abbreviations: S1, S2, S3, spiny stellate cells; NS, nonspiny stellate cell. After Szentagothai (1975). Adapted by permission of Elsevier Science.

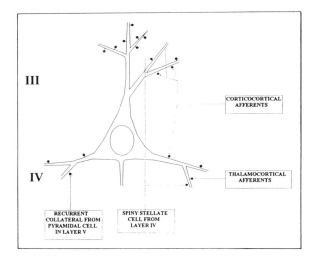

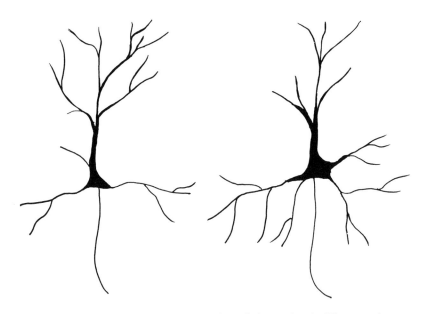

FIG. 2.3.   Top: Schematic illustration of the regional differences in afferents to different parts of the neuron. After Morrison and Hof (1992). Bottom: Schematic illustration showing how neurons can have similar dendritic material but it can be distributed differently in the apical and basilar regions of the dendritic tree. Differences in dendritic growth can therefore reflect growth in different types of inputs.

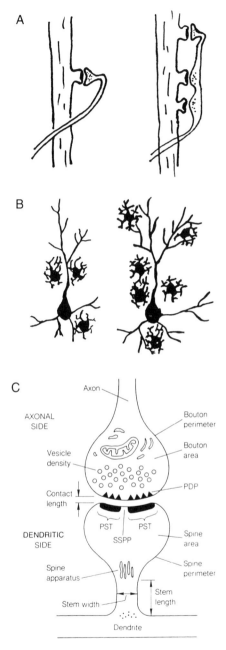

FIG. 2.4. Schematic illustrations of changes in the axons, glia, and synapses in brain plasticity. (A) Axons may develop new connections en passant. (B) Glia may grow in size or in number. (C) Synapses may show many different changes, including at the postsynaptic thickening (PST), subsynaptic plate perforation (SSPP), and presynaptic dense projection (PDP).

development the cortex appears uniform across its extent as it lacks much of the specificity in cytoarchitecture and connections of the adult cortex, suggesting that it may have the capacity for greater plasticity in development than later in adulthood. Various researchers have shown that the developing neocortex is remarkable in its flexibility, and many cortical areas appear to be capable of assuming the structure and functions of virtually any other area (e.g., Kennedy & Dehay, 1993; O'Leary, 1989) . However, as the cortex develops its adult input–output characteristics its plasticity decreases and it becomes constrained by its gross connectivity. Thus, in the developing brain it is possible to influence the connectivity radically, but once the general input–output organization is determined it is more difficult to reorganize it in a major way. On the other hand, it is possible to increase the number of connections that existing inputs make into a given area. This, in turn, can lead to changes in the intrinsic wiring.

CORRELATES OF CORTICAL PLASTICITY

The three most obvious correlates of cortical plasticity are changes in the axon, dendrite, and glia. It is important to realize that changes in the structure of any one of these will require alterations in the production of the structural proteins of which they are composed. The instruction to the cell to produce proteins comes from genes, so there must also be a change in gene expression. Changes in gene expression necessarily involve the cell body. Thus, although changes in the cell body are not normally correlated with functional recovery, it is implicit in any measure of axons or dendrites that some change must have occurred in the cell body too.

Axonal Growth

Most new synapses likely are formed by the development of new contacts on axons as they pass by dendrites *en passant* (Figs. 2.1 and 2.4). There is a tendency to assume that most synapses that result from axon growth occur at the end of the axon, but this is probably an uncommon form of synapse formation. Axon growth therefore does not usually imply that axons have actually grown very far, although during development this may occur as abnormal connections may form after injury. Evidence of an increase in axon terminals is normally taken as evidence of the formation of new synapses, which has been verified using electron microscopic techniques. One difficulty with measuring axonal growth is that it is very difficult to find and to quantify using light microscope procedures, although it is sometimes possible to do so using specific immunohistochemical stains.

There is another type of axonal growth that involves merely an increase in the amount of transmitter available. That is, the axon terminal could increase (or decrease) its production of a transmitter or one of the enzymes that regulate transmitter activity. This can be measured relatively easily using various assay procedures, but it is not as easy to identify which neurons have actually changed.

Dendritic Growth

Dendritic growth refers to the expansion of the dendritic surface, which again implies the formation of new synapses. Dendritic expansion can occur by the growth of more dendritic material or by the increase in the number of dendritic spines (Horner, 1993). Increased dendritic growth can be seen in changes in the length or diameter of particular branches or in the growth of new branches, both of which allow for increased space for synapse formation. It is relatively easy to measure dendritic growth. The most used method is some variation on the Golgi technique, in which a small percentage of all cortical cells (usually about 5%) is stained by a precipitate of a heavy metal such as silver or mercury. It is assumed that the staining is random, although this has been a source of debate for nearly 100 years. Another way to stain cells is to inject them with some type of dye that shows the entire cell body. It has recently become possible to inject cells post-mortem with various dyes, which is a potentially very useful procedure, but this is very time-consuming and has not yet been used much in studies of behavior and brain. Once cells are stained, it is merely necessary to use some sort of procedure to estimate the total amount of dendritic material. In our studies we measure various aspects including the dendritic length, the number of dendritic branches, and the number of spines per length of dendrite (i.e., spine density).

Just as it is possible to consider transmitter production as an aspect of axonal growth, it is possible to consider receptor activity as an aspect of dendritic growth. An increase or decrease in receptor density would clearly alter post-synaptic sensitivity to transmitter release and thus alter dendritic activity. It is relatively easy to measure receptor density, but like transmitter production, it is not easy to localize which neurons actually show the changes in receptor density.

Glial Changes

The central nervous system has two major categories of glial cells: the macroglia and the microglia. The macroglia include astrocytes and oligodendrocytes (Fig. 2.5). Astrocytes are intimately associated with both neurons and with blood vessels (Fig. 2.5). Astrocytes actively produce factors that influence plastic processes, and increase in astrocyte activity is associated with plasticity. Astrocytes can be identified by specific immunohistochemical stains that stain for proteins that are normally only seen in astrocytes (e.g., glial fibrillary acidic protein [GFAP], vimentin). Astrocytes increase in size when they are especially active, so it is possible to measure the extent of their fibrous protrusions in order to quantify astrocytic activity. The number of astrocytes observed in a particular

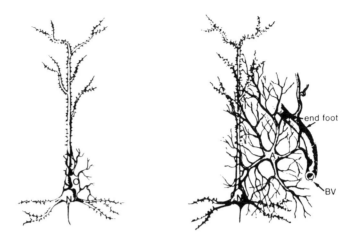

FIG. 2.5. Illustrations of the relationship between oligodendroctyes (left, O) and astrocytes (right, A) and neurons (N). Astrocytes have extensive fibrous outgrowths that can contact both neuropil and blood vessels. After Steward (1989). Adapted by permission of Springer-Verlag New York, Inc.

cortical region also changes with plasticity, although the reason is not clear. It could reflect migration of astrocytes, especially from the white matter into the gray matter. It could also reflect mitosis of astrocytes or a change in the expression of specific proteins, such as GFAP, which makes them visible.

Microglia are macrophage-like scavenger cells. Unlike macroglia, the microglia are physiologically and embryologically unrelated to other elements of the nervous system but rather are related to blood cells. Microglia increase dramatically after the brain is injured, a phenomenon that can be seen in certain immunohistochemical stains such as one known as OX-42.

In sum, glial cells play a basic role in synaptic plasticity. Astrocytes play a central role, appear to have receptors for certain neurotransmitters, and subsequently can produce various trophic factors that can function to provoke or sustain plasticity.

Measuring Synapses

Measurements of axons, dendrites, and glia are indirect measures of the likelihood of synapse growth. In principle, it would make sense to measure synapses directly using electron microscope procedures, as illustrated in Fig. 1.2. Synapses vary along a number of dimensions, including the length of the postsynaptic thickening, the size of the spine, and the size of the pool of presynaptic vesicles (Fig. 2.4). In addition, there are inhibitory and excitatory synapses, and these can be distinguished by the details of their ultrastructure.

There are problems with direct measurement of synapses, however. Electron microscopic procedures are expensive and very time-consuming. In order to analyze the tissue it is necessary to photograph regions of cortex, usually at magnifications in the order to 45,000× or more. Thus, there must be multiple photographs of even a small region of cortex (e.g. 0.5 mm width × the thickness). It is impractical to analyze large regions of the cortex, so one must have a very good idea of exactly where to look and what to look for. It is also impractical to use large numbers of animals that are normally required for studies of behavior, making direct correlation of brain and behavioral change in the same animals difficult. Thus, for most studies of brain plasticity and behavior, synaptic change is not measured directly but is inferred from measurement of changes in axons, dendrites, and glia.

EXAMPLES OF SYNAPTIC PLASTICITY IN THE NORMAL BRAIN

Synaptic Turnover

The stability of neurons and their connections in normal mature animals is an unresolved issue. A common view is that once neurons are generated and they develop their adult complement of connections, then they are relatively static in morphology until there is some perturbation that alters the neural network. An alternate view is that neural change arises from continually changing patterns of connections. In the former case one would expect that neurons would appear to be relatively constant in morphology over time, whereas in the latter case they would be constantly changing. It would seem relatively simple to determine which view is correct by simply watching a set of neurons over an extended period of time in the living animal. The trick is to do it. Recently, an interesting technique that was developed by Purves and his colleagues has provided a means to follow individual neurons and their connections over intervals of weeks and months in living animals. In this procedure nontoxic dyes are injected into neurons and the neurons are imaged using video microscopy (Purves & Voyvodic, 1987). It is then possible to return the animal to its normal routine and relabel and reimage the neuron for analysis (Fig. 2.6). When Purves and his colleagues analyzed the dorsal root ganglion of the mouse in this manner for periods up to 3 months, they found that the dendritic branches of these neurons change continually. Because the majority of synapses on dorsal root ganglion neurons occur on the cell dendrites, it is likely that the changes in dendritic morphology reflect commensurate changes in synaptic inputs. Thus, it appears that at least some neurons show dynamic changes in synaptic elements in the absence of any obvious major perturbations. This is important because it bears directly on the way the adult nervous system generates long-term change. The

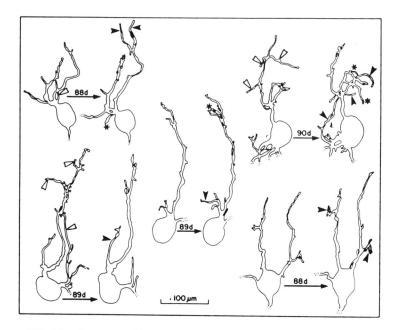

FIG. 2.6. Camera lucida reconstructions of portions of the dendritic arbors of five mouse superior cervical ganglion cells visualized at an interval of 3 months. Changes involving both the extension and retraction of particular branches are evident. Open arrowheads show examples of branches that appear to have retracted; closed arrowheads show examples of branches that appear to have extended; asterisks mark examples of branches that have formed de novo in the interval. The black arrows indicate the appearance after the specified number of days. After Purves and Voyvodic (1987).

functional consequences of spontaneous remodeling of neuron structure are unknown, but it may provide the flexibility in neuronal structure that can subsequently be shaped by the environment.

Experience-Dependent Changes

Hebb first reported in 1947 that rats raised in his home showed an increased learning ability relative to laboratory-reared rats. Hebb's work led to a large number of studies on the effects of a stimulating environment on behavior and on the brain. It is now clear that environmental treatments can profoundly alter the structure of the cortex (Table 2.1). For example, there are changes in the total dendritic length and the structure of the dendritic arbor, the number of synapses per neuron, and even neuron size. Furthermore, there are changes in nonneuronal elements, too, as the number of capillary vessels increases as does the size of astrocytes. Surprisingly, these changes can occur quite rapidly, in the order of days. Wallace, Kilman, Withers, and Greenough (1992) showed significant structural modifications to dendritic length and structure after only 4 days of experience in an "enriched" environment. This observation raises intriguing questions about the necessary and sufficient experience for demonstrating cortical plasticity.

One of the common assumptions of experience-dependent changes in plasticity is that all measures of synaptic growth will provide the same type of information. This need not be the case, however. When my colleagues and I analyzed the dendritic changes in rats reared in complex environments, we replicated the often-found result that the enriched experience increased dendritic growth (Fig. 2.7). However, when we measured the dendritic spines we were surprised to find that the spine density had decreased in the enriched animals (Fig. 2.7). Thus, the plastic changes in the cortex were not merely growth of more connections, but rather we found a remodeling of the dendrites with the synapses further apart. We have not yet discovered what this type of change might mean, but one could speculate that the decrease in spine density provides a space for further experience-dependent synapses to form. Because these synapses could be *en passant* and require no further growth of dendritic branches, we can speculate further that animals with "enriched neurons" ought to be able to change more quickly as animals learn new things. For example, we might predict

TABLE 2.1

Principal Cellular Differences in the Occipital Cortex between Rats
Raised in Enriched Condition (EC) and Impoverished Condition (IC)

Cellular Variable	Environment	Reference
Neuron size	EC > IC	Diamond et al. (1967)
Neuron density	IC > EC	Turner and Greenough (1985)
Dendritic branching	EC > IC	Volkmar and Greenough (1972)
Dendritic spine density	EC > IC	Globus et al. (1973)
Number of unmyelinated axons in splenial corpus callosum	EC > IC	Juraska and Kopcik (1988)
Size of unmyelinated axons in splenial corpus callosum	EC > IC	Juraska and Kopcik (1988)
Number of synapses per neuron	EC > IC	Turner and Greenough (1983)
Size of synaptic contact	EC > IC	West and Greenough (1972)
Synaptic plate perforations	EC > IC	Greenough et al. (1978)
Percentage of total tissue volume Capital vessels	EC > IC	Black et al. (1987)
Astrocytic nuclei	EC > IC	Sirevaag and Greenough (1987)
Oligondendrocytic nuclei	EC > IC	Sirevaag and Greenough (1987)
Mitochondria	EC > IC	Sirevaag and Greenough (1987)

From Juraska (1990). Reprinted by permission.

ENRICHED

ISOLATED

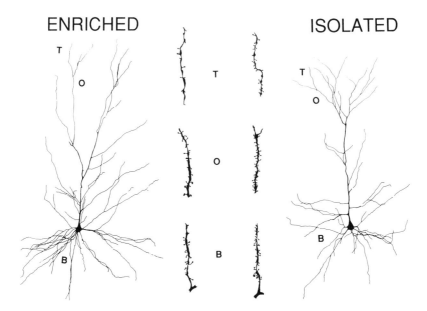

FIG. 2.7.   Camera lucida drawings of a layer III pyramidal cell from parietal cortex of a rat housed for 3 months in an enriched or isolated condition. The enriched neurons have more dendrites but the spine density is reduced. From Kolb, Gorny, and Gibb (1995). Reprinted by permission.

that enriched animals would learn cognitive tasks more quickly than their un-stimulated peers. Viewed in this way, the effect of the experience has been to remodel the brain to make it more responsive to subsequent experiences. Stated differently, plastic changes have made the brain more plastic. This type of explanation accounts for the generalized effects of various experiences, such as attending kindergarten or university, that are alleged to make people more adaptable.

Although the first experiments showing experience-dependent changes in cortical structure and behavior used global experiences, such as rearing in large enclosures filled with "toys," runways, and other animals, later studies have shown that specific learning experiences can affect specific cortical regions. For example, when Greenough, Larson, and Withers (1985) trained rats to reach into a tube to obtain food reward they found an increase in dendritic branching in layer V pyramidal neurons in the motor cortex controlling forelimb movement. These changes were specific to the motor neurons in the hemisphere controlling the reaching paw and were not seen in the motor cortex on the opposite side. My colleagues and I wondered whether the changes in the motor neurons in Greenough's experiments might also occur in bimanual tasks. We investigated this possibility by comparing the brains of rats that were trained in two specific motor skills. In the first task, which was similar to Greenough's experiment, we used a version of the Whishaw reaching task to train rats to use one paw to reach (Fig. 2.8). In the second task, which was developed by Tomie and Whishaw (1990), rats were trained to pull up a string using both paws in order to obtain food reward. A control group was merely exposed to the training platform each day. When we analyzed the brains we found that the rats who learned to reach with a single paw showed a 15% increase in dendritic material in the cortical forelimb area opposite the trained paw relative to the same region opposite the untrained paw. In contrast, rats trained to pull the strings up with both paws showed an increase in both hemispheres that was equivalent to the growth seen in the trained paw of the reaching rats (Fig. 2.9).

It is difficult to perform dendritic experiments on human subjects with specific training, but a recent study by Pascual-Leone and colleagues (1993) suggests that similar changes do occur in humans. These authors used focal transcranial magnetic stimulation to map the motor cortical areas for the fingers in blind braille readers and blind controls. Because braille is read with the left hand, the authors were able to compare the effect of extensive braille training on the left and right hemispheres. The braille readers had learned braille as children and used it daily for 5 to 10 hr. The controls had learned braille as adults and used it less than 1 hr per day. In the controls there was no significant different in the finger representations in the two hands. In contrast, the proficient braille users had a significantly

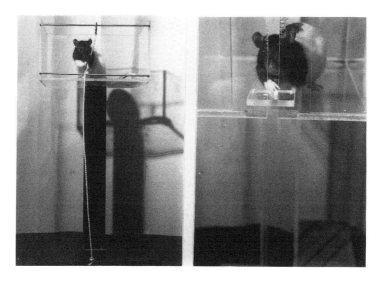

FIG. 2.8. Photographs of rats in the string pulling task (left) or the Whishaw reaching task (right). Rats in the string pulling task used both forelimbs to retrieve food whereas rats in the reaching task used only one paw. From Kolb, Tomie, and Ouellette (1995). Reprinted by permission.

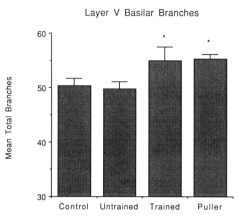

Layer V Basilar Branches

FIG. 2.9.   Summary of the dendritic data from layer III pyramidal cells in the forelimb area of
the rats in the string pulling and
reaching tasks. The bilateral
task increased dendritic branching bilaterally, whereas the unilateral task increased branching
only in the neurons contralateral to the trained limb. Control
refers to both hemispheres of
animals who were placed on
the testing platform but were
not trained to do any task. Untrained refers to the hemisphere
ipsilateral to the limb trained to
reach for food. Trained refers
to the hemisphere contralateral
to the limb trained to reach for
food. Puller refers to both hemispheres of the rats trained to pull
strings with both paws. From
Kolb, Tomie, and Ouellette (1995).
Reprinted by permission.

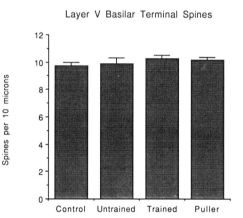

Layer V Basilar Terminal Spines

larger representation in the right hemisphere, which controls the left hand, than
in either their left hemisphere or in either hemisphere of the controls. This result
implies that the cortex of the braille readers had undergone a plastic change in
response to the training, which resulted in increasing the size of the brain area
that represents the braille-reading digit.

Perhaps one of the best known sets of experiments on environmentally induced plasticity in the cortex has been done on the visual cortex of the cat.
Exposure to a restricted range of stimulus orientations during early postnatal life
alters the distribution of orientation preferences of cells in primary visual cortex.
For example, cats raised with selective exposure to lines oriented vertically have
a vertical bias in the orientation preference of visual cortical cells. Of particular
interest here is that the dendritic morphology of cortical neurons is related to their
preferred orientations (e.g., Tieman & Hirsch, 1982). In other words, the experi-

ence of the cat alters the orientation of the dendritic fields in a consistent way, thus providing a morphological basis for the observed physiological differences (Fig. 2.10). These changes were specific, however, as they occurred only in pyramidal cells in visual cortex and not in the adjacent stellate cells. Experience-dependent changes in visual cortical neurons are not only seen in developing animals. Greenough and his colleagues have also shown that training rats to learn visual mazes produces specific changes in neurons in visual cortex (e.g., Greenough, Juraska, & Volkmar, 1979), which suggests that many forms of learning will be associated with changes in the structure of cortical neurons in the sensory cortex.

It is not yet known if primary sensory areas, which are the regions that receive the most direct input from the sensory receptors (e.g., area 17 for vision), or "higher" sensory areas will show more plastic changes in response to experience. In a preliminary study Robbin Gibb and I measured the dendritic extent of pyramidal cells in area 17 and area TE (a higher visual area) in rats from isolated and enriched environments. Our results showed a clear effect of enrichment in area 17 but none in area TE. This result was unexpected, but it implies that

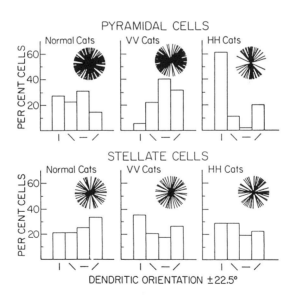

FIG. 2.10. Summary of the orientation of the dendritic fields of neurons from the brains of cats raised with selective exposure to either vertical lines (VV Cats) or horizontal lines (HH Cats). Cats raised in a normal environment had a random distribution of dendritic fields. VV Cats showed a bias to horizontally oriented dendrites, whereas HH Cats showed a bias to vertically oriented dendrites. Stellate cells showed no such bias. After Tieman and Hirsch (1982).

primary areas may be more responsive to general enrichment effects than higher order areas. Perhaps the higher order areas are more affected by specific experiences. It is known, for example, that extensive training on specific visual patterns will alter the firing characteristics of neurons in area TE in the monkey. Thus, Tanaka (1993) found that the selectivity of TE neurons is not determined by genes or early experience but rather by the visual environment in the adult. He trained monkeys to discriminate 28 different moderately complex shapes for a year. In trained monkeys 39% of the neurons in TE gave a maximum response to some of the visual stimuli used during training whereas only 9% of neurons in untrained animals gave a similar response. In view of the Tieman and Hirsch experiment described earlier, it seems likely that the area TE neurons changed their morphology (and synaptivity) in some manner in response to the training.

Aging-Related Changes in Plasticity

As the brain ages it shows considerable histological evidence of degeneration (Coleman & Flood, 1987). In particular, there is a loss of neurons, although the extent of loss may vary considerably from region to region and in different species. Because it is a common observation that most old people are not demented and are capable of learning new things, it follows that there must be some way for the brain to compensate for the neuronal loss. One mechanism appears to be to increase the number of synapses per neuron. Buell and Coleman (1981) measured the dendrites of layer II pyramidal neurons in the parahippocampal gyrus of adult (age 51 years) and normal aged (age 80 years) humans. The dendritic trees were longer and more branched in the aged people, suggesting that there were plastic changes in the neurons to accommodate the neuronal loss. When Buell and Coleman similarly analyzed the brains of aged people with senile dementia, they found dendritic trees that were smaller than in the younger adult brains. We did a similar analysis of rat brains in which we compared layer II/III pyramidal cells in the parietal cortex of 28-month-old ($n = 8$) and 6-month-old ($n = 5$) Long-Evans rats. As in the Buell and Coleman study, there was an increase in dendritic branching in the aged rats, although it was restricted to the basilar field.[1]

CONCLUSIONS

There are six conclusions to draw from this discussion. First, the crucial feature that determines cortical function is its afferent and efferent connections. It follows that in the absence of appropriate connectivity, a given cortical area will not

---

[1]Analysis of variance on the basilar branches was significant ($F = 6.39, p < .05$), whereas it was not for the apical it was not ($F = 0.23, p > .6$).

be able to compensate for the loss of another, regardless of how many synapses are formed. The analysis of information and the subsequent action on that information require the connections that specify cortical function. This is major constraint on the capability of the cortex to support recovery of function. Second, there is a canonical intrinsic circuit in the cortex. This circuit is responsible for the bulk of cortical connections and is thus the most likely location for cortical plasticity. Third, the three most studied measures of cortical plasticity are axon terminal growth, dendritic growth, and glial change. It is likely that the glial cells play a key role in stimulating plasticity in the neuron. Synapses are seldom studied directly because this requires electron microscopic analysis, which is expensive and time-consuming. Fourth, evidence of synaptic plasticity can be seen in the effects of both general and specific training, as well as in the aging brain. Fifth, plastic changes in the nervous system likely occur on a background of continual change in neuronal morphology, rather than on a static system. This continual change in neurons may provide a mechanism for the rapid changes needed to support learning. Finally, experience may not only change the synaptic organization of the cortex but it may also alter the dendritic morphology such that future plastic changes can occur more quickly.

II BRAIN INJURY AND BEHAVIOR

One way to investigate brain plasticity is to use what could be called the "sledgehammer approach." That is, in order to find the changes in the brain when it changes, we use dramatic experiences that produce massive changes. One way to do this is to injure the brain and then to investigate the changes that subsequently occur. The advantage of this approach is that the phenomena are reliable and the onset and nature of the experience can be specified precisely. Another advantage is that the study of the injured brain provides us with a window on the treatment of one of the leading causes of death and disability in the modern world, namely, brain injury. However, before we can begin to look at brain plasticity after cerebral injury we must first examine the nature of behavioral change after brain injury. Thus, by determining the conditions under which functions do and do not recover after injury, we are in a position to begin to consider what the neural correlates of this recovery might be. Because one of the major determinants of recovery form cerebral injury is developmental age, injury to the adult and developing brain are considered separately. The adult is considered first (chapter 3) because an understanding of functional change after injury in adulthood provides us with the necessary tools to consider the more difficult problem of the effects of injury to the developing brain (chapter 4).

3 Is There Really Recovery from Brain Damage?

The brain can be damaged in many ways (stroke, disease, trauma), and it is rare indeed for a family not be affected by one of them. For example, it is estimated that about 400,000 people with new head injuries are admitted to hospitals each year in the United States. This figure is a conservative measure of the incidence of head injuries, because there is clear neuropathological and neuropsychological evidence that significant damage to the central nervous system can also result from minor head injury or concussion that does not lead to hospitalization (e.g., Levin, Eisenberg, & Benton, 1989). Estimates of the number of people who have mild head injuries, without hospitalization, vary widely, but in the United States it is probably in the order of at least an additional 100,000 per year. An additional 100,000 people die from head trauma and are not included in most statistics. Overall, it appears that the frequency of closed head injuries in industrialized countries ranges from about 300 to 450 per 100,000 population per year. Projected over one's life span, the chances of such an injury are high indeed. It has been estimated that a child's chances of having a significant closed head injury are 1 in 30 before the child is old enough to drive! Similarly, it is estimated that there are about 400,000 new cases of stroke every year in the United States (about 1.3% of the population), and most surviving stroke victims experience significant cognitive loss. As the number of stroke survivors in the United States now approaches 2 million, we can begin to understand the strain on support services. When we add the toll from neurological diseases (e.g., Parkinson's, Alzheimer's) we reach a very high probability of having a behavioral disorder, or of having a close relative with a disorder, related to brain injury or disease. The estimate in the United States is that about 48 million people (or about 15%) have some sort of neurological disorder, exclusive of "mental diseases" such as schizophrenia, which is also clearly a result of neural dysfunction.

The high incidence of brain injury and disease thus poses perhaps the most perplexing clinical neurological problem in the 1990s, which is the question of how to repair the damaged brain. Because recovery from brain damage is a practical example of brain plasticity, the incidence and processes of recovery are of considerable interest in the context of research on brain plasticity. Before one can investigate the relationship between brain plasticity and recovery of function, it is necessary to consider the conditions under which recovery is most likely to occur and to review the way in which functional recovery is measured. This chapter reviews (a) the methods of studying functional recovery in both human patients and laboratory animals and (b) the evidence of functional recovery in adult humans and laboratory animals. Recovery in the developing animal is reviewed in the next chapter.

STUDYING THE BROKEN BRAIN TO UNDERSTAND THE NORMAL BRAIN

It may at first seem paradoxical that one would damage the brain in order to understand the nature of plastic processes of the normal brain. Indeed, it seems logical simply to study the plasticity of the normal brain as it learns new material or changes with experience. After all, if brain plasticity is responsible for behavioral change, then changes in the brain should be apparent when behavior changes in the normal person. This is a reasonable perspective, but there are some complications. In particular, there is the problem of knowing where to look for plastic changes in the billions of cells and trillions of synapses. Thus, practically, it is going to be necessary to study brain plasticity in situations in which we can expect large and unambiguous changes in particular locations and in which a time of onset can be specified. A fundamental assumption I am making, therefore, is that the easiest way to produce and to locate large changes in cerebral organization is to perturb the brain directly, and then to study the nature of the neural and behavioral changes that follow. This is the "sledgehammer" approach to studying behavioral change, but once we have found changes in brain and behavior it will be possible to try more subtle approaches.

It is now well documented that there are systematic changes in the brain after injury (e.g., Nieto-Sampedro & Cotman, 1985), and, although behavioral changes are less well characterized, there is now sufficient evidence to suggest that there are specific and predictable changes in behavior in the weeks and months following cerebral injury. Thus, both the brain and behavior change over time after injury. If the changes in the brain are meaningful with respect to the observed behavioral changes, then the temporal sequences of change in the brain and behavior should be consistently related. That is, if we propose that a particular form of neural plasticity is responsible for recovery of function, then we ought to find recovery only when that neural change occurs first. In addition, it should also be possible to manipulate the neural plasticity and to show that the behavioral changes are also modified in some way. These manipulations might take the form of pharmacological or behavioral treatments, and they may act to enhance or to retard recovery. In either event, however, the correlations between brain and behavioral changes should endure.

In sum, I am assuming that damaging the brain is an especially good way to investigate mechanisms of brain plasticity and behavior. Although we run the risk that plastic changes following brain injury are unique and play no role in other forms of plasticity, I have assumed that the nervous system is conservative and will use many of the same mechanisms in most forms of plasticity.

WHAT DOES RECOVERY OF FUNCTION MEAN?

As we begin to consider the nature of recovery after brain injury we must be wary of potential traps. It is tempting to assume that if behavior improves after injury, then there is recovery of the original behavior. In this case it should be a simple matter of seeing how the brain changes and then concluding that the functional restitution results from the observed neuronal changes. Unfortunately, it is not so straightforward. Consider the following personal example. One morning in January 1986, I awoke to discover that I was was unable to see anything in the left half of visual space. In fact, everything appeared absolutely black (a condition known as hemianopia). In view of my age at the time (38 years) and a history of classic migraine, it seems likely that I had experienced what is known as a migraine-induced stroke. This is a condition in which certain blood vessels contract and restrict blood flow, which is known as a spasm, and stay closed long enough to deprive neurons of oxygen and glucose, leading to cell death.

Within a few hours the left visual field began to change. The lower quadrant of my visual world began to return, and within a few more hours my vision appeared to be fairly normal in the lower left field. The upper quadrant was very slow to change, however, and a computed tomography (CT) scan revealed damage to the lower bank of the right calcarine fissure (Fig. 3.1), which is the region in the occipital lobe containing the primary visual area. As the field defect slowly resolved it became clear that I had lost pattern vision in one-fourth of the foveal representation, which is the central region of the retina that is used for fine vision such as in reading, and I had reduced acuity in the remaining upper left quadrant. There were changes in my vision over the next weeks and months, however, that could be described as "recovery." I was initially unable to read because when I looked at words the left-hand portion of the word fell in the abnormal visual field (Fig. 3.1). Similarly, I had difficulty recognizing faces, as people were "missing" much of the left side of their faces. This made looking at people's faces quite

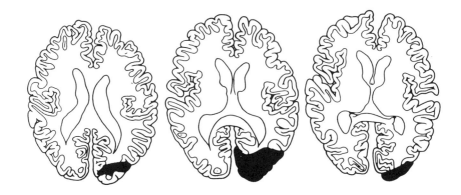

INTRODUCTION

Damage to the visual systems is manifested in a great variety of symptoms. Thus, although complete central blindness is possible, damage to neocortical regions produces only relative blindness such that form perception, for example, is lost but light detection is maintained. Similarly, the relative blindness may be for a single feature of visual perception, such as colour, or may be manifested as an inability to know or understand the meaning of visual stimuli, as in an agnosia. (For a review of visual perceptual symptoms, see ▆▆▆▆▆▆▆▆shaw, 1990, Chapter 12).

Although the principal ▆▆▆▆▆▆▆g visual organization in the first part of this c▆▆▆▆▆▆▆▆▆▆▆▆l cases with anatomical verification ▆▆▆▆▆▆▆▆▆▆▆▆e last 50 years has seen an emph▆▆▆▆▆▆▆▆▆▆▆▆e effects of surgical ▆▆▆▆▆▆s and the activity of single units in different cortical regions. Nonetheless, the investigation of clinical disturbances of vision remains a powerful tool in understanding the nature of visual disturbances and especially in understanding the changes in visual symptoms after a cerebral injury, which I shall refer to as 'recovery'. One difficulty in studying human cases with damage to the visual cortex, however, is that in view of the location of this tissue, which is buried deep within a sulcus on the medial surface of each hemisphere, it is rare to have access to patients whose damage is restricted to just the primary visual region. Hence, when such patients become available it is significant and worth studying in some detail (e.g. Weiskrantz, 1986).

Symptoms of damage to the primary visual cortex

FIG. 3.1.   Top: Extent of the occipital infarct in case B. K. Bottom: Illustration of the Extent of the residual scotoma. If the reader fixates on the bottom right corner of the darkened area, it is possible to appreciate the difficulty in reading, or in other visual functions. After Kolb (1990b).

disturbing because they had only one eye and I often found myself staring as I "played" with this symptom. Finally, I made many visual errors when I reached for objects. Eight years later, I now read as quickly as I did before the stroke, people have two eyes again, and although I do not believe that my facial memory is as good as it was before, I can recognize people quickly and accurately. It would appear that I have "recovered."

It would be an error to assume that my brain has reorganized in some way to allow me to regain my lost vision, however. A more likely explanation is that, like a cat reduced to walking with three legs, I have compensated for the loss. I am able to read not because I can see in the left upper fovea again but because I do not try to use this region to read with. Rather, I have learned to fixate so that parts of words that once fell in the left upper fovea now fall in the lower fields. I am told by observers that I do this by tilting my head to one side, although I am not conscious of doing this. I should note that I did not specifically set out to learn this strategy but I apparently developed this strategy "spontaneously." This change in fixation also makes facial recognition easier because people are missing only part of their forehead, which likely has little effect on face recognition. My development of a strategy illustrates one of the real difficulties in studying recovery of function. That is, just because a behavior appears to recover does not mean that the lost behavior has returned. Thus, the problem is to determine when recovery has actually occurred as opposed to reflecting compensation.

We can identify at least three outcomes that could occur after brain injury. First, as in my case, there may be compensation resulting from an adaptation to the loss. This could reflect a change in strategy, or it may represent a substitution of a new behavior for the lost one. For example, a person who has a deficit in moving the eyes can be expected to have difficulty in reading. This difficulty can be solved, however, by moving the head, which allows restitution of function (reading) by substitution of one behavior for another. It should be clear, however, that compensation does not reflect a return of the lost function.

A second outcome might be partial restitution of the original behavior. This could reflect recovery from some sort of nonspecific effect of the injury, such as swelling, or it may reflect a genuine return of function. In my case it is likely that the short-term loss of the lower left visual field resulted from some sort of vascular or metabolic abnormality caused by the stroke. The rapid return of vision over a few hours merely reflected the fact that the brain responsible for this vision was not actually damaged, so its function could return. Behaviors that return over a period of months are more likely to reflect a partial restitution of function. This is most clearly seen in patients with significant language disturbances in which the severe deficits in making the movements of the tongue and mouth necessary to speak may dissipate, leaving the person with only a subtle language disturbance, such as in finding words (anomia).

Third, there is the possibility that there could be a complete restitution of the original behavior. Because I have assumed, in chapter 1, that the structural properties of the brain are important to its function, it follows that any permanent injury will affect function permanently. Although it is at least theoretically possible for lost functions to completely return in a plastic brain, careful behavioral analysis shows that this is rarely, if ever, the case in either laboratory animals or human patients. Claims of "recovery" must therefore be evaluated critically with the expectation that the most likely outcome is a partial recovery of function along with considerable substitution of function.

There is one final issue related to the use of the word *recovery*. It is often claimed that a particular treatment produced recovery. In view of the keen interest that people have in getting better, we need to ask what such a claim might mean. It might mean that by taking some type of treatment, such as a drug, there was a return (or partial return) of some behavior, and that this return would not have occurred without the drug. The key point here is the idea that the drug-induced recovery would not otherwise have occurred. There is another interpretation, however. That is, although the behavioral endpoint was the same, there was a faster recovery process than there would be in the absence of the drug. This is quite a different conclusion. Finally, there is a very different perspective. There is an axiom in neuroscience that says "use it or lose it." The implication here is that if behaviors are not used, they are lost. Note that the loss is not due to brain damage directly, but may be due to a failure to use certain behaviors after injury. Consider a person with a stroke that makes it difficult to use the left hand. The person may be capable of making some movements of the fingers, but by failing to use the affected hand, the person may actually lose the ability to use the residual finger ability. Thus, a treatment may make it easier to use the compromised limb, and prevent further loss. In this case recovery actually means less behavioral loss! Indeed, this may be a major role for physiotherapy after cerebral injury. In sum, even once we have agreed on a definition of recovery, we must be careful when we evaluate claims about the efficacy of specific treatments.

RECOVERY FROM BRAIN DAMAGE
IN ADULT HUMAN PATIENTS

Although neurologists and neuropsychologists have been studying behavioral symptoms in patients for well over 100 years, there are very few systematic studies of recovery of function over time. Rather, the emphasis has been on the nature of the chronic behavioral symptoms that patients exhibit, presumably because of an overriding interest in the organization of cerebral processing. Nonetheless, although the most important factors influencing the recovery have yet to be clearly delineated, there is enough evidence from various patient populations to suggest that partial recovery is possible in many patients with cerebral injury. Although stroke patients have been the most extensively studied neurological population, there are several other types of brain injuries that are well suited to studies of recovery. These include patients with closed head injuries, penetrating war injuries, and surgical excisions. I consider each of these patient populations separately. My goal is not be comprehensive but to give a flavor for the nature of recovery that is seen and to illustrate the limitations in recovery with pertinent examples.

Recovery from Stroke

Stroke is a general term that includes any event that results in neuronal death because of an interruption of blood flow. Because the primary symptom of stroke is usually behavioral, it is hardly surprising that people with strokes usually have significant chronic behavioral loss. What is intriguing, however, is the common observation that the severity of behavioral loss frequently declines noticeably over at least the first year. For example, in an extensive survey of aphasia in stroke patients, Kertesz (1979) showed that most patients showed some improvement over time (Table 3.1), and the likelihood of improvement was related to the severity of the initial deficits. Thus, patients with global aphasia, which is a severe language impairment in which patients neither understand nor produce language, showed the least recovery, whereas patients with anomic aphasia, which is a mild language impairment in which there is an inability to give the names of objects, showed the best recovery. Patients with intermediate forms such as Broca's (a primary difficulty in producing speech) or Wernicke's (a primary difficulty in comprehending speech) showed an intermediate level of recovery. The severity of symptoms is almost certainly related to the extent of the lesion, as the global aphasics presumably had much larger infarcts than those patients with anomic aphasia, who undoubtedly had the smallest lesions.

Recovery from stroke is not limited to language functions, as many damaged

TABLE 3.1
Final Outcome of Aphasia

| Group | Outcome | | | |
	Poor (0–25)	Fair (25–50)	Good (50–75)	Very Good (75–100)
Global	81	13	0	6
Broca	0	46	46	8
Wernicke	31	46	23	0
Anomic	0	0	23	77

Note. Numbers represent percentage of patients showing a particular outcome. The outcome was determined by performance on objective tests of language production and comprehension. Outcome scores are percentiles. After Kertesz (1979).

functions will improve. For example, there is overwhelming evidence that patients with right hemisphere lesions show a consistent evolution of behavioral symptoms over time. Thus, people with right superior parietal strokes fail to respond to stimulation in the contralateral (i.e., left) part of their world, but this symptom rarely persists. Most patients eventually begin to respond to the formerly neglected hemiworld, although their responses are not normal. Recovery passes through two stages. The first is characterized by the person's beginning to respond to stimuli on the neglected side, but doing so as if the stimuli were on the good side. The person responds to and orients to visual, tactile, or auditory stimuli on the left side of the body as if they were on the right. The second stage, known as simultaneous extinction, occurs when the person responds to stimuli on the hitherto neglected side unless both sides are stimulated simultaneously, in which case he or she notices only the stimulation on the side ipsilateral to the lesion.

Closed Head Injury

Patients with closed head injuries represent a variable patient population, as the extent and location of the injury may vary with the severity of the head trauma, the precise angle of the head blow, and so on (see Table 3.2). Nonetheless, it is possible to reach several conclusions from the available evidence. First, the prognosis for extensive recovery from a coma lasting more than a few days is

TABLE 3.2
Primary and Secondary Brain Injury after
Closed Head Trauma

Primary brain injury
  Macroscopic lesions
    Contusions underlying the site of impact
    Contrecoup contusion frequently in the undersurfaces of
      the frontal lobes and tips of the temporal lobes
  Microscopic lesions
    Widespread shearing or stretching of nerve fibers
Secondary mechanisms of brain injury
  Intracranial hemorrhage
  Edema in white matter adjacent to focal mass lesions
  Diffuse brain swelling
  Ischemic brain damage
  Raised intracranial pressure
  Brain shift and herniation
Secondary insult from extracerebral events
  Effects of multiple injuries
    Hypoxia
    Fat embolism

Note. After Levin, Benton, and Grossman (1982).

TABLE 3.3
Comparison of Outcome in Survivors of Severe Head Injury
at Different Centers

Series	Good Recovery	Moderate Disability	Severe Disability	Persistent Vegetative State
Galveston	37	44	19	0
Glasgow	45	34	16	5
Los Angeles	28	28	35	9
Netherlands	57	31	11	1
Richmond	51	35	10	4
San Diego	66	16	12	6

Note. Numbers represent percentage of patients in each series. Patients who died are excluded. After Levin et al. (1982).

poor and the degree of recovery is highly variable (Table 3.3). For example, Levin, Grossman, Rose, and Teasdale (1979) summarized the outcome of severe head injury in young adults and found that only 44% were employed a year after injury. Only 33% of their patients were categorized as having made a "good recovery."

Second, in his studies of recovery from aphasia, Kertesz was struck by the fact that patients with closed head injuries showed much more complete and rapid recovery from aphasia than did his stroke patients. This is likely because the strokes damaged larger regions of both cortical and subcortical tissue than did the closed head injuries, and the injuries in strokes were more complete within the language areas. Nonetheless, it is interesting that after awakening from extended comas patients would be aphasic and then would recover, because it seems unlikely that the recovery of language could be due to factors such as a reduction of edema (i.e., swelling), which would likely have resolved well before the patients awakened.

Third, although there are few studies of the long-term consequences of mild closed head injuries, there is accumulating evidence that even concussions with periods of amnesia of only a few seconds or minutes may be correlated with a long-lasting, and likely permanent, cognitive loss (e.g., Gronwall, 1989). In a study of graduate students with a history of a mild head injury (i.e., concussion), Bryan Fantie and I found that even this select group of above average intelligence subjects could be shown to differ significantly from matched controls on tests of interhemispheric transfer in the tactile, auditory, and visual modalities (Fantie & Kolb, 1988, 1989). When subjects had to feel complex tactile patterns, which were out of sight, with one hand and then choose an appropriate match from a group of four others with the other hand, the mild head injury subjects were significantly poorer. Thus, we can see that even apparently "trivial" head injuries can produce long-term consequences. One of the curious questions in the current context is why the brain fails to compensate from what would appear to be a relatively minor insult. Indeed, most of the subjects in our study had had several years to recover. Of course, we do not know how poorly the subjects might have performed had we studied them within days of the concussion. Perhaps there was substantial recovery.

Recovery from Penetrating Head Injury

One of the most intriguing investigations of recovery from cortical injury comes from studies of World War II and Korean War veterans by Teuber and his colleagues (e.g., Teuber, 1975). These patients are excellent subjects for study because they received standardized tests after induction into the army, the subjects were relatively young at the time of injury, and the kind and extent of recovery can be documented through prolonged follow-up by veterans' services. In the initial studies Teuber compared war veterans on tests given 1 week after injury with those given 20 years later. A summary of results is shown in Table 3.4. They reveal that about 40% of subjects showed some type of functional improvement, although the likelihood of improvement declined with age at the time of injury. Perhaps the most discouraging result was the observation that 75% of the patients showed no recovery from aphasia. A similar study of Vietnam War veterans by Mohr et al. (1980) found similar results, although Mohr found somewhat better recovery from aphasia (34%).

More recently, Corkin and her colleagues (Corkin, 1989) have shown that the veterans studied by Teuber may have paid a price for their recovery. Corkin looked at the changes in test performance of the veterans as they approached old age and found a marked decline in performance relative to age-matched veterans who had war injuries outside the brain (Fig. 3.2). That is, relative to their scores in the 1950s, the head-injured veterans with head injuries showed a greater decline in performance in the 1980s than did those veterans with nerve injuries outside the brain. This result suggests that as the brain compensates for neuronal

TABLE 3.4
Recovery in Soldiers with Penetrating Head Injuries

Symptoms	Age at Injury (years)		
	17–21	*22–25*	*26+*
Motor deficits	58	41	26
Somatosensory deficits	46	31	22
Visual field deficits	67	43	14
Aphasia[a]	29	16	

Note. Numbers indicate percentage of sample improved 20 years later in 167 cases from Korean campaign. After Teuber (1975).

[a] Age categories are actually 17–22 and 23+.

FIG. 3.2. Comparison of the long-term consequences of head injuries in World War II veterans. Veterans with head injuries showed a greater decline in performance on the Army General Classification Tests (AGCT) and the hidden figures test than did those veterans with nerve injuries outside the brain. There may be a limit to recovery and a price to pay for early recovery during aging. After Corkin (1989).

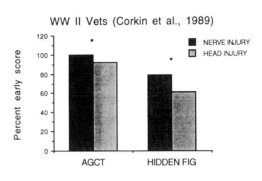

loss during the normal aging process, the brain may use the same mechanisms that it used to support recovery from injury. Thus, the fact that the veterans showed more rapid deterioration as they aged than did the control subjects suggests that there is a limit to the duration of plastic changes in the brain that can support recovery. This may also partly account for the fact that recovery appears to be related to lesion size. It presumably takes more plastic changes to compensate for larger than smaller injuries. Corkin's results are also significant because they represent the only study that makes the point that recovery may be transient after brain injury. The recent return of polio symptoms in "recovered" victims of the polio epidemic in the 1940s and 1950s may provide another example of the limitations of recovery mechanisms and the transient nature of recovery in the aging brain.

Recovery from Surgical Excision

Patients who undergo surgical removals of cerebral tissue for the treatment of intractable epilepsy of various etiologies (e.g., vascular abnormalities, tumor, closed head injury) provide a unique group from which to study recovery of function because it is possible to do neuropsychological evaluations prior to as well as after surgery. Studies of excision patients allow us to draw at least three conclusions.

1. Cerebral injury may produce some general symptoms that are related to factors such as edema. For example, in her extensive studies of patients over the past 45 years, Brenda Milner has consistently found a postoperative drop in intelligence quotient that recovers over time. Curiously, the drop in IQ occurs independent of the lesion location (temporal, frontal, parietal), which suggests that the brain may be responding to some nonspecific insult, such as edema. This hypothesis is consistent with the observation that cortisone, which reduces the edema, lessens the drop in IQ. In this case, the recovery would not be due to compensatory change in the brain.

2. In the case of stroke patients, patients with lesions to the language zones show rather good recovery from their dysphasias. Indeed, the recovery from even near total removals of Broca's area has led some to question the necessity of this classical speech area for language (e.g., Zangwill, 1975).

3. In contrast to their general recovery of intelligence quotients, surgical excision patients may show virtually no change in other sorts of neuropsychological functioning. For example, Milner (1975) has also shown that although right temporal lobe patients show a marked improvement in intelligence quotients, they show no improvement whatsoever in their ability to recall complex visual material such as geometric figures.

The failure to see any improvement in memory functions is somewhat surprising in view of the recovery from aphasias but appears to be a consistent finding on other tests of complex cognitive function. For example, Laughlin Taylor, Brenda Milner, and I studied patients with unilateral frontal lobe excisions on a series of tests measuring: (a) the ability to copy sequences of arm or facial movements, (b) the recognition of facial expressions, and (c) the production of facial expressions. Patients with unilateral frontal lobe lesions were studied either 2 weeks after their surgery or a year or more later and were compared to normal control subjects (Kolb & Milner, 1981a, 1981b; Kolb & Taylor, 1981, 1988). The patients were studied at Montreal Neurological Institute, where they were undergoing unilateral frontal lobe surgery for the relief of intractable epilepsy (for representative brain maps, see Kolb & Milner, 1981b). The frontal-lobe patients were young (mean age around 25 years) and were of average intelligence. There was no difference in the effects of left versus right hemisphere removals on the measures I am reporting, so patients with left- and right-side lesions were considered as a single group. The patients were compared to normal control subjects who were matched for age and education.

Movement Copying. It was our expectation that because aphasic patients with frontal strokes show improvement in the control of language-related movements (see earlier), it seemed likely that patients with surgical removal of frontal lobe tissue would also show improvements in movement control. This was not the case.

Subjects were asked to copy a sequence of arm or facial movements, and their accuracy in making the movement sequences was scored (Fig. 3.3; see Kolb & Milner, 1981b, for details of the procedure). Patients with frontal lobe excisions had little difficulty in making the individual movements, such as sticking out the tongue or making a closed fist, but they were poor at copying the movement sequences, especially facial movement sequences. What was surprising, however, is that the patients were equally impaired at 2 weeks versus several years after surgery (Fig. 3.4). Indeed, we had the opportunity to test a small number of

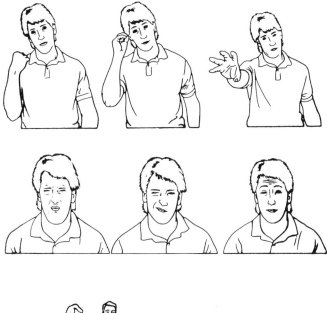

FIG. 3.3.   Tasks used in the copying of arm movement sequences (top) and facial movement sequences (middle). The bottom cartoon illustrates an example of the test of production of facial expression. The subject's task is to produce the appropriate expression for the faceless character.

subjects more than 10 years after their surgeries and they performed no better than the acute patients.

Production of Facial Expressions.   One of the most salient symptoms of frontal lobe injuries in primates is the marked reduction in the production of facial expressions (Kolb, 1990a). This reduction can be seen in the spontaneous production of facial expressions (Kolb & Milner, 1981a) or in the ability of

A.   Producing facial expression

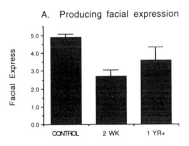

B.   Perceiving facial expression

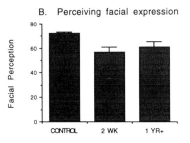

FIG. 3.4. Summary of the performance of frontal lobe patients 2 weeks versus 1 year or more after unilateral frontal lobectomy. Values indicate means and standard errors. In all cases the lesioned patients differed significantly from the normal control subjects but did not differ from one another.

C.   Copying facial movement sequences

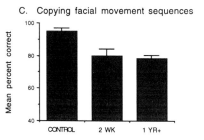

patients to produce facial expressions that are appropriate to the situation (Kolb & Taylor, 1988). In one test we showed patients a series of cartoons in which one character was faceless (Fig. 3.3). The subjects' task was to make a facial expression that was appropriate for the situation depicted in the cartoon. We videotaped the subjects' behavior and then scored the expressions using several different scoring procedures. One scoring procedure was based on Eckman's facial affect scoring system (FAST), in which different parts of the face, such as the forehead, nose, eyes, and mouth, were scored separately according to a series of criteria derived from the study of normal subjects. The results showed that even though frontal lobe patients could mimic facial expressions shown to them, they made very few facial movements in the faceless cartoon test (Fig. 3.4). Furthermore, as in the copying of arm and facial movement sequences, there was no improvement over recovery time.

Recognition of Facial Expressions.   Laughlin Taylor and I had shown that patients with frontal lobe lesions are not only impaired at producing facial expressions, but they are also poor at recognizing the facial expressions in others. Thus, we took the opportunity to see if the ability of frontal-lobe patients to recognize facial expressions might change over recovery time. In one task subjects matched a series of photographs from *Life* magazine with key photographs of one of six distinct emotions (sad, fear, happy, anger, disgust, surprise). In a second task, the subjects choose the key photograph that was appropriate for the faceless character in cartoons like those used in the movement task. The results showed a significant effect of frontal lobe injury on both the face-matching and cartoon tests, but there was no difference between the short-term and long-term recovery times on either task (Fig. 3.4).

In sum, we found no evidence of any recovery of frontal lobe functions in our patients, even with several years of postoperative recovery. Milner (1964) made a similar observation on the performance of frontal lobe patients on several other frontal lobe tasks including the Wisconsin Card Sorting Test.

Conclusions

It is possible to reach six conclusions regarding recovery from brain damage in human patients.

1. There is little doubt that partial recovery does occur after many forms of brain injury.

2. There is marked variability in the extent to which recovery occurs in different patients and after different forms of injury.

3. Recovery appears to be more extensive for language functions than for most other cognitive functions.

4. Some instances of recovery can reasonably be ascribed to processes such as the reduction of edema, whereas other examples of recovery appear to be unrelated to such changes.

5. There appear to be limits to recovery, and there is clear evidence that recovery does not always occur. Indeed, it appears that there is rather little recovery of specific cognitive functions in epileptic patients undergoing cortical excision to relieve the seizures. This lack of recovery in the epileptic patients may represent the long-standing nature of the preexisting brain injury, the possibility that epileptic brains are somewhat different in their plastic properties, or some other factor. It should be noted, however, that the lesions in the epileptic patients are normally restricted to neocortical tissue, whereas the injuries in naturally occurring injuries, such as strokes, usually include subcortical damage. This difference may prove to be important in understanding the "rules" predicting recovery. However, I note too that even in the case of stroke-induced infarcts to the sensory areas there may be limited recovery of function.

6. There is reason to suspect that recovery may be reversible. Thus, as patients age it appears that the mechanisms that promote recovery from brain damage earlier in life may be called on to compensate for neuronal deterioration associated with aging, which in turn may lead to a return of the symptoms of the earlier brain injury.

RECOVERY FROM BRAIN DAMAGE IN ADULT
LABORATORY ANIMALS

Although there are hundreds of studies that purport to describe recovery of function in laboratory animals with cerebral injury, few have actually shown that a particular behavior is lost after an injury and then it returns some time later. Rather, the typical experiment examines the effect of some treatment, such as a drug or experience, on the behavior of animals that receive a cerebral injury. This behavior is then compared to that of other animals that received some type of "control" treatment. If the group with the specific treatment performs better than those without it, it is inferred that some form of recovery process has been influenced by the treatment in question. This type of experiment is legitimate, but it is not the optimal design to make inferences about the loss and subsequent return of the ability to perform particular behaviors or solve problems. Similarly, many studies have looked at the effect of particular preoperative events on the later severity of symptoms, but again, this is not directly relevant to the question of how behavior changes after cerebral injury and how the changes are related to brain plasticity. It is the evolution of behavioral change after injury that is of special interest to me here, for it is possible to correlate the emergence of behaviors with neuronal changes. My review of recovery from cortical injuries will therefore be selective and will emphasize those studies that bear most directly on the investigations of plasticity to follow in later chapters. I will begin, however, with some general comments on the nature of behavioral investigation in the laboratory rat.

Analysis of Behavioral Change in the Rat

A detailed description of the analysis of behavior in the rat is beyond the scope of this discussion, but the way behavior is analyzed is fundamental to the nature of the inferences that we can make about behavior and brain relationships. In the 1920s there developed a notion that laboratory animals should be tested in a single behavioral task and then sacrificed, whereas additional animals were tested in other tasks. Thus, as Lashley and others began to do lesion studies in animals, they were influenced by the view of behaviorism that the behavior of animals was uniquely influenced by experiences and that intersubject variation was due largely to differences in environmental experiences. In this context it was reasonable to suppose that studies of decorticated rats would best be done on subjects with no previous experiences in psychological studies. Behavioral study of the naive animal usually involved a single test of learning, with little attention paid to other behaviors that the animal might exhibit. Although behavioral neuroscience is now long removed from the behavioristic bias prevalent into the 1950s, the idea that the way to study cortical function is to give an animal some sort of neuropsychological learning test remains. One of the strong biases that my colleagues and I bring to behavioral analysis is the idea that single behavioral measures provide very biased estimates of behavior, especially if the behavioral measure is the performance of some sort of learned task (e.g., Kolb & Whishaw, 1983b; Whishaw, Kolb, & Sutherland, 1983). It is our view that although such tasks can be useful in teasing out subtle behavioral effects of cerebral injury, such analyses ignore most of the behaviors that the cortex evolved to support (e.g., Warren, 1972). Thus, we have developed a neuropsychological assessment battery (Table 3.5) that assesses a wide variety of species typical and learned behaviors. This battery is analogous to those developed for studying human patients (e.g., Kolb & Whishaw, 1990). It is worth noting that most of what has been learned about recovery in human patients comes from studies using bat-

TABLE 3.5

Behavioral Assessment of the Rat: A Partial Summary of Features
of Behavior for Examination

Measure	Specific Feature
Appearance	Body weight, core temperature, eyes, feces, fur, genitals, muscle tone, pupils, responsiveness, saliva, teeth, toenails, vocalizations
Sensory and sensorimotor	Response to stimuli of each sensory modality presented in both home cage and in novel place such as open field
Posture and immobility	Behavior when spontaneously immobile, immobile without posture or tone; tonic immobility or animal hypnosis; environmental influences on immobility
Movement	General activity, movement initiation, turning, climbing, walking, swimming, righting responses, limb movements in different activities such as reaching or bar pressing, oral movements such as in licking or chewing, environmental influences on movement
Species-typical behaviors	All species-typical behaviors such as grooming, food hoarding, foraging, sleep, maternal or sexual behavior, play, and burying
Learning	Operant and respondent conditioning and learning sets, especially including measures of spatial learning, avoidance learning, and memory

Note. After Whishaw, Kolb, and Sutherland (1983).

teries of tests and studying the same patients repeatedly over time, so it makes sense to use the same procedure in the study of laboratory animals.

One of the advantages of measuring behaviors other than the learning of neuropsychological tasks is that it is possible to study a particular behavior repeatedly and to note changes over time. For example, one behavior that rats engage in is the trimming of their toenails (Whishaw, Kolb, Sutherland, & Becker, 1983). This is a complex behavior, for it requires that the animal hold the paw still and make fine biting movements to trim the claw. This behavior emerges fairly late in adolescence and continues throughout adulthood until old age, at which time the behavior declines. Indeed, we have seen many aged rats (24 months or older) with claws that are more than three times longer than that usually found in a normal middle-aged animal. In the course of studying claw cutting in rats with frontal cortex injury we found that even relatively small lesions disrupted this behavior permanently (e.g., Kolb, 1987; Whishaw et al., 1983). In fact, many frontal-decorticated rats appeared to completely stop claw cutting even though they were otherwise clean and healthy looking. This motor loss is not unique, however, as frontal operates are also chronically impaired at other fine motor skills such as using their forepaws to reach for food. Nonetheless, the same animals often show marked recovery of many other abilities such as the performance on tests of spatial navigation through mazes. The contrasting recovery on some types of tests and not on others is important not only for reaching inferences about the nature of recovery of function, but also for studies in which plastic changes in the brain are being studied in the same animals.

Recovery of Movement

Until recently, the definition of the motor and somatosensory cortex of the rat was handicapped by: (a) the failure to determine the correlation between the maps defined by electrical stimulation and those defined anatomically and (b) the failure to properly recognize and characterize the motor abilities of the rat. Indeed, until recently it was common for researchers to believe that motor cortex lesions in rats had little effect on motoric behavior. It is now clear, however, that there are clear effects of motor cortex lesions on: (a) the ability to reach with the forelimb and grasp objects such as food (Whishaw, O'Connor, & Dunnett, 1986), (b) the ability to protrude the tongue to lick food (Whishaw & Kolb, 1983), and (c) the ability to use the limbs for walking (e.g. Gentile, Green, Nieburgs, Schmelzer, & Stein, 1978; Kolb & Whishaw, 1983a). These behaviors provide good models for recovery, because they allow us to study the execution of the same behavior repeatedly over time and to characterize the nature of the recovery and/or compensation. Consider the following examples.

Forelimb Reaching.   Ian Whishaw and his colleagues have developed a procedure for assessing the ability of rats to reach using the forepaws (see Fig. 3.5) (e.g., Whishaw, Dringenberg, & Pellis, 1992; Whishaw, O'Connor, & Dunnett,

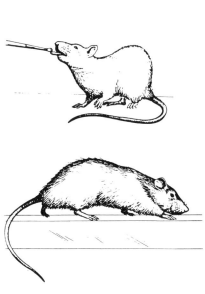

FIG. 3.5. Illustration of three behaviors of the rat. Top: The reaching behavior of the rat in the Whishaw reaching task. The animal must reach through bars (not shown) to grasp a piece of food and retrieve it. Middle: The licking behavior of a rat. The length of tongue extension can be measured by various means, such as by requiring the animal to lick through a slot. Bottom: Walking on a narrow beam. Task difficulty can be varied by making the beam progressively narrower.

1986; Whishaw & Pellis, 1990; Whishaw, Pellis, Gorny, & Pellis, 1991). The essential features of the task are that (a) rats learn to reach through bars to retrieve small pieces of food, and (b) the animals can be forced to use just one paw by placing a bracelet around the wrist of the other arm so that it does not fit through the bars. Reaching ability can be assessed by measuring endpoint success such as accuracy of reaching (i.e., percent of reaches in which the animal successfully retrieves food) or by videotaping the animal's behavior and doing more refined kinematic analyses on different aspects of the actual movements. I have used Whishaw's procedure to examine the recovery of reaching behavior in rats that were given either unilateral or bilateral lesions of the motor cortex. (The animals with unilateral lesions were forced to use their paw contralateral to the injury.) An example of the results of such an experiment is illustrated in Fig. 3.6. It can be seen that reaching was virtually abolished by the lesions and showed a slow improvement over the recovery time.[1] Thus, over a period of 6 weeks the

---

[1]Analysis of variance showed a significant main effect of group [$F(4,48) = 69.35$, $p < .001$] and time [$F(4,16) = 238.8$, $p < .001$] as well as an interaction of group and time [$F(16, 192) = 526.7$, $p < .001$].

A. Forelimb Reaching

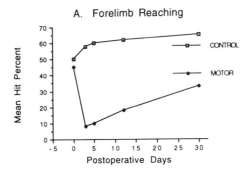

B. Tongue Extension

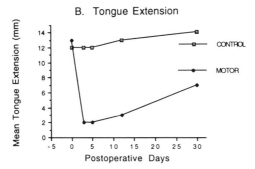

FIG. 3.6.   (A) Summary of recovery of forelimb reaching behavior in rats with bilateral lesions of the motor cortex. (B) Summary of recovery of tongue use in rats with bilateral lesions of the motor cortex.

animals slowly recovered their ability to obtain food. Note, however, that the lesioned animals were still impaired after 30 days. Subsequent measures over the following months showed very little additional improvement.

One of the questions that my experiment did not answer was how the animals managed to improve. This question has been addressed by Whishaw and his colleagues in a series of elegant experiments. By using sophisticated behavioral analyses (Eshkol-Wachmann movement notation and video kinematics) they have been able to show that there are two types of behavioral change that vary with lesion size. First, in their studies, rats with small unilateral motor cortex injuries eventually were able to reach almost normally and had only mild impairments in lifting, aiming, and advancing the limb. Thus, they appeared to show substantial "recovery" of the original behaviors. Second, in contrast, rats with larger unilateral motor cortex lesions that included all of the forelimb representation showed a chronic loss in the ability to pronate and supinate the forearm in order to obtain the food. The animals compensated for this loss by a variety of whole-body movements that indirectly guide the limb movements and allow the animals some success in reaching for food. This compensation does not allow accurate guidance of the forelimb, however, and the animals are impaired at the endpoint measure of success in grasping food. The distinction between the recovery from small, subtotal lesions of the forelimb representation and the compensation after larger complete lesions of the forelimb area has important implications for understanding the neural mechanisms underlying the recovery. In particular, we can predict that in the case of small lesions there may be changes in the remaining motor cortex that could underlie the recovery of function. In contrast, in the case of the larger lesions there may be changes in other cortical regions that allow the compensatory movements to become more efficient with practice.

Although the reaching behavior of rats with motor cortex lesions may not be normal, it is somewhat surprising that the animals are as good as they are, because many rats with complete removal of one hemisphere are incapable of reaching at all (Whishaw & Kolb, 1988). Similarly, human patients with large strokes that include motor cortex also show rather poorer recovery. In order to examine this question we have studied rats with middle cerebral artery strokes that remove most of the motor and somatosensory cortex. Thus, in collaboration with Claudio Cuello and his colleagues at McGill University we have studied the recovery of motor abilities in rats given large unilateral strokes that removed most of the motor and somatosensory cortex. These animals show very poor reaching with the contralateral paw, even after several months of retraining. Indeed, many of the animals were never able to reach successfully again. This observation accords well with studies of humans with middle cerebral strokes and provides another model for studying processes of recovery. I return to this paradigm later, for we have been able to show that certain treatments, such as infusion with nerve growth factor, markedly enhance reaching ability in our rats with strokes.

Tongue Extension.   Like all mammals, rats are able to stick their tongues out to obtain food items (Fig. 3.5). This can be quantified by various means, such as has having the animals lick soft food from a ruler held against their cage bars. By using this procedure it is possible to measure the ability of rats to stick out their tongues and to get a quantification of this ability (Whishaw & Kolb, 1983). This is a sensitive measure of the integrity of the motor cortex, in large part because more neurons are devoted to moving the tongue than any other part of the body. When rats are given motor cortex lesions that include the tongue representation there is very little recovery of this function, and even after several months of testing they rarely can extend their tongue much past the teeth (Kolb & Gibb, 1991; Kolb & Whishaw, 1983a; Whishaw & Kolb, 1989). It appears that the brain cannot compensate for the loss of the cortical neurons projecting to the cranial nerve nuclei that control voluntary tongue protrusion. It is worth noting, however, that rats with motor cortex lesions that spare part of the tongue representation have a lesser deficit in tongue extension, which shows some recovery over time. Thus, when we tested our animals with large motor cortex lesions we found a transient deficit in tongue use that had cleared in about 3 weeks after the surgery (Fig. 3.6).[2]

Walking. One of the most striking observations of rats with motor cortex lesions is that they appear to be far less debilitated at walking than human patients with middle cerebral strokes. This difference does not represent a difference in the cortical control of walking so much as it reflects a fundamental difference in the manner in which humans and rats walk. That is, humans walk on two legs and rats walk on four legs. More careful analysis of walking in rats with motor cortex injuries has shown that there is a severe deficit in being able to walk along a relatively narrow beam (e.g., Gentile et al., 1978; Kolb & Whishaw, 1983a). Thus, when the walking task becomes more difficult and requires careful steps and control of balance, rats are impaired to the point of simply being unable (or unwilling) to move at all. I studied the recovery of beam walking in the animals with motor cortex lesions whose reaching and tongue extension behaviors were discussed earlier. The animals were trained to walk preoperatively along a 4-cm-wide beam to obtain food reward. The day after surgery those animals with bilateral lesions could not be encouraged to move once they were placed on the beam, but by the fourth postoperative day they were able to move on the beam and they were nearly as good as controls a month later.[3] However, although the animals now negotiated the beam to obtain reward, their posture did not appear to be normal and the animals with bilateral lesions tended to grasp the edge of the beam rather than walk along its center. This chronic deficit in gait has been studied in more detail by Gentile and her colleagues, who have shown that rats with sensorimotor cortex lesions show compensatory changes in the angle that the body is carried relative to the ground (Gentile et al., 1977). Thus, it appears that recovery from large motor lesions involves compensatory changes in posture for both walking and forelimb reaching. Gentile did not study animals with small lesions, however, so it is possible that like reaching, walking may show some restitution of function if the damage is subtotal.

Postural and Motor Asymmetry. Jones and Schallert (1992) used another interesting paradigm to study recovery of movement. They noticed that rats with small unilateral lesions of sensorimotor cortex favored the contralateral forelimb when investigating a novel environment. Thus, as the animals stopped to investi-

---

[2]Analysis of variance showed a significant group effect [$F(4,48) = 31.15, p < .001$], effect of time [$F(4,192) = 669.8, p < .001$], and a significant interaction [$F(16, 192) = 12.44, p < .001$].

[3]Analysis of variance on the number of abnormal steps taken on the beam showed a significant main effect of lesion group [$F(4,48) = 14.65, p < .001$] and recovery time [$F(16,192) = 26.9, p < .001$], as well as a significant interaction [$F(4,192) = 4.31, p < .001$].

gate the environment they tended to support their weight with the paw ipsilateral to the injury and to hold the contralateral paw off the floor close to the body. As the animals recovered, they slowly began to reuse the affected limb. This is an interesting behavioral paradigm, because it is possible to study compensation by the ipsilateral (unaffected) limb at the same time as observing recovery in the contralateral limb. As a twist on the Jones and Schallert experiment, Mike Melynchuk and I repeated the original study but added three more groups. One group received bilateral sensorimotor lesions, a second group received a unilateral sensorimotor lesion followed 15 days later with a similar lesion on the opposite side, and a third group received a unilateral lesion followed 15 days later by an expansion of the original lesion. We had noted that by 15 days the animals had begun to show recovery of the postural asymmetry, so we hoped that the second lesions would tell us which hemispheres were involved in this recovery. Our expectation was that the animals with a two-stage bilateral lesion would show a sudden reversal of the postural asymmetry and the animals would now favor the paw contralateral to the newly injured hemisphere. This would suggest that the originally damaged hemisphere had partially recovered and was capable of supporting the animals' behavior. If the animals showed no asymmetry, which was what we found in the one-stage bilateral animals, we could conclude that there had been little recovery in the originally damaged hemisphere. Finally, we also anticipated that if the damaged hemisphere was involved in the recovery from the original injury, then an expansion of the injury would reverse the recovery. On the other hand, if some other structure (i.e., the normal hemisphere or a subcortical structure) were responsible for the improvement in behavior, then there would be no change in the pattern of behavior. The results confirmed the hypothesis that the originally injured hemisphere was involved in the recovery (Fig. 3.7). In order to statistically analyze the results of our experiment we calculated an asymmetry score for each rat, in which we counted the total number of times that each animal favored each forelimb and then used the following formula: (left − right)/(left + right). This analysis confirmed what is evident from Fig. 3.7:

1. Lesions of sensorimotor cortex produced a significant postural asymmetry that slowly recovered over time.
2. A second lesion in the normal hemisphere reversed the asymmetry as the animals now favored the most recently injured side. Thus, there must have been some form of plasticity in the originally damaged hemisphere.
3. Increasing the lesion size potentiated the deficit. This suggests that the region around the lesion may play some role in the recovery process and again suggests some form of plastic change in the damaged hemisphere. If the recovery were entirely dependent on the normal hemisphere, we would not have expected such a severe reinstatement of the original asymmetry.

FIG. 3.7. Postural asymmetry after unilateral sensorimotor lesions in the rat. The deviation from zero represents a bias in the use of one paw over the other. On the day after surgery the animals with one-stage unilateral lesions (UN-1) showed a strong tendency to use the paw opposite the normal hemisphere. This slowly improved over the next 29 days. Rats that had the original injury expanded (UN-2) on day 14 had an exaggeration of the original deficit. Rats that had a second-stage lesion to the previously normal hemisphere on day 14 (BI-2) showed a reversal of the asymmetry, as the animals now favored their paw opposite the originally injured hemisphere.

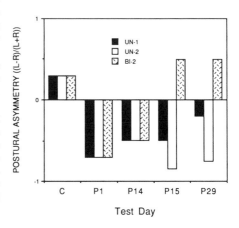

Recovery of Tactile Sensitivity

Tim Schallert and his collaborators devised a test of tactile sensitivity that has proven useful in understanding recovery (Schallert, 1983). In this task, small bits of sticky tape are placed on the ulnar surface of an animal's forearm. Normally, rats remove this tape almost instantly. In contrast, rats with parietal or frontal cortex lesions are slow to remove the tape and, in extreme cases, may appear to ignore it completely (e.g., Kolb & Elliott, 1987; Schallert & Whishaw, 1985). A test analogous to a test of simultaneous extinction can be given to the animals by placing tape on both forearms. Normal animals will remove the tape from each side, and will remove the first piece from either side, more or less at random. Rats with unilateral lesions will always remove the tape contralateral to the normal hemisphere first and will be slow to attend to the tape contralateral to the injured side.

Another way to test tactile sensitivity is to touch the skin (or fur) with a fine piece of nylon or a stiff hair. Animals will have a much higher threshold for detecting the stimulus on the body side opposite a lesion. In one beautiful experiment, Schallert took advantage of the asymmetry in response to fine hairs after unilateral injuries in order to study the process of recovery. He gave rats unilateral lesions to the region of the lateral hypothalamus and found that the animals initially showed a dramatic asymmetry in their responses (Fig. 3.8). Over time, however, the asymmetry vanished, and by 60 days postinjury they responded equally well to both sides. Schallert continued to test the animals for nearly 2 years and, like Corkin's findings with head-injured veterans who grew worse as they aged, he found that the tactile asymmetry reemerged in the elderly brain-injured rats. In other words, it again appears that as the brain ages it is unable to cope with processes necessary to compensate for aging and brain injury. It follows from this logic that elderly animals may not be able to compensate well for brain damage sustained in a brain that has already initiated plastic processes required to cope with aging. In order to test this possibility, we gave rats bilateral frontal cortex lesions at about 2 years of age. The animals were trained postoperatively either on a spatial navigation task (see later) or on Whishaw's reaching task. The old brain-injured animals were unable to acquire either task, even though the normal-aged control animals performed nearly as well as middle-aged control animals. Taken together, the results of our experiment and Schallert's and Corkin's experiments imply that there is a limit to plasticity that the brain can show, and it may be possible to cope with aging or with brain injury but not with both.

Recovery of Spatial Navigation Ability

Perhaps the most common type of experimental paradigm in which recovery in brain-damaged rats is studied is a neuropsychological task in which some type of cognitive performance is believed to be assessed (for a review see Finger & Stein, 1982). Two types of tasks have proven especially popular. In the first, which is known as spatial alteration, rats are trained in a maze that is shaped like a capital T. The animals are placed in the bottom of the T and the task is locate food in one of the two arms forming the cross of the T. Once food is located in one arm, the animal is returned to the start point and is allowed to search again except that the food is now located in the arm opposite to where the animal found the food on the first trial. Thus, the animal must keep track of where food was found on the previous trial and alternate from trial to trial. The task can be made more difficult by imposing a delay of a few seconds between the consumption of

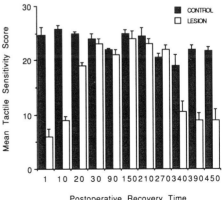

FIG. 3.8. Recovery and loss of tactile function in rats with unilateral lateral hypothalamic lesions. The lesioned animals showed recovery of tactile recognition ability over the first postoperative month, and this was maintained for nearly a year. There was then a progressive loss of function as the animals aged. After Schallert (1983).

the food and the beginning of the next trial, which is known as delayed spatial alternation. Rats with various types of cerebral lesions (e.g., prefrontal cortex, entorhinal cortex, hippocampus) have difficulty learning this task, but most can eventually acquire it. I am not aware of any studies looking at the improvement in performance in this task over time, but there are now many studies showing that different treatments, such as nerve growth factor, reduce the deficit seen after different cerebral lesions. It would be interesting, however, to see how performance on this task changes with postoperative recovery time.

A second popular task was invented by Richard Morris (1980). In this task rats are trained to swim to a platform that is located just under the surface of the water in a large tank (Fig. 3.9). The water is tinted with a bit of powdered milk, and thus the platform becomes invisible to the animal in the tank and can be located only by learning its location relative to a constellation of cues in the extramaze environment. Rats are aquatic animals and learn to find the platform with only a few trials of practice. Performance on this task can be measured by recording the time taken to swim to the platform, measuring the distance swum, or measuring the accuracy in heading directly to the platform (e.g., Sutherland, Whishaw, & Kolb, 1983; Whishaw, 1989). Rats with various cortical or hippo-campal lesions are severely impaired at learning the location of the platform (e.g., Kolb, Sutherland, & Whishaw, 1983a; Sutherland et al., 1983), and in

FIG. 3.9.   Illustration of the Morris water task. The rat's task is to lo-cate a submerged escape platform by using cues available in the room.

many cases the animals are unable to acquire the task, even with extensive training. These deficits are not due to problems in swimming or standing on the platform, because even totally decorticated rats can learn to swim to a visible black platform in the swimming tank. Rather, the problem is one either of learning the location of a hidden platform or of navigating to it. One can draw a simple analog to the problem of finding one's vehicle in a large parking lot when it is the only black one in a sea of white ones versus finding a white car in a lot full white cars. The former problem can be solved by visually locating the black car and walking to it. The latter problem requires knowledge of the spatial location of the car relative to a constellation of cues beyond the lot.

My colleagues and I took advantage of the sensitivity of the Morris task to study the effects of cortical lesions to look at various aspects of the recovery process. I focus on three aspects of our results. First, we considered the non-specific effects of cortical injury on performance of the Morris task. Rats were given lesions of the motor cortex and were trained in the Morris task beginning 3 days after surgery. Rats with motor cortex lesions would not be expected to have chronic deficits on a spatial navigation task, so a transient deficit on this type of task would suggest a "nonspecific" lesion effect, much as Milner found in her IQ results in human patients with cortical lesions. The results were clear: Even unilateral motor cortex lesions impaired the acquisition of the Morris task in the first few postoperative days. This impairment was not due to difficulties in swimming or climbing on the platform, because the animals were capable of swimming to a visible platform. The animals did learn the task, however, and by the end of 2 weeks of recovery they were performing as well as normal control subjects. The results of this experiment are informative, for they imply the assessment of recovery from performance on neuropsychological tasks must exclude the possibility that the improvement in behavior merely reflects the recovery from processes such as ischemia or edema rather than actually reflecting some type of reactive change in the brain.

Second, we considered the long-term recovery of spatial navigation ability in rats with prefrontal lesions. In view of our findings of transient nonspecific effects of lesions in the early postoperative period, Tom Comery and I waited for a month after surgery and then trained rats in the Morris task for eight trials per day for 5 days. We then waited for 6 months before retraining the animals in the same task. The behavioral difference over the 6 months was stunning (Fig. 3.10). Whereas the animals were grossly impaired at learning the location of the plat-form on the initial testing, they were much better 6 months later, and eventually learned the location of the platform. This result suggested that some plastic process, which may have taken weeks or months, had occurred over the 6-month recovery period and this neural change was supporting the behavior. We have evidence that dendritic changes follow such a time course and could, in princi-ple, support recovery (see Chapter 5).

Finally, it appears that there is a poor correlation between the recovery ob-

FRONTAL LESIONS: MORRIS TASK

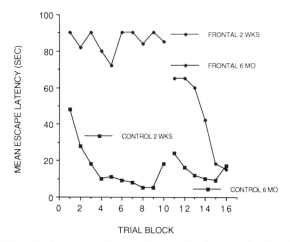

FIG. 3.10.   Performance of rats with frontal lesions on the Morris water task. When first trained a month after surgery the lesioned animals
failed to learn the task. When retested 6 months later the frontal rats
acquired the task.

served in neuropsychological tests and recovery in other tests. For example,
whereas we have evidence that rats show improvement over time in learning
spatial navigation tasks after prefrontal lesions, there is little improvement in
motor tasks such as reaching or in measures of species-typical behavior, such as
food hoarding or social behavior. Thus, the rats who showed improvement over
the 6-month recovery period showed virtually no recovery of forepaw reaching
over the same period. This type of result leads me to three conclusions:

1. It is important to make multiple measures of behavior in studies purporting
to relate brain plasticity and functional recovery. Single measures of behavior
may be misleading.

2. There may be a fundamental difference in the processes underlying recovery of performance on neuropsychological tests and tests of motor or species-
typical behavior.

3. Because the life expectancy of a rat is probably on the order of 2 years, it
is tempting to think of long recovery times in the rat as being on the order of
month. We have evidence that recovery processes continue much longer in the
rat, and Finger, Hart, and Jones (1982) reported that after somatosensory cortex
lesions there was little improvement of tactile discrimination ability at 1 or 6
months later, but there was improvement after 1 or 2 years. The time course of
these changes is similar to those seen in people and may suggest that plastic
processes underlying recovery from cerebral injury may take far longer in the rat
than is generally appreciated.

Serial Lesions

I have already alluded to the fact that larger lesions allow less recovery than do small lesions. In general, if a lesion removes an entire functional system, there typically is far less recovery than if the lesion is partial. Of more interest, however, is the *serial lesion effect,* which refers to the observation that lesions incurred in multiple stages appear to allow more recovery than do single-stage removals of the same size (Finger & Stein, 1982). The serial lesion effect has been seen as a model of slow-growing lesions in humans and would seem to provide an ideal model to search for recovery–plasticity correlations. Unfortunately, despite considerable study, the behavioral phenomena are still controversial (Kolb, 1990c). For example, I know of no instance in which a behavior that is completely lost from a single-stage lesion has been protected by a serial lesion. In general, the serial lesion effect appears to be restricted to performance on neuropsychological tests in which the brain-injured animals are impaired relative to normal control animals, but the lesioned animals do eventually acquire the task. For example, Patrissi and Stein (1975) gave rats one- or two-stage removals of the medial frontal cortex, with a 2-week interoperative period. The animals were trained later in a spontaneous alternation task, a task at which rats with medial frontal lesions are slow to learn, but that they eventually can master. Patrissi and Stein found a significant beneficial effect of the two-stage procedure, a result that Stein and his colleagues found in many other similar studies (see Finger & Stein, 1982). In contrast to the results of Stein's experiments, we have found repeatedly that there is absolutely no benefit in the acquisition of the Morris water task by rats with seriatum removal of the medial frontal cortex. Thus, when I gave rats unilateral medial frontal lesions, followed by a second lesion 2 weeks later, the performance of the animals in the Morris task a month later was indistinguishable from animals given bilateral lesions in one stage. I should note that Arthur Nonneman and I replicated the Patrissi and Stein experiment, which suggests that their result is reliable, but we also found that the same animals did not show a serial lesion advantage on other measures such as food hoarding (Nonneman & Kolb, 1979). The apparent task-dependent nature of the serial lesion effect suggests that either the protective effect of serial lesions is due to some form of compensation, rather than a plastic change in the brain that allows a restitution of the original function, or that the plastic changes in the brain are capable of supporting only a limited range of behaviors.

Conclusions

As with human patients, there is little doubt that partial recovery occurs after cerebral injury in laboratory rats. Several factors appear to modulate this recovery.

  1. The observed recovery recovery is task dependent. Thus, the same animals may show recovery on one behavioral measure and not on another. The

task-dependent nature of the recovery needs further study, because it will likely provide a key to understanding the basis of recovery when it occurs. In general, cognitive behaviors show better recovery than species-typical behaviors, but the performance on some cognitive tasks shows very slow, or no, recovery.

2.   There is little doubt that a relatively lengthy postoperative recovery time is crucial for some types of behavior but not for others. It is not immediately obvious what accounts for this difference.

3.   Lesion size may play an important role in recovery. Thus, lesions that spare part of a functional zone are likely to allow more recovery than complete lesions of the zone. This may reflect the fact that it is easier to reorganize a fragment of a functional area than to reconstruct one in an adjacent region.

4.   There is reason to suspect that as in human patients, recovery in laboratory animals may be reversible. Thus, rats that recover from brain damage in young adulthood may once again show the same symptoms as they age. This result is intriguing because it implies that plastic changes in the brain may have a finite limit and that the same mechanisms may be used for coping with aging as are used in recovery from brain damage.

GENERAL CONCLUSIONS

Is there really recovery after brain damage? The answer to the question posed by this chapter must be, "Yes, under some circumstances." Studies of both human patients and laboratory animals show evidence of at least partial restitution of some types of motor symptoms as well as some cognitive functions. The major difficulty is in the interpretation of the functional recovery. The improvement in the capacity of a brain-injured subject to perform a neuropsychological test does not mean that the original function has, or has not, returned. Many behavioral problems have more than one solution, although some solutions may be more efficient than others. I believe that there needs to be a recognition that adequate behavioral analysis does not mean reporting the number of errors to criterion on some task. There needs to be a careful determination of how behaviors are changed initially by the injury and how they evolve over time. This type of analysis has rarely been applied rigorously to the study of either human patients or laboratory animals, which makes the correlation between functional recovery and brain plasticity difficult.

4 Brain Development and Recovery

Consider the following case histories. P. B. is a 22-year-old business school graduate who was struck by a car and suffered a serious head injury in which the posterior part of the right hemisphere was damaged, requiring emergency surgery to repair the skull and to relieve the pressure from subdural bleeding. In view of the severity of her injury, it proved to be necessary to remove a large region of posterior temporal-parietal cortex during surgery. After the accident she had a left visual field defect but was able to return to her job as a typist/clerk. Upon neuropsychological examination 6 years after the injury, she obtained an average IQ score, although she was relatively better at verbal tests than those requiring manipulation of pictorial information. She had particular difficulty drawing and remembering pictorial information, including faces. Her motor skills were good, and although she initially had difficulty reading because of the visual loss, she overcame this handicap and could read as well as IQ-matched controls. Thus, P. B. had symptoms that were typical of injury to the right posterior cortex in adulthood.

S. S. is an 18-year-old woman who had a difficult birth and forceps delivery. There was a concern that she might have suffered a cerebral injury during the delivery but her early development appeared to be normal. She suddenly began having epileptic seizures at 14 years of age. These seizures were almost certainly a result of her forceps delivery. Neurological examination in adulthood revealed a right parietal cyst that subsequently was removed, and the seizures were arrested. S. S. was an average student in school but had difficulty in Grade 12, especially with English and mathematics. Her neuropsychological assessment at age 18 revealed an average IQ, but she was relatively better at pictorial tests than verbal ones. Furthermore, she had a poor vocabulary score considering her education, IQ, and socioeconomic group, and she had a difficult time with arithmetic. She also had difficulty in repeating sequences of movements shown to her by the examiner, especially those of the face, and had difficulty on various tests that are typically sensitive to frontal-lobe injury. In contrast, she had no difficulty on tests of drawing or visual memory. Thus, S. S. had a right posterior injury at birth but she had symptoms more commonly associated with damage to the frontal lobe.

P. B. and S. S. had similar brain damage, but at different ages, and the consequences could not have been much more different. Several questions arise from the comparison of these two cases. Why were the symptoms of brain damage to the same region different in the two cases? Was the age at which brain damage was sustained responsible for the behavioral differences? Is there an age at which brain damage is likely to allow better recovery of function than at other ages, or are the effects of brain damage at different ages simply different? It is issues such as these that I address in this chapter.

BRAIN DEVELOPMENT

The mammalian brain follows a general pattern of development, beginning as a hollow tube, which surrounds a single ventricle where cells are generated along the ventricular wall and then migrate out to their proper location (Fig. 4.1). The development of the brain includes several stages: cell proliferation, cell differentiation, dendritic and axonal growth, synaptogenesis, cell and synaptic death, and gliogenesis (Fig. 4.2). The order of these events is similar across species, but because the gestation time varies dramatically across different mammalian species, the timing of the events relative to birth varies considerably. This can be seen in the common observation that whereas kittens and puppies are born helpless and blind (their eyes do not open for about 2 weeks), human babies are born somewhat more mobile and with their eyes open, and calves at birth are able to stand and walk about and, of course, have their eyes open. I note, parenthetically, that although I suspect few readers have observed baby rats, they are born less mature than kittens and their eyes do not open until postnatal day 15 (P15). Thus, we can see that birth date is a poor marker of brain development. Rather, we must consider the embryological state of the nervous system with respect to the various stages of development. Because I intend to emphasize behavioral outcome in developing infants and rats, I briefly compare the development of the cortex of the human and the rat.

Neural Generation and Migration

Brain cells are generated along the ventricular wall and then migrate out to their proper location in the cortex. This is not a simple event, because the migrating

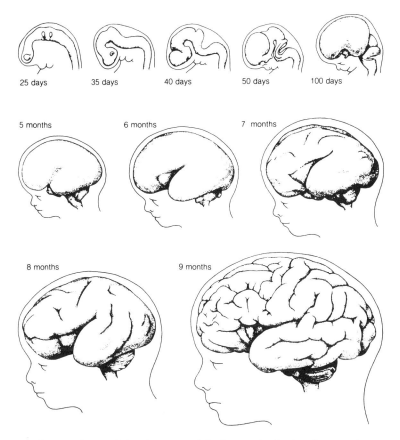

FIG. 4.1.   Prenatal development of the human brain showing a series of embryonic and fetal stages. From Cowan (1979). Adapted by permission.

neurons must form different layers and dozens of functional regions. In humans, approximately 10^9 cells are required to form the mature cortex of a single cerebral hemisphere (Rakic, 1988). This is a lot of neurons, and according to Cowan (1979), during the time of peak growth of the human brain, neurons must be generated at the rate of more than 250,000 neurons per minute! There is some disagreement over how long cells destined for the cortex divide, but cell proliferation appears to be largely complete by the fifth month of gestation. Cell migration proceeds for several months after this time, possibly continuing postnatally, and the cortical lamination continues to develop until after birth. Marin-Padilla (1970a, 1970b) studied the sequential lamination of the human motor cortex in ontogenesis and found that by the fifth embryonic month, cortical layers V and VI are visible, although not yet mature in appearance until birth.

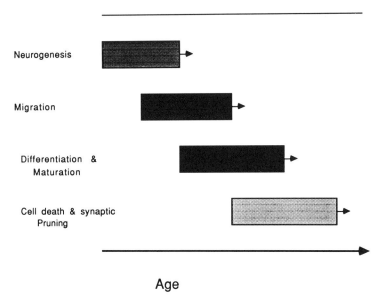

Neurogenesis

Migration

Differentiation &
Maturation

Cell death & synaptic
Pruning

Age

FIG. 4.2.   Schematic illustration of the stages of development in the brain. Each successive stage begins before the completion of the previous one.

More superficial layers develop later; they are first visible at about 7 months, and are not mature in appearance until after birth. Various types of local-circuit neurons appear in all cortical layers during the late prenatal period, but all are formed by birth.

In contrast to the 9-month gestation of the human, the rat is born after only 3 weeks of gestation. Neural proliferation continues in the cortex until birth, and neuronal migration continues for at least 5–7 days postnatally (Fig. 4.3). Thus, on the basis of neural division, a newborn rat would appear to be equivalent to

FIG. 4.3.   (opposite page) Top: Diagram of tritiated thymidine-labeled cells in the rat brain that originated on the 17th (ovals) or 20th intra-uterine day (black). Notice that by the day of birth migration is not yet complete but continues until about the fifth day in the frontal cortex. The mature pattern is illustrated in the 3½ weeks stage. After Hicks and D'Amato (1970). Bottom: Schematic illustration of rate of development of basal and apical dendrites of the pyramidal cells of the superficial and deep layers of the cerebral cortex of the rat. Note that the cells in the deep cortex are well differentiated relative to the more superficial cells that have just completed migration. The superficial cells are especially sensitive to the effects of early cortical lesions. Numbers indicate postoperative age in days. After Berry (1974).

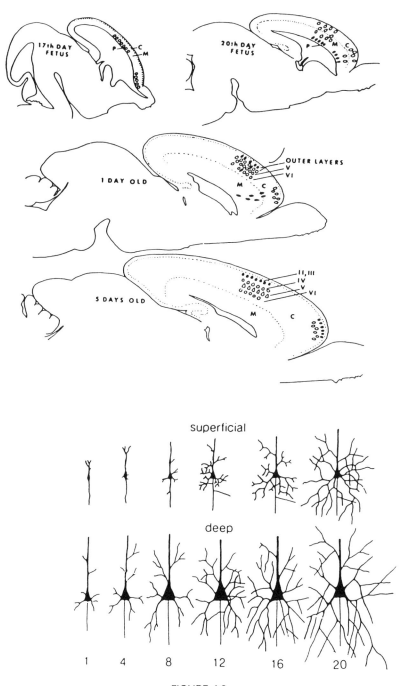

FIGURE 4.3.

about a 5-month-old human fetus. Or, on the basis of neural migration, the newborn human may be equivalent to about a 5-day-old rat (Fig. 4.4).

Until recently it was assumed that once neurons had migrated to the cortex and other structures during development, cell division was complete and no further neurogenesis occurred. There is accumulating evidence, however, to indicate that at least in some species of mammals, such as the rat, neurogenesis continues along the ventricular wall throughout the life of the animal (Craig, Morshead, Roach, & van der Kooy, 1994; Morshead et al., 1994; Reynolds & Weiss, 1992). It appears that these cells do not normally leave the ventricular zone. When Reynolds and Weiss (1992) harvested and placed these neurons in a culture medium with epidermal growth factor (EGF) they were able to show that the cells were capable of dividing and differentiating into neurons and glia. Reynolds and Weiss have also shown that stem cells from the ventricular zone in humans are also able to differentiate in the right culture conditions. The observation that neurons can differentiate in adulthood is important because it opens the possibility that the mammalian brain has the capacity for regrowing neurons lost to injury.

Because cortical cells are born along the ventricle and must migrate to the cortical plate, it is reasonable to ask how this occurs, particularly for the cells traveling to the superficial cortical layers, because they must traverse the cells and fibers of the inner layers. Rakic (1972) first showed that neurons migrate to the appropriate laminae within the cortex along specialized filaments, known as radial glial fibers, which span the fetal cerebral wall at early stages. Although it is now clear that not all neurons migrate along radial glial fibers, this is certainly a major method for most neurons in all species studied. One special feature of radial glial fibers has important implications for the possibility of neurogenesis in

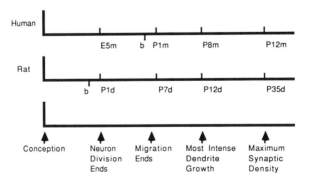

FIG. 4.4. Schematic illustration of the comparable developmental ages of the brain of the rat and human. E, embryonic day; P, postnatal day, b, day of birth. Note that the day of birth in the rat is much earlier in embryonic development than the day of birth in the human.

the adult brain. After cell migration is complete, radial glial fibers disappear and may actually be transformed into another class of glia, namely, astrocytes. The fact that neurons normally migrate along radial glia and the fact that the radial glia are not present in the mature brain present an obvious problem for neural repair or regrowth. Any dividing stem cell will not have a way of reaching an injured area. On the other hand, it is possible that after cerebral injuries during early development the radial glia may still be in place or possibly may remain in place longer than normal, thus providing a route for the replacement of cortical neurons. In fact, Whishaw and I have been consistently frustrated in our attempts to make cortical lesions in infant rats. It seems that if we restrict our lesions to the grey matter, especially along the midline, the tissue appears to have returned. Larger lesions that invade the ventricular zone do not produce this outcome. In view of the evidence for the presence of stem cells in the ventricular zone of even adult animals, it is reasonable to propose that our surgical problems are in fact due to the brain regrowing the lost region. This is an unexpected possibility that we return to in chapter 6.

Axon and Dendrite Development

As cells migrate along the radial glial fibers, they begin to develop axons that run to subcortical areas or other cortical areas. The rate of axon development is extremely rapid, apparently on the order of 1 mm/day. In addition to axons of cortical cells growing out, axons from the thalamus enter the cortex after the principal cortical target cells complete their migrations and assume the appropriate positions within the developing cortex. In the rat, axon development begins by about gestational day 16 but most cortical axon formation is postnatal, especially between days 6 and 18.

Dendritic development begins prenatally in the human, with the age of onset varying with the cortical layer and location. There is considerable complexity to the dendritic growth in the deepest layers (V and VI) by the seventh fetal month, and by birth these layers have reached about 60% of maximum growth. In contrast, the superficial layers are only about 30% maximum growth (Becker, Armstrong, Chan & Wood, 1984; Marin-Padilla, 1970a, 1970b). Elongation of dendritic branches in the visual cortex appears to end by about 18 months, but it continues for some time in other areas such as the frontal cortex, where dendritic growth is only about 50% of maximum at 2 years (Schadé & van Groenigen, 1961).

In the cortex of the rat, dendritic growth is virtually all postnatal, with the peak of development being between about postnatal days 8 and 20. Maximum dendritic growth is achieved by day 30, and regional differences do not appear to be as extreme as in the human. It is difficult to identify comparative ages for the maximal period of dendritic growth or for the age at which the dendritic growth is mature, in large part because in the human cortex there is such marked variation in dendritic growth in different regions. Nonetheless, it appears that the most intense period of dendritic growth in the human is in the postnatal months, possibly lasting until 18 months, whereas in the rat the most intense period runs from about postnatal day 10 to 20.

In contrast to the development of axons, dendritic growth usually commences after the cell reaches its final position in the cortex and proceeds at a very slow rate, on the order of micrometers per day. The disparate developmental rates of axons and dendrites are important because a faster growing axon can contact its target cell before the dendritic processes of that cell are elaborated, suggesting that the axon may play a role in dendritic differentiation. We can speculate that if the axon plays such a role in development, then it may play a similar role in processes of plasticity in adulthood.

Synaptic Development

In the human cerebral cortex, dendritic spines, on which most synapses are likely to form, begin to develop in the deepest pyramidal neurons (layer V) in the seventh fetal month. After birth, spine development spreads rapidly, which is reflected in a rapid increase in synapses. In the visual cortex synaptic density almost doubles between the second and fourth month and then continues to increase until 1 year. After 1 year synaptic density begins to decline to adult values, which occur around age 11 (Huttenlocher, 1990). In the frontal cortex synaptic density also reaches maximum levels at about 1 year, but this density is far higher than in visual cortex and does not begin to decline until about 5–7 years of age. It then takes until about 16 years of age to decline to adult levels (Huttenlocher, 1984). During the peak of maximum synaptic loss in humans it has been estimated by Pasko Rakic that as many as 100,000 synapses may be lost per second! It is little wonder that children seem to change moods and behaviors so quickly.

In the rat, synaptogenesis is almost all postnatal. The first synaptic spines begin to appear between P10 and P20 but they do not appear adult-like until about P30. Synaptic density appears to reach its peak about day 35 in sensory and motor cortex, and declines thereafter (e.g., Blue & Parnavelas, 1983a, 1983b; Uylings, van Eden, Parnavelas, & Kalsbeek, 1990). My own observations on frontal cortex are incomplete but, like the human, it appears that synaptic growth and elimination are later in the prefrontal regions than in posterior cortex.

The elimination of synapses during development coincident with the emergence of increasing motor and cognitive skill is intriguing. It suggests that the process of synaptic elimination is an important feature of behavioral development. This synaptic elimination can be seen in measures of synaptic density, spine density, and in some cases dendritic length and neuron death. Thus, there may be a general principle in plasticity that there is an overgrowth and subsequent pruning of synapses. One reason for this overgrowth may be that it provides a mechanism whereby environmental stimulation can influence cerebral growth. Synapses that are used may be kept, whereas those that are not used are eliminated. The loss of unused connections may provide another benefit as well. There are undoubtedly errors of connection during development, in which inappropriate connections are formed. For example, we have observed connections from the visual thalamus to the somatosensory cortex in newborn rats. If these connections are not used, they would be lost, which would be an important advantage to the process of brain development. It also seems likely that hormones or other growth factors could play a role in the details of synaptic pruning, thus providing a mechanism for the brain to show sexual dimorphism.

Conclusions

All mammalian brains go through a series of parallel developmental stages from neuronal birth to synapse formation and elimination. The plasticity of developing brain must vary with the particular developmental stage. In particular, it is reasonable to expect that a brain perturbation during the period of cell migration might have a different outcome than one during the period of synaptogenesis. Indeed, it might be reasonable to expect that there would be more plasticity during the period of overproduction of synapses, as the large number of synapses might lead to an enhanced capacity to adjust to the injury. One of the difficulties in preparing animal models of early brain injury is that it is very difficult to determine the equivalent developmental stages in different species. A working timetable is given in Fig. 4.3 with several important times as tentative markers. These include the completion of neurogenesis, the completion of cell migration, the time of maximum dendritic growth in the superficial and intrinsic neurons, and the point of maximum synaptic density. For the human, I took values for visual cortex because there is such a large range in different human regions.

THE KENNARD PRINCIPLE

Hebb (1980) made the point that it takes 50 to 100 years for scientific findings to become common sense and then 100 years to change that common sense if it is wrong. One of the ideas that has become common sense was called the Kennard Principle by Hans-Leukas Teuber. Kennard was studying the effects of motor cortex lesions in infant monkeys and she reported that infant monkeys appeared to have a better behavioral outcome than adult monkeys with similar injuries. Teuber's conclusion from Kennard's result was that "if you are going to have brain damage, have it early," which is what Teuber dubbed the Kennard Principle. The Kennard Principle has some intuitive appeal, because it is a common observation that infants seem to recover quickly from many maladies, and because their brain is developing it seems reasonable to expect that it would be able to compensate better than the adult brain. In fact, it is rare for children to experience lasting aphasia, which is a major problem for adults with left hemisphere injuries, and various authors have used this observation as evidence for plasticity in the infant brain (e.g., Lenneberg, 1967).

There are two fundamental problems with the Kennard Principle. First, the idea assumes that all developing brains are equivalent. We have just seen, however, that the brain goes through several stages in development, and it is a very different brain in each stage. It seems likely, therefore, that brain injuries will have different consequences at different stages of brain development. Second, the Kennard Principle ignores the fact that development of the brain is much like building a house. You must begin with a foundation, then progress to the framing, and so on. If the foundation is inadequate, there is nothing in the framing that will help. The idea that there is an important, and necessary, sequence in both brain and cognitive development was first clearly stated by Hebb, and thus I take the liberty of calling his idea the Hebb Principle. Hebb was studying children with damage to the frontal lobes in infancy, and he concluded that brain damage early in life may be worse than later damage because some aspects of cognitive development are critically dependent on the integrity of particular cerebral structures at certain times in development (Hebb, 1949). In other words, if certain structures are not working properly during critical periods in development, it may be that cognitive development is adversely affected and the child is never able to adequately compensate. One could imagine, for example, that if the auditory cortex is injured early in life, then language development could be compromised. Indeed, abnormal auditory processing has been proposed as an important cause of learning disabilities (e.g., Tallal, Stark, & Mellits, 1985a, 1985b). Thus, although it seems to be common sense that early brain injury will allow better recovery than later injury, there is a substantial body of evidence that suggests just the opposite. Nonetheless, the common view of most basic textbooks in psychology is that Kennard Principle is correct. It may take 100 years to reverse this perception.

THE EFFECT OF BRAIN DAMAGE IN INFANTS

Recovery from Aphasia

Perhaps the most dramatic evidence of recovery from early childhood brain injury comes from the observations that children with damage to language areas rarely have aphasia later in life. In fact, shortly after he published his observations on the nature of aphasia in adults, Broca noted that children did not appear to be aphasic after damage to the third frontal convolution on the left (i.e., Broca's area). More recently, in his comprehensive theory of language, Lenneberg (1967) proposed that language processes in the left hemisphere developed rapidly from ages 2 to 5 years and then more slowly until puberty, by which time development was complete. He reasoned that if brain damage occurred during this time of rapid development it would be possible to shift language functions to the intact right hemisphere, and there would be no chronic aphasia. Damage after this time would not permit reorganization and the prognosis for recovery would be poor. Although Lenneberg believed that plasticity in language processes would be possible until age 10–14 years, it seems more likely that the upper age limit for significant reorganization of language to the opposite hemisphere is about 5 years. Rasmussen and Milner (1977) found that although childhood injuries before 5 years would allow a shift of language processes to the right hemisphere, injuries after 6 years would not allow transfer to the opposite hemisphere but there was a shift of language within the left hemisphere, which could still support some recovery. There is a price to pay for the recovery of language, however. Woods and Teuber found that children with left-hemisphere injuries in the speech zones showed unexpected deficits in right-hemisphere functions as well as an overall drop in IQ (Woods, 1980; Woods & Teuber, 1973). Furthermore, there is a general finding that lesions occuring before the age of 1 year produce more severe impairments in IQ than those occuring later in life (e.g., Riva & Cazzaniga, 1986).

The possibility that children with injuries to the language areas, and subsequent reorganization of language functions into the right hemisphere, might pay a price for their "recovery" can be seen in a study by Brenda Milner and me. In the course of studying the ability of patients with focal cortical removals for the treatment of intractable epilepsy to copy sequences of arm or facial movements, we had the opportunity to study a group of 10 patients who had early left-hemisphere injuries and subsequently developed bilateral speech. That is, the early injury induced some of the language functions to shift to the right hemisphere, but some functions remained in the left hemisphere. Thus, when the patients had each hemisphere anesthetized, in turn, using Wada's sodium amobarbital procedure, the patients could be shown to have some language representation in each hemisphere. These patients subsequently had the left temporal lobe removed in adolescence or adulthood to treat their seizure disorder, which presumably was related to the early injury. We had previously shown that left temporal lobectomies in people with normal left-hemisphere speech representation had very little effect on the patients' ability to copy arm movement sequences (Kolb & Milner, 1981b). Patients with left parietal or left frontal lesions were impaired, however, which confirmed Kimura and Archibald's (1974) suggestion that the left hemisphere played a special role in the organization of certain types of motor programs. In contrast to our findings in patients with normal speech representation, we found that all of the bilateral speech subjects with left temporal lobectomies were impaired at the copying task, making about three times as many errors as normal control subjects. In sum, it appears that the reorganization of language did more than simply affect speech functions. Functions of the left hemisphere that were not normally affected by left temporal lobe lesions were now impaired. This type of observation is reminiscent of patient S. S. described earlier. Recall that she showed symptoms of right frontal-lobe injury even though her injury was in the right parietal cortex.

Emergence of Deficits

One of the difficulties in assessing the effects of early brain injury in children is the problem of knowing when to investigate the behavior. After all, it is pointless to try to investigate the extent of language loss in a 1-year-old infant. In an interesting and important study, Banich, Cohen-Levine, Kim, and Huttenlocher (1990) studied the development of performance on two subtests of the Wechsler Intelligence Scale for Children, namely, vocabulary and block design, in children with congenital cerebral injuries. The authors found that at 6 years of age there were no differences in performance, but as the children aged, significant deficits emerged in the brain damaged children relative to matched normal controls (Fig. 4.5). It thus appears that the children's brains matured, they "grew into deficits." This observation appears to confirm the Hebb Principle and is especially problematic in making predictions regarding the prognosis for children with cerebral injuries.

Further evidence for the emergence of deficits during development comes

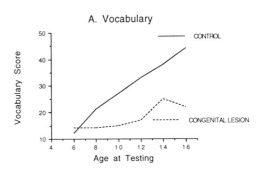

FIG. 4.5. Summary of the developmental changes in performance on two subtests of the Wechsler Intelligence Scale for Children–Revised. Note that children with congenital lesions are equivalent to normal children at age 6 years, but they fail to improve and thus fall progressively behind as they age. After Banich et al. (1990).

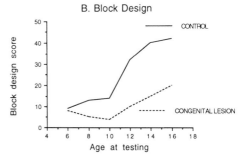

from the work of Patricia Goldman-Rakic and her colleagues. In her early studies she was impressed with apparent recovery of functions after frontal lobe injuries in infant monkeys (e.g., Goldman, 1974). As she continued her investigations it became clear that she and others had overestimated the extent of recovery because the animals were tested when still young. Thus, she found that as animals with dorsolateral prefrontal lesions developed they became progressively more impaired at cognitive tasks such as delayed alternation (Goldman-Rakic, Isseroff, Schwartz, & Bugbee, 1983).

In order to test directly the idea that the prefrontal cortex becomes progressively more important to the solution of particular cognitive problems, she used a technique in which she could make reversible lesions at different ages. She took advantage of the observation that when the cortex is cooled it does not function properly but when it returns to normal temperature it can function normally once again. She therefore implanted cooling probes into the prefrontal cortex of infant monkeys and studied the effect of cooling that cortex on the performance of a delayed response test. In this task the subject is shown the location of food reward on a board, the board is hidden from view for a brief period, and then the subject is allowed access to the board. Monkeys with dorsolateral prefrontal lesions in adulthood are impaired at this task. When she cooled the prefrontal cortex at 9–16 months of age the animals performed as well as they did in the uncooled state. However, when tested at 19–31 months the animals were impaired, and this impairment became progressively larger as they grew older (Fig. 4.6).

This type of experiment is important because it shows us that behavior may appear virtually normal early in life but become progressively less normal as animals develop. Ian Whishaw and I made a similar observation in hamsters with prefrontal lesions. We removed the cortex on the day of birth and then began to study nest building and food hoarding, which are important behaviors in adult hamsters, and found that although brain-injured and normal hamsters performed equally well in adolescence, the normal animals improved markedly over the ensuing weeks whereas the frontal animals showed no improvement and thus appeared to "grow into their deficits" (Kolb & Whishaw, 1985a).

Effects of Frontal Lesions in Children

I noted earlier that Hebb concluded that damage to the frontal lobe in children could have consequences that were more severe than similar injuries in adulthood. There is now accumulating evidence that this may indeed be the case. In my own studies I found the mean IQ of children with frontal lobe injuries in the first 5 years of life to be around 85 (Kolb & Fantie, 1989). Although there are likely differences in etiology and extent of injuries in the children in different studies, the overriding conclusion that intelligence is compromised by the early frontal injuries is inescapable (e.g. Vargha-Khadem, Watters, & O'Gorman,

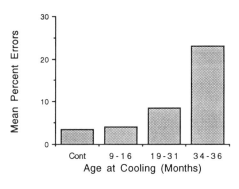

FIG. 4.6. Performance of monkeys on a delayed response test at different ages during development. A cooling probe was inserted into the frontal lobe, which produced reversible lesions at different times during development. As the animals grew older, the effects of the cooling became more pronounced. This can be taken as evidence that the frontal lobe progressively was assuming those functions necessary to solve the delayed response task. After Goldman-Rakic et al. (1983).

1985). Furthermore, although the numbers are small and age breakdowns vary from study to study, it would appear that the effects on IQ are worse if the injury is in the first year of life (or prenatal) than if the injuries are later.

In the preceding chapter I discussed the recovery by adult frontal lobe patients on tests of making or perceiving facial expressions (see Fig. 3.3). Laughlin Taylor and I also had the opportunity to study the performance of frontal lobe patients whose original frontal lobe injury occurred at different ages. We grouped patients into those who had injuries before their first birthday, those whose injuries occurred after the first birthday but before age 12 years, and those whose injuries occurred in adulthood. As in our earlier study we combined patients with left or right frontal lobe injuries, because side of lesion did not appear to make a difference. Our results showed that the although the subjects with early injuries were impaired relative to normal control subjects at making or perceiving the appropriate facial expressions, they performed significantly better on the test of making expressions than the adult frontal patients (Fig. 4.7).

In sum, it appears that children with frontal lobe injuries may show some recovery of function, but they are by no means normal after injury at any age and appear to have a significant depression of general intelligence. One important complication in understanding the effects early brain injury in human subjects is the fact that children with early brain injuries frequently have seizure disorders, whereas this is much less common in adults, and is virtually absent after stroke in adults. I am not aware of any systematic study in which children with and without seizure disorders after early cerebral injury are compared, but it seems likely that there might be some difference. In particular, it is known that the effects of brain stimulation of nonepileptogenic tissue in the epileptic brain may be markedly different than in normal brains, so one might expect that plastic processes may be compromised, or at least different, in the epileptogenic brain. The problem of seizures after early lesions in humans further complicates com-

A. Making the appropriate expression

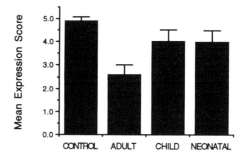

B. Perception of appropriate expression

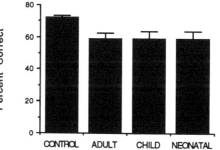

FIG. 4.7. Performance of children on tests of production and perception of facial expression. The subjects included controls and patients with unilateral frontal lobe lesions in adulthood (Adult), childhood (Child), or before age 2 years (Neonatal).

parisons with studies of laboratory animals, because laboratory animals do not have seizures after surgical injuries at any time in life.

EFFECTS OF FRONTAL LESIONS IN INFANT LABORATORY ANIMALS

Although there are considerable data on the effects of cortical injuries to most cortical regions and in a variety of species, I concentrate my comments here on studies on the frontal cortex, which is my most studied region. Because my own work has been with rats, I focus on this species but I make comparisons to studies in cats and monkeys. For the purposes of the following discussion the frontal cortex includes the prefrontal cortex, which is the projection field of the dorsomedial nucleus of the thalamus, as well as the premotor and supplementary motor cortex. In studies on the developing rat, it is virtually impossible to make lesions that are restricted only to the prefrontal cortex, because the brain is so small at birth. Thus, in most of my studies the lesions also include damage to the premotor cortex and the bordering motor cortex. In monkeys and cats, species that have much larger brains at birth, the lesions are normally restricted to the prefrontal cortex, and in the case of monkeys, to the dorsal or ventral (orbital) prefrontal subregions.

Effects of Frontal Lesions in Developing Rats

In my initial studies of recovery of function after frontal lesions in infancy I was impressed by the remarkably normal adult behavior of animals with frontal removals at about 7 days of age. In these studies the animals were virtually indistinguishable from normal control animals when they were tested in a variety of neuropsychological tasks in adulthood (e.g., Kolb & Nonneman, 1976, 1978; Kolb, Sutherland, & Whishaw, 1983c). Unfortunately, it is an unwritten rule in science that the longer one studies a phenomenon the smaller it seems to become. As we began to study the effects of earlier lesions and to use a broader battery of behavioral tests, our evidence of beneficial effects from early lesions appeared to evaporate and led me to question if we had ever actually seen recovery! After 20 years of study, a story has begun to unravel.

There are dramatic differences in outcome after damage at different times in the first 2 weeks of life. Thus, we found that removal of the frontal cortex prior to 5 days of age led to far worse behavioral impairment than similar removal in adulthood. In contrast, removal of the same frontal region at 7–10 days of age allowed substantially better behavioral outcome than in adulthood (e.g., Kolb, 1987; Kolb & Whishaw, 1981b, 1985b). Fig. 4.8 illustrates this result on the tasks illustrated in Chapter 3, namely, the Morris water task and Whishaw's reaching task. On both tests the rats with lesions around day 10 perform better than the other lesion groups, whereas those rats with lesions on the day of birth are far worse than the other brain-injured groups. We also found that damage in adolescence allowed only a small improvement in outcome relative to adult operates. Thus, it appears that cerebral injury during the time of cell migration is particularly damaging, whereas injury later, during the time of dendritic growth, allows better recovery. This general observation was not confined to studies of frontal cortex injury, for we found virtually identical results with posterior parietal and motor cortex lesions as well (Kolb, Hewson, & Whishaw, 1993; Kolb, Holmes, & Whishaw, 1987).

Our test battery allowed us to study recovery on different kinds of tests. There is far better recovery on tests of cognitive function, as measured by various neuropsychological tasks such as mazes, than on tests of species typical behavior such as food hoarding or nest building (Kolb & Whishaw, 1981b, 1985a; Whishaw, Kolb, Sutherland, & Becker, 1983). For example, when Whishaw and I studied rats with frontal lesions on postnatal day 7 we found that although they

Morris Water Task

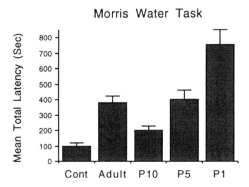

FIG. 4.8. Top: Performance of rats in the Morris water task. Animals were given bilateral frontal lesions in adulthood (Adult) or on postnatal day 10 (P10), postnatal day 5 (P5), or postnatal day 1 (P1). Rats with lesions on P10 showed recovery of function relative to adult operates, whereas rats with P1 lesions were far worse than adults. Bottom: Performance of rats in the Whishaw reaching task. Rats with frontal lesions in adulthood or on P1 were very poor at the task, whereas rats with lesions on P10 showed relative recovery.

Whishaw Reaching Task

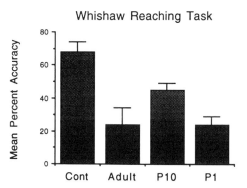

performed rather well on tests of spatial navigation, they were grossly impaired on various tests of species typical behavior. Pinel and Treit (1983) devised a test of natural avoidance behavior in rats in which a noxious stimulus, such as an electrified prod, was introduced into a rat's living quarters. Pinel and Treit found that rats, being curious, approached this stimulus but they were "stung" by it, and when they recovered from the immediate startle of the experience, they began to bury the stimulus. This highly reliable behavior could be quantified with measures such as the depth of sawdust piled on the electric prod. When Whishaw and I used this test with our rats with day 7 frontal lesions, we found that they failed to bury the prod at all, although they clearly learned that the prod was noxious because no animal was shocked a second time; they simply avoided it. These same subjects were also abnormal on other tests of species-typical behavior: They failed to hoard food, build nests, or to trim their claws. The fact that species-typical behaviors show such poor recovery was noted in the last chapter, too, where I suggested that cognitive tasks may show better recovery because there may be alternate, although possibly less efficient, strategies to solve cognitive problems, whereas there may be only one way for the cortex to control relatively inflexible innate behaviors. The importance of these innate behaviors should not be ignored, because it is these very behaviors that have been selected by evolution. These behaviors must play a central role in the survival of the animals, and the inefficiency of plastic processes to compensate is puzzling and no doubt important.

Recovery is directly related to lesion size: If the lesions at postnatal days 1–5 are large enough to include all of the prefrontal cortex, the behavioral outcome is very dismal indeed (Kolb, 1987; Kolb & Whishaw, 1981a; Nonneman, Corwin, Sahley, & Vicedomini, 1984; Vicedomini, Corwin, & Nonneman, 1982). In contrast, lesions restricted to a portion of the prefrontal cortex have a far better prognosis, and behavioral symptoms are similar to rats with similar lesions in adulthood (Kolb & Nonneman, 1976; Kolb, Petrie, & Cioe, 1995; Kolb & Whishaw, 1985b). This result suggests that the plastic processes underlying recovery make use of the remaining cortical regions after subtotal lesions.

Even restricted frontal lesions on postnatal days 1–5 produce a wide range of behavioral abnormalities not observed following similar lesions in adulthood (Kolb, 1987; Kolb & Holmes, 1983; Kolb & Whishaw, 1985b). In fact, the new deficits are often observed coincidentally with recovery on other tests normally impaired in rats with lesions in adulthood. This result is reminiscent of case S. S., who had novel deficits after her perinatal parietal injury. We have seen similar results after damage to prefrontal, motor, and parietal cortex (Kolb, 1987; Kolb, Hewson, & Whishaw, 1993; Kolb, Holmes, & Whishaw, 1987). The observation of new behavioral deficits underlines the importance of having a thorough test behavioral test battery, especially in experiments aimed at correlating brain function with anatomical plasticity.

Behavioral deficits may emerge with maturation, or they may actually disappear. We considered the first result just mentioned, but the second one was somewhat more surprising. We gave rats large frontal lesions either on day 1 or day 10 of life and then began testing them in the Morris water task on postnatal day 19, which is the earliest that infant rats can solve the problem (Rudy, Stadler-Morris, & Albert, 1987). To my surprise, rats with lesions at day 1 or 10 both were impaired at the task (Kolb & Gibb, 1993). On the basis of all earlier experiments I had expected that the day 10 operates would be normal. We decided to give the animals more recovery time and to retest the animals in adolescence. We then retested the animals at day 56 and we found that although the day 1 rats were still severely impaired at the task, the day 10 rats performed as well as normal control animals. In other words, the animals had "grown out of their deficits." Stated differently, it seems likely that whatever plastic process supports the recovery seen in adult rats with lesions on day 10 continues well after the injury, just as it does in adulthood. I had not expected this, because I naively thought that the developing brain could "simply" modify its development to support recovery. It appears that the genetic program is less flexible than this and the recovery process may occur largely during the period of synaptic pruning, rather than synaptic growth.

Unilateral lesions allow substantially more recovery relative to adult operates than bilateral lesions, even when the lesions are rather large. A similar effect has been observed in cats as well (Villablanca, Burgess, & Sonnier, 1984). The relatively small effects of unilateral lesions suggest that as long as one functional system is intact, the brain is able to recruit recovery mechanisms to support behaviors, especially cognitive behaviors. In contrast, when there is even subtotal damage to both hemispheres there is no longer a complete functional system, leaving the brain with a more difficult task.

Prenatal lesions produce surprisingly small behavioral deficits in rats. Deborah Muirhead and I exposed fetal rat pups at embryonic days 16–18 and either removed or vigorously disturbed the tissue that occupied the region of the medial prefrontal cortex. Although these lesions produced very peculiar brains, the behavior of most of the animals was surprisingly normal (Kolb & Muirhead, 1995). Thus, when we studied the performance either in the Morris water task or in Whishaw's reaching task, the majority of the animals were indistinguishable from normal control animals. Animals with gross hydrocephaly did not do as well, and some of these animals performed nearly as poorly as neonatally decorticated rats (Kolb & Whishaw, 1981a; Whishaw & Kolb, 1984). Nonetheless, aside from severely hydrocephalic animals, the behavior of animals with grossly abnormal brains was remarkable.

These results are difficult to interpret for a couple of reasons. We made the lesions well before mitosis was complete, so it is difficult to be certain just what was removed, especially because the cytoarchitecture developed so abnormally. This makes it rather difficult to make comparisons to animals with lesions later in life. In addition, it is quite possible that because mitosis continued after the injury, the animals may have regrown the lost regions. Such a result has some precedent, as Hicks and D'Amato reported similar results in animals with x-radiation–induced lesions on embryonic day 12 (e.g., Hicks, 1954). Indeed, in some of the Hicks and D'Amato experiments it appeared that the animals virtually grew a new brain after the x-radiation–induced damage! The remarkable finding in our results, as well as in the Hicks and D'Amato studies, was that such abnormal-appearing brains could be associated with such apparently normal behavior. To our knowledge, this is the earliest that restricted cortical lesions have been made in any species of laboratory animal. If our results prove reliable it would suggest that although cortical injury during the period of cell migration is devastating, cortical injury during the period of neurogenesis may be far less disruptive and it might be possible to show significant functional savings.

Effects of Prefrontal Lesions in Developing Monkeys and Cats

In her studies of monkeys with frontal lesions, Kennard (e.g., 1938, 1940) first showed that small motor cortex lesions in infants allowed significant recovery of function relative to adult monkeys with similar lesions. Kennard's behavioral measures were crude, and it now seems likely that the extent of recovery was far less than she had believed; in fact, Passingham, Perry, and Wilkinson (1983) suggested that there may be virtually no difference between the effects of motor cortex lesions in infant and adult monkeys when an entire system is damaged. Kennard's lesions were subtotal, whereas Passingham's were larger. Again, it appears that lesion size may be an important predictor in recovery from early injury.

Harlow was probably the first to make prefrontal lesions in infant monkeys, and he reported that these animals were far less impaired at cognitive tests than were adult operates, which was consistent with the *zeitgeist* of the time (Harlow, Akert, & Schiltz, 1964). As I described earlier, subsequent work by Goldman-Rakic and her colleagues showed that age at behavioral testing is important, and it now appears that like motor cortex lesions in infant monkeys, there is rather little recovery after prefrontal lesions in infant monkeys (e.g., Goldman-Rakic et al., 1983). I note parenthetically that Goldman-Rakic has shown that there is recovery in infant monkeys with restricted orbitofrontal lesions, even when behavior is assessed in adulthood (for reviews see Goldman, 1974; Goldman-Rakic et al., 1983), but this appears to be an exception to the general finding of poor recovery. Monkeys are born very late in embryological development relative to rats, and in fact are even embryologically older than humans. It therefore is reasonable to wonder what might happen if frontal lesions were made in monkeys at a developmental time more similar to our 10-day-old rats, which is likely equivalent to a prenatal injury in monkeys. Indeed, when Goldman and Galkin (1978) made prenatal frontal lesions in monkeys they found a dramatically better behavioral outcome than they had previously found in monkeys with lesions in early infancy, suggesting that there may be a prenatal developmental period in monkeys that allows better recovery of function than does injury later in life.

Villablanca and his colleagues conducted an extensive series of studies on the behavior of cats with frontal or prefrontal injuries (e.g., Villablanca et al., 1984, Villablanca, Hovda, Jackson, & Infante, 1993). Cats provide an interesting comparison to the rat and monkey studies because they are embryologically older than rats at birth with a gestation period of about 65 days, but they are much younger at birth than monkeys. Overall, Villablanca has found that although cats with prefrontal lesions shortly after birth show good recovery relative to animals with lesions later in life, cats with prenatal lesions have greater behavioral impairments than do animals with later lesions.

Taken together, the results from our studies in rats, Villablanca's studies in

When is it best to have brain damage?

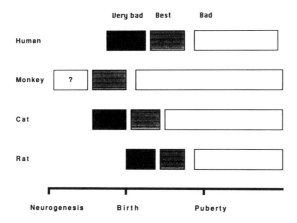

FIG. 4.9.   Summary of the outcome of cortical lesions at different ages in humans, monkeys, cats, and rats. Dark black bars indicate very poor outcome, grey bars indicate good recovery, and open bars indicate an outcome that is similar to that seen in adulthood. Relative to day of birth there are marked differences in the different species. Comparison with Fig. 4.4 indicates that the worst outcome occurs when mitosis and migration are still in progress. The best outcome occurs when neurons are developing dendrites and synapses.

cats, and Goldman-Rakic's studies in monkeys lead to the conclusion that behavioral outcome varies directly with the developmental stage of the cortex at the time of injury (Fig. 4.9): There appears to be a time early in development of rats and cats when cortical injury is devastating, and a later time in all three species when there is substantial recovery of function. As I noted earlier, the preliminary results from our studies of even earlier lesions in rats suggest that there is yet another time period very early in development during which there is a also very good recovery. One could also predict that if Goldman and Galkin had made their prenatal lesions earlier in development, they would have found a period during which there was a very poor behavioral outcome.

EFFECTS OF HEMIDECORTICATION

During the course of treatment for severe and often life-threatening neurological disorders it has sometimes proven necessary to remove an entire hemisphere (hemispherectomy) or all of the cortex of one hemisphere (hemidecortication). (For the present discussion I treat these procedures as equivalent as there is little evidence of any significant behavioral difference.) The behavior of people with such removals is especially interesting, for there is remarkable behavioral recovery, especially in children. Perhaps the most striking result is that regardless of age, after complete removal of the left hemisphere most people are capable of some language and do not experience the dense global aphasia seen in patients with large left hemisphere strokes. There are, however, significant behavioral sequelae of hemidecortication (e.g., Vargha-Khadem & Polkey, 1992). Full-scale IQ is usually at least one standard deviation below normal, but it is surprisingly high in view of the extent of the removal. There is also rather dramatic variability in the outcome, as several patients have been reported to have IQs that are above average (e.g., Smith, 1984). The outcome of hemidecortication varies with the etiology. Children with early seizure onset (before 1 year) have a very poor outcome (IQ less than 70) relative to those with later disease onset. Left-hemisphere "recovery" is more complete than right-hemisphere "recovery." Indeed, although most left-hemisphere patients show surprisingly good language functions, visuospatial and constructional capacities are compromised in most patients with removal of either hemisphere. In contrast to most patients with restricted lesions, there is much higher variation in the extent of behavioral dysfunction after hemidecortication. This may be related to the severity of residual seizure or other neurological disorders. Finally, functional recovery is very slow and may continue for many years. Overall, it seems likely that recovery from hemidecortication is the slowest of all injuries in humans, but this may not be surprising in view of the severity of the brain damage.

The first studies of neonatal hemidecorticates in laboratory animals were done by Hicks and D'Amato (1968, 1970, 1975). They found that both adult and infant lesions led to (a) a loss of tactile placing contralateral to the ablation, (b) a loss of visual discrimination ability, and (c) loss of the ability to gauge variable jumping distances visually. There was some recovery relative to adult operates, however, as the stride of neonatal operates was normal whereas that of the adult operates was not. In subsequent studies on hemidecorticates we have found that although hemidecortication at all ages produces behavioral changes, the neonatal hemidecorticates generally perform much better than adults on sensorimotor behaviors such as walking, swimming, and reaching (Kolb & Tomie, 1988; Whishaw & Kolb, 1988). The extent of recovery is clearly greater on some tests than others however, as illustrated in Fig. 4.10. Like Hicks and D'Amato, we found that walking was much better in the early operates, whereas we also found that reaching was only marginally better. Performance on the Morris task was also much better in the early operates.

As we varied the age at hemidecortication in our studies we had anticipated that, like animals with restricted frontal lesions, there would be a clear relationship between age at injury and the extent of recovery. We were surprised on two counts. First, the effect of age during the first 2 weeks was much smaller than in our previous studies of animals with frontal or parietal injuries. Second, the age

A. Walking

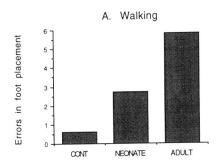

B. Forelimb Reaching

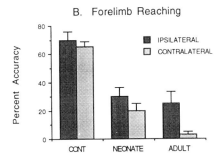

C. Morris Water Task

FIG. 4.10. Summary of the adult performance of hemidecorticate rats on tests of walking, the Whishaw reaching task, and the Morris water task. Rats with hemidecorticates in infancy show a better outcome on all measures than do rats with hemidecortications in adulthood.

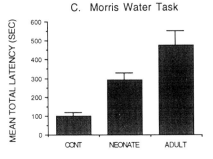

relationship was reversed! That is, the behavioral outcome was best in the animals with the earliest lesions, which was on the day of birth. In hindsight such a result should not have been too surprising, because we believe that the most likely explanation for the very poor behavioral outcome after frontal lesions on day 1 is that the rest of the hemisphere's growth and development is seriously compromised. In the case of the hemidecorticated brain there is no parallel compromise because there is no remaining hemisphere. Rather, it appears that the absence of the hemisphere early may have some "beneficial" effect on the growth and development of the remaining, normal hemisphere. This leads to a clear prediction: It is likely that any perturbation of the remaining hemisphere could be very disruptive. In order to examine this possibility, we hemidecorticated animals at birth and then made either stab wounds or very small sensorimotor cortex lesions in the remaining hemisphere (Kolb, Gibb, & Muirhead, 1995). The results were clear: The second lesion compromised the recovery, as the animals were as impaired behaviorally as animals with hemidecortications in adulthood. Animals with only a small stab wound in an otherwise normal brain were indistinguishable from normal controls. We have not varied the age of the hemidecortication, but it is likely that the effect of the small contralateral injury will decline in older animals.

Our finding that small perturbations of an otherwise normal hemisphere can compromise recovery from a more substantial injury in the opposite hemisphere has a clinical precedent. Vargha-Khadem et al. (1985) showed that children with perinatal lesions of the language zones in the left hemisphere do not show a shift in language to the right hemisphere if there is a small right hemisphere injury. Evidently recovery is dependent on the complete integrity of the hemisphere contralateral to a large lesion.

CONCLUSIONS

The mammalian neocortex develops through a series of stages from the generation of neurons, the migration of the neurons to the appropriate location, axonal and dendritic growth, synapse formation, and synapse pruning. It therefore comes as no real surprise that the functional consequences of cortical injury vary with the developmental stage at the time of injury. With this in mind, it is possible to reach several conclusions.

1. Cortical injury during at the end of the mitotic phase or during neuronal migration leads to a very poor behavioral outcome. In rats this period ranges from birth to about 6 days of age. In humans it likely begins midway through the third trimester and continues through part of the first year.

2. Cortical injury during the period of maximal dendritic differentiation and synapse formation is associated with the most complete recovery of function observed at any time in life. (I note as well that this period is also associated with maximal astrocyte development, which may turn out to be critical.) In rats, this begins at 7–10 days and probably continues into early adolescence, although this has not been determined. In humans this period probably includes the second year of life, but the endpoint probably varies considerably with the area injured. Because visual cortex develops more quickly than frontal cortex, there is likely a shorter window for recovery after visual cortex injury.

3. Estimates of recovery vary with the behavior measured. In general, cognitive behaviors show better recovery than species-typical behaviors.

4. Recovery of function may have a price. I began the chapter with a discussion of case S. S., who clearly paid a price for her recovery of parietal lobe

function. Rather than having symptoms of parietal lobe injury, she had symptoms more typical of frontal lobe injury.

5. The estimation of the extent of recovery varies with the age at assessment. Cortically injured subjects may "grow into deficits" or "grow out of deficits," depending on the area damaged, the behavior measured, and the extent of injury. It is also seems likely that as animals with early brain damage approach old age there will be a loss of the some of the recovered functions, much as we saw for adults in the last chapter.

6. The extent of injury influences the likelihood of recovery. Thus, lesions that remove an entire functional area are less likely to allow recovery than lesions that leave part of a functional region intact. In addition, unilateral lesions allow better recovery than bilateral lesions, which may reflect the fact that a unilateral lesion removes only one half of a functional system.

7. In general, it appears that recovery is better in laboratory animals with damage to the developing cortex than to human infants. This is almost certainly due to the nature of the injury in humans, because natural lesions do not reflect functional boundaries and the lesions are very likely to be larger. In addition, naturally occurring lesions tend to leave a lot of abnormal brain, which is likely to interfere with the normal functioning of the remaining, intact brain. This abnormal functioning is often reflected in the presence of seizures, which are rarely seen in laboratory animals with surgical or chemical lesions of the developing cortex.

In sum, the damage to the developing brain provides a good opportunity to examine processes underlying brain plasticity, especially because the functional outcome varies from very poor to very good. One would predict that whatever plastic change is supporting recovery therefore will be present, or more extensive, when recovery is present versus when it is not. As we return to our consideration of cases P. B. and S. S., we can speculate that the plastic processes that followed the injuries to their brains must have been very different. P. B. showed recovery of some right posterior functions, suggesting some sort of change in either the damaged right hemisphere or, less likely, in the left hemisphere. S. S. showed even better recovery of her right posterior functions but she lost some right frontal functions. This is probably not some atypical result of a single case, as Whishaw and I have found that early posterior parietal lesions in rats also lead to frontal lobe symptoms in adulthood. Thus, the plastic processes underlying recovery by S. S. may have included the frontal lobe, and although these changes were beneficial in one regard, they interfered with the development of frontal lobe functions. The slower development of the frontal lobe is almost certainly an important variable here. An important message here is that not all plasticity is beneficial.

III RECOVERY AND BRAIN PLASTICITY

Brain injury provides one of the most powerful stimuli to change the brain. This section deals with the relationship between brain injury and the plastic processes that we have identified in the normal brain and in the developing brain. Chapter 5 reviews the evidence for plastic changes after injury in the adult brain. Chapter 6 then considers the plastic changes after injuries at different ages in the developing brain. Chapter 7 goes yet a step further. Brain plasticity is influenced by hormones, neurotrophic factors, neuromodulators, and experience. This chapter examines the relationship that these factors have with functional recovery and brain plasticity.

5 Brain Plasticity and Recovery of Function in Adulthood

When the brain is damaged, many neurons that are not directly injured lose their normal synaptic inputs. This synaptic loss leads to three possible fates in the deafferented neurons: (a) death; (b) survival with reduced total input; and (c) reinnervation, either in whole or in part. In most cases all three events occur after injury. Although reinnervation was once thought to be a rare event, a view has emerged in the last decade that the replacement of damaged connections following neural injury is actually the rule in the central nervous system. What is less clear, however, is whether reinnervation is functionally advantageous or whether it might actually interfere with normal functioning.

Behavior also changes when the brain changes. When behavior changes, experience changes too. Consider an example in which a person has a stroke that renders her unable to move one arm. The likely effect of this functional loss will be the increased reliance on the other limb, which means the brain controlling that limb will be more active. We saw in Chapter 2 that when animals are trained to use a specific limb, there are changes in the neurons controlling the limb. It is therefore reasonable to expect that the brain will change after our hypothetical stroke because the behavior has changed. Thus, a brain injury can change the behavior, which in turn changes the brain. These behaviorally induced changes need not be in the vicinity of the injury and very often are not even on the same side of the brain as the injury. The possibility that behavior can change the brain after injury is not normally appreciated in studies of plasticity, but it is fundamental to understanding the brain–behavior correlations during recovery. It is also crucial to the issue of establishing behavioral therapies to assist restitution of function. I return to this issue later.

In this chapter I focus on the changes in the brain in response to cortical injury. The best known work on cortical reorganization after injury is the work on the effects of unilateral entorhinal lesions on hippocampal structure and function. I begin by briefly reviewing this model, in part because it provides us with a framework for discussing work on the neocortex, but also because it provides some more general principles. The synaptic reorganization that results from denervation of the hippocampal formation has been reviewed in detail elsewhere (Cotman & Lynch, 1976; Cotman & Nadler, 1978; Lynch & Cotman, 1975; Steward, 1991), so the main goal here is to provide a general overview.

REMODELING THE HIPPOCAMPUS AFTER ENTORHINAL INJURY

The hippocampal formation has provided a good model to study synaptic replacement. The hippocampus has a clearly laminated arrangement of neuron types that makes it especially easy to study (Fig. 5.1). Most neocortical regions have many more types of neurons, and these neurons are not as neatly organized in easily recognized rows. Hippocampal neurons also have a discrete and relatively simple pattern of afferents in which changes are relatively easily observed (Fig. 5.1). Consider, for example, the granule cells in the dentate gyrus. They receive a massive excitatory projection from the ipsilateral entorhinal cortex (via the perforant path), which terminates in the outer 70% of their apical dendritic field (Fig. 5.1). This dendritic zone also receives a crossed projection from the entorhinal cortex on the contralateral side. This crossed projection overlaps with the ipsilateral entorhinal pathway, which means that if connections from either pathway are lost, there are appropriate afferents already in place that could expand to fill the void. The granule cells also receive a projection from the pyramidal cells forming the hilus of Ammon's horn (CA4). This projection includes inputs from both the ipsilateral and contralateral hemisphere and synapses in a narrow band proximal to the cell body (Fig. 5.1). Finally, there is a cholinergic input from the septum. This septal input terminates throughout the dendritic field of the granule cells, but it is heaviest in the region of the granule cell bodies. This septal projection does not overlap the projection area of the pyramidal cells. Thus, we can see that the granule cells receive distinct bands of inputs that can be visualized easily using appropriate stains. The advantage of this arrangement for the student of plasticity is that it is a simple matter to see if injury to any part of the input systems might alter the pattern of connectivity on the granule cells.

When the entorhinal cortex of rats is removed unilaterally, there is a loss of 86% of the synapses from the distal 70% of the ipsilateral granule cell dendrites (Mathews, Cotman, & Lynch, 1976). This massive denervation of the dentate gyrus, and subsequently of much of Ammon's horn, leads to a reorganization of the connections of the dentate gyrus (for detailed reviews see Cotman & Lynch,

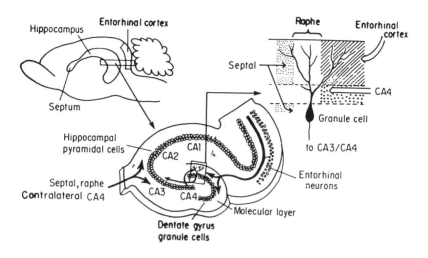

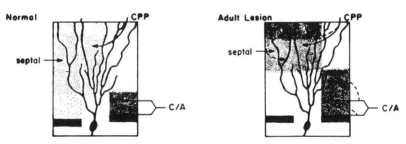

FIG. 5.1.   Illustration of the anatomy of the hippocampal formation and the effects of unilateral ablation of the entorhinal cortex. Granule cells receive a stratified input that is altered after entorhinal injury. The CA4 input and the septal inputs expand, as does the crossed input from the entorhinal cortex. CPP, crossed perforant path; C/A, commissural and associational (CA4) fibers. After Cotman and Nadler (1978), Nieto-Sampedro and Cotman (1985), and Steward (1991).

1976; Cotman & Nadler, 1978; Lynch & Cotman, 1975; Steward, 1991). In particular, there is an expansion of the connections from the contralateral entorhinal cortex and from the hippocampal pyramidal cells (Fig. 5.1). During the first 4 postinjury days there is a degeneration of the affected presynaptic terminals and a deterioration of the dendrites and their spines. The loss of dendritic elements is easily seen in Golgi-stained material and reflects a major loss of synapses on dendritic spines (Fig. 5.2).

The axon terminals begin to proliferate new presynaptic processes on about day 4, and this continues at a rapid rate for about a week. Dendritic growth may begin somewhat later than axon terminal growth, but it is clearly visible in Golgi material by 10 days (Steward, 1991). Dendritic growth continues for at least a

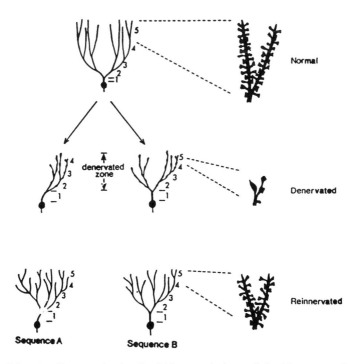

FIG. 5.2.   Changes in the dendritic morphology of the hippocampal granule cells after denervation. The dendrites initially retract and then regrow. The regrowth is not the same as the original growth, and the dendrites remain somewhat stunted. After Steward (1991).

month. Curiously, the dendritic growth is not identical to the original morphology; the dendrites have more branches but a shorter vertical extent (Fig. 5.2). This alteration in the dendritic morphology, which I call *remodeling,* implies a change in the biophysical properties of the dendrites, which will obviously reflect a change in neuronal excitability and possibly in function.

In addition to neuronal changes, there are also glial changes. Hence, at the same time that neurons are changing, there is a proliferation of microglia within the denervated zone and a hypertrophy of the astrocytes. The microglia function to remove the degeneration debris, especially the dead presynaptic elements, and the astrocytes may also play a key role in the reinnervation process, possibly through the production of trophic factors, such as nerve growth factor.

Although I have emphasized the changes in the dentate gyrus after its denervation, pronounced transneuronal changes may also take place in associated areas that were not directly denervated. For example, Hoff (1986) showed that unilateral entorhinal injury leads to a loss of synapses in the ipsilateral CA4 region, which normally receives input from the dentate gyrus. Over time, these synapses are replaced and actually show an overall increase relative to normal levels. Thus, the remodeling occurring after cortical injury may include regions that are removed from the site of injury. Also, it appears that the total number of synapses can be increased significantly over preinjury levels. Such increases in synapses do not represent a "simple" reinnervation but must reflect an innervation that was not previously present.

A key question regarding the remodeling of the hippocampus after entorhinal lesions is whether it makes a difference functionally. After all, the mere presence of connections does not mean that they are functional nor that they are necessarily helpful. The simplest way to address this issue is to examine the behavior of animals with entorhinal lesions and to compare the time course of behavioral and anatomical change. Loesche and Steward (1977) therefore gave rats either bilateral or unilateral lesions of the entorhinal cortex and then looked at recovery of performance on a delayed alternation task. Bilateral entorhinal cortex lesions produced a persistent deficit on this task that did not recover after 50 days of training (but see later). Animals with unilateral lesions exhibited an initial deficit that recovered over the first 10–12 days postlesion. The authors hypothesized that this recovery was dependent on the reinnervation of the dentate gyrus by the contralateral entorhinal input. In order to test this hypothesis, they cut the fiber tract from the contralateral side. This reinstituted the deficit, which implies that the contralateral projection was necessary for the behavior. The correlation between the recovery and the dentate reinnervation is provocative and has important implications for understanding recovery of function. One difficulty, however, is that correlation is not proof of causation. The critical experiments require an attempt to enhance or retard anatomical change and then to determine what happens functionally. One way to do this might be to try to slow down the dentate reinnervation and see if the recovery is slowed. For example, one could study old animals, because they appear to have a slower anatomical response to injury. Another way might be to use a drug like alcohol or diazepam, both of which are alleged to block recovery and plasticity (e.g., Schallert, Hernandez, & Barth, 1986; Tjossem, Goodlett, & West, 1987).

One puzzling aspect of the brain–behavior correlation in the entorhinal-hippocampal model is that the synaptic remodeling continues far longer than the 12 days that it takes spatial alternation behavior to return to normal level. We must therefore ask why the remodeling continues and whether the extended synaptic change has functional consequences. It would be valuable to do a more thorough examination of the behavior of the entorhinal lesion animal and to determine if the improvement of other behaviors might correlate with the longer term synaptic changes. After all, the hippocampus did not evolve to solve spatial alternation tasks. Furthermore, it has been proposed that aberrant reinnervation of the hippocampal formation may play a role in Alzheimer's disease, so one might wonder what the long-term consequences of dentate gyrus injury might be (Hyman, Kromer, & van Hoesen, 1987). For example, is it possible that there is a period of behavioral "recovery" that is followed some time later by a return, and perhaps worsening, of the functional deficits? This hypothesis would be consistent with the clinical observations of returning deficits in aging that were discussed earlier.

Reinnervation from the contralateral entorhinal cortex is possible after a unilateral entorhinal injury, but it is obviously not possible after a bilateral removal. Nonetheless, there is still reorganization of the hippocampus after a bilateral lesion. In this case the reorganization is limited to changes in the connections from the septum and pyramidal cells of Ammon's horn (Lynch & Cotman, 1975). These changes are particularly interesting because they bear no relationship with the afferents that were destroyed by the lesion. It is therefore particularly interesting to know if there is a correlation between behavioral change and the remodeling. Several studies have looked at the evolution of the behavioral impairments after entorhinal lesions (e.g., Ramirez, Labbe, & Stein, 1988; Steward, Loesche, & Horton, 1977), with the general consensus being that although there are chronic deficits in many behaviors, there is an improvement in performance at about 12 days after the lesion, which correlates with the remodeling. Because the remodeling is fundamentally different than the original organization, the implications of this finding are provocative and require careful attention.

In sum, when the major afferents to the hippocampal system are damaged, there are changes in both behavior and neural connectivity that are correlated in time. This correlation is not proof of causation, so the next step is to try to prevent either recovery or the synaptic remodeling and see if the correlation is maintained. That is, if recovery is dependent on the observed synaptic changes, then a blockage of the synaptic changes ought to prevent recovery.

PLASTICITY AFTER NEOCORTICAL INJURY

It has been assumed until recently that the most likely effect of neocortical injury was cellular atrophy. The first clear evidence supporting this view came from a study by Jones and Thomas in 1962. They cut the olfactory tract input into the pyriform cortex and showed a dramatic atrophy of the dendrites in the pyriform neurons. Indeed, when my colleagues and I began to search for evidence of neocortical change after cortical injury, we fully expected that rats with lesions in adulthood would show either atrophy or no change at all. For example, when we gave rats large unilateral strokes of the sensorimotor cortex we found very poor recovery of sensorimotor behaviors such as forelimb reaching, and this was correlated with a significant atrophy of dendritic branching throughout the injured cortex, even with a prolonged recovery period of 4 months (Fig. 5.3). We have been pleasantly surprised to discover that such atrophy is not an inevitable result of cortical injury, however, as both prefrontal and motor cortex lesions can

A. Reaching after MCA stroke

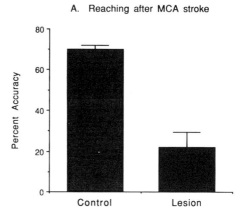

B. Layer III pyramidal cells after stroke

Fig. 5.3. Unilateral cerebral stroke impairs reaching in the Whishaw reaching task (top) and causes dendritic atrophy in remaining cortical neurons (bottom). After Kolb, Ribeiro-da-Silva, and Cuello (1995).

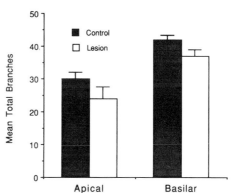

be associated with synaptic remodeling. It now appears that although neocortical remodeling may be much slower than it is in the hippocampal formation, it may be a more common outcome of cortical injury than was hitherto appreciated.

Recovery from Frontal Lesions

In the mid 1980s Robbin Gibb and I began to look at the effect of large frontal lesions, which included both medial prefrontal and adjacent motor cortex, on dendritic branching in the sensorimotor, visual, or temporal cortex. In our initial study we allowed animals to recover for about 4 months before sacrifice (Kolb & Gibb, 1991a). We then measured the dendritic arborization in the adjacent parietal cortex and in the more distant visual cortex. The results were clear: There was a significant increase in dendritic branching in parietal cortex but not in the

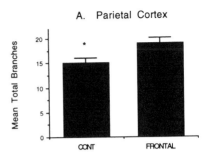

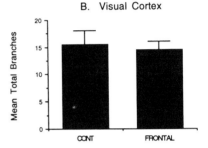

FIG. 5.4. Frontal lesions provoke a growth in dendritic arborization in (A) the parietal but
(B) not the visual cortex. After
Kolb and Gibb (1991).

visual cortex (Fig. 5.4). Thus, we had found a selective increase in dendritic
branching, which correlated with the improvement in forelimb reaching and
spatial learning that we had seen in other parallel experiments (see Chapter 3).
Our results were without precedent but we subsequently replicated our anatomical finding in animals with larger lesions that included the entire cingulate cortex
(Kolb & Whishaw, 1991). The question that remains puzzling, however, is how
changes in the sensorimotor cortex could support functions normally subserved
by the prefrontal cortex. After all, the sensorimotor cortex does not have the
same afferent and efferent connections as the prefrontal cortex. The sensorimotor
cortex does have corticospinal projections, however, and these could have altered
to compensate for the loss of the corticospinal projections in the anterior cingulate and premotor regions that were removed in the injury. The improvement in
spatial learning is more difficult to account for, however, and this behavioral
improvement could have been due to other synaptic changes that we did not
measure. Possible candidate structures might be the posterior parietal cortex,
posterior cingulate cortex, or hippocampal formation.

    In view of the time-dependent nature of recovery of spatial navigation behav-
ior after frontal lesions (see Fig. 3.10), we decided to sacrifice animals at shorter
postoperative recovery times. Animals were given medial frontal lesions and
trained on the Morris water task and retrained at the Whishaw reaching task
beginning either on postoperative day 2 or 30. They were sacrificed at the end of

training, which was 5 days later, and their dendritic arborization in the parietal cortex was compared to control animals. Neither group showed evidence of behavioral recovery on either task. Although all of the control animals learned to swim more or less directly to the hidden platform in the Morris task, the frontal lesioned animals took an average of about 60 sec to find the platform, and none of them consistently swam in the general direction of the platform. Similarly, on the reaching task the performance was 9 ± 1.9% and 18 ± 3.3% accuracy for the day 2 and day 30 groups, respectively. This performance compared to a pre-operative performance of 66 ± 5% for the same animals. Thus, the behavioral results show little recovery of function over the 35-day recovery period. Comparison of these results to the performance of animals with over 4 months of recovery, which were described in Chapter 3, is striking. The animals with 4 months of recovery all learned the location of the platform by the end of training, and their reaching was also better as they reached with about 35% accuracy.

Analysis of the layer III pyramidal cell dendrites in the adjacent sensorimotor cortex showed a pattern of change that is reminiscent of the changes in hippocampal cells. There was an initial drop in dendritic branching, which reflected a retraction of terminal branches, followed by an increase in branching over time. Fig. 5.5 summarizes the dendritic results from animals sacrificed 7, 35, or 200 days after surgery. There was a significant drop in both basilar and apical

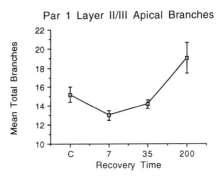

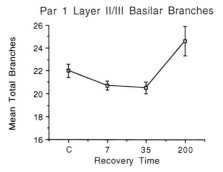

FIG. 5.5. Time course of dendritic changes after frontal cortex lesions. There is an initial atrophy of dendritic branches, followed by a growth of new branches.

branches on day 7, an increase in apical branches on day 35, and a large increase in both branch types by 200 days.

In sum, our behavioral and dendritic data show a general correlation between recovery of both a cognitive behavior (spatial learning) and a motor behavior (reaching) and the postinjury changes in dendritic branching. We have not established the time course of the dendritic and behavioral changes, but it is clearly longer than reported for behavior and plasticity in the entorhinal model.

Dendritic Remodeling After Motor Cortex Injury

Rats with subtotal bilateral motor cortex lesions show an initial severe impairment in various motor abilities, including reaching for food, protruding the tongue, and walking on narrow beams. These deficits reduce over time, but there are always significant residual behavioral deficits. This behavioral outcome is associated with a remodeling of the remaining sensorimotor cortex 200 days after injury (Kolb, Hewson, & Whishaw, 1993). Analysis of layer III pyramidal cells showed an 11% increase in branching of the basilar dendrites but a 16% decrease in branching of the apical dendrites (Fig. 5.6). In other words, the same neurons showed an increase in synapses on one part of the dendritic field and a decrease on another part. This means that the inputs to these cells were remodeled in a significant manner. In addition, when we analyzed the spine density on dendrites of the layer V neurons we found a decrease in the number of dendritic branches but an increase in the spine density on the remaining branches. Thus, there were more synapses in less space after the lesions. This must represent a change in the biophysical properties of the neurons, and presumably the function, of the remaining motor cortex neurons. It is difficult to conclude that the dendritic changes were supporting the behavioral improvement, because we have no proof that the layer V neurons we studied were actually projecting to the spinal cord.

FIG. 5.6. Partial removal of the motor cortex leads to a chronic remodeling of the layer V pyramidal cells in remaining motor cortex. There is an increase in apical branches and a decrease in basilar branches. There is also an increase in spine density in both types of branches (not shown). After Kolb, Hewson, and Whishaw (1993).

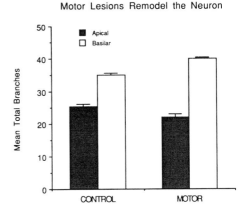

Nonetheless, a parallel study is supportive of this possibility (Whishaw, Pellis, Gorny, Kolb, & Tetzlaff, 1993). In this experiment we cut the pyramidal tract and found no recovery on the Whishaw reaching task, even with extensive training: The operated animals stayed at 10%–15% accuracy over 180 days of postoperative training. We also found no significant changes in either branching or spine density of the basilar dendrites of layer V pyramids. Thus, when we obtained partial recovery in the cortical lesion study we saw remodeling, whereas when we obtained no recovery in the pyramidal tract experiment we saw no evidence of remodeling. These results are complementary and provide support for the general idea that the cortical changes are necessary for functional recovery.

Plasticity After Hemidecortication

There have been very few systematic studies of recovery of function in humans with hemidecortications (or hemispherectomies) in adulthood, but there are now several case reports of surprisingly good functional outcomes (e.g., Damasio, Lima, & Damasio, 1975; Ellingson & McBeath, 1967; Ogden, 1988; Smith, 1966, 1969). Similarly, although there are many studies of hemidecorticated or hemispherectomized rats (e.g., Hicks & D'Amato, 1970; Kolb, MacIntosh, Sutherland, & Whishaw, 1984), there are few studies of recovery of function. Most experiments only assess behavior at a single time point after the hemidecortication. Perhaps the most extensive study is by Schallert and Whishaw (1984), who found that hemidecorticated rats showed a slow recovery from contralateral tactile neglect over a period of 3 months to a year. Taken together, the sparse behavioral data suggest that significant behavioral recovery is possible after hemidecortication. With this in mind, my colleagues and I have assessed the dendritic changes in the sensorimotor cortex of rats with hemidecortications in adulthood (Kolb, Gibb, & Muirhead, 1995). The animals were given about 120 days to recover, were administered several behavioral tests, and were sacrificed about 200 days postsurgery. Analysis of the layer V pyramidal cells in motor cortex showed a 20% increase in basilar dendritic branches. Analysis of layer III pyramidal cells showed 16% increase in basilar branches but no significant change in the apical branches. Thus, once again there is a remodeling of the dendritic fields of the pyramidal cells that correlates with improved function.

Plasticity and Brain Damage in Aged Rats

As the brain ages it must continually compensate for the loss of neurons. If we presume that there are limits to the extent of compensatory plasticity that is available, which seems reasonable because a single enormous neuron could not compensate for the loss of millions, then the aging brain may have a difficult time in coping with injury. To test this possibility we performed two experiments on 28-month-old rats (Kolb, Gibb, & Winocur, unpublished results, 1993). In the first experiment we placed rats in complex environments for 60 days, and then compared their dendritic arbors with littermates that were housed in standard laboratory cages over the same period. The enriched animals showed a significant increase in dendritic arborization, which told us that the brain of the 28-month-old rat could show plastic changes. In the second experiment, 28-month-old rats were given frontal lesions and were tested in the Morris water task after 60 days of recovery. The animals performed very poorly and showed no evidence of any learning of the task at the end of training. When we examined their dendritic arbors, we found that in contrast to younger animals, these aged rats showed a significant atrophy in dendritic arborization, much like we had seen in the stroke rats. The contrasting effects of enrichment and cortical injury on the remaining cortical neurons implies that although the aged brain can change in response to experience, it may not be able to compensate for significant brain injury. The obvious experiment is to see if enrichment might have provoked the aged brain to grow new connections. This experiment would have obvious clinical implications in the treatment of elderly people with cerebral injuries.

Conclusions

In summary, our results to date show that after prefrontal or motor cortex lesions or after hemidecortications there is some functional restitution, and this is correlated with a remodeling of the pyramidal cell dendritic fields, with an overall increase in synaptic space per neuron. An increase in dendritic branching is not always the end result of cortical injury in adulthood, however. For example, when we made large visual cortex lesions, we found no recovery of either visual discrimination learning or visually guided spatial navigation learning. When we analyzed dendritic arborization about 200 days after the injuries, we found a significant decrease in somatosensory pyramidal cell dendritic fields (Kolb, Ladowsky, Gibb, & Gorny, 1994). Thus, in this study we found no recovery and found the neuronal atrophy that we had expected in our original experiments. Similarly, we have found that after large unilateral cortical stroke, which allows little recovery of function, there is also a decrease in dendritic fields of pyramidal neurons in the ipsilateral hemisphere (Kolb, Ribeiro-da-Silva, & Cuello, 1995). There is no change in contralateral hemisphere and no change in the spine density in either hemisphere.

Taken together, the results of our prefrontal, motor cortex, visual cortex, pyramidal tract, hemidecortication, and stroke studies suggest that when there is significant restitution of function there is a remodeling of cortical circuitry that correlates with the recovery. In contrast, when there is no restitution of function either there is no obvious remodeling of cortical circuitry or there is an atrophy of the dendrites of the remaining neurons.

Our demonstration of a correlation between dendritic change and behavioral outcome does not prove that the dendritic growth and remodeling supports the behavioral recovery. The recovery could be due to some other neuronal change that we have not measured, or it could be that the behavioral recovery causes the dendritic changes. Nonetheless, it is a reasonable hypothesis that because dendritic growth is correlated with recovery and dendritic atrophy is correlated with nonrecovery, the dendritic growth may be necessary for the recovery.

A reasonable question that we might ask is how an increase in dendritic space could allow an increase in synapses. After all, there must be presynaptic (axonal) input as well. One way to conceive of the increased synapses is to focus on the likely ways that axons would form new synapses. Steward (1991) proposed two ways for the hippocampal model, and similar mechanisms are likely in the cortex as well (Fig. 5.7). In one type of synapse formation the axons that travel past vacant postsynaptic sites could form a new presynaptic apparatus and make connections, *en passant* (Fig. 5.7). This type of synapse formation requires very

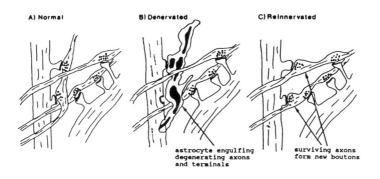

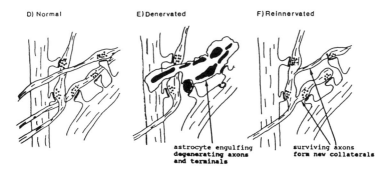

FIG. 5.7.   Two ways that new synapses may be formed after a loss of afferents. In the top sequence there is a growth of new axon terminals in existing axon branches. In the bottom sequence the axons form new collaterals, which synapse on the dendrites. In the latter case, there could be growth of new dendrites to accommodate the growth of the axon collaterals. After Steward (1991). Adapted by permission of Plenum Publishing Corporation.

little growth in the presynaptic side and none in the postsynaptic side. This type of synapse formation probably would not be observed as an increase in dendritic material. A second type of synapse formation is somewhat different. In this case, the axons form new branches, known as collaterals, and these synapse on the dendrites. In this case we could imagine an increase in dendritic arbor, which would allow these new synapses to form.

Even if we accept the dendrite–behavior relationship as causal, we are left, of course, with the many significant questions. What are the actual changes in the connections that are reflected in the dendritic reorganization? That is, what are the new connections and where do they come from? I have suggested that the changes reflect some type of change in the intrinsic connectivity of the cortex, but this is not proven. What are the signals that trigger the synaptic changes? That is, why do the changes occur? There are changes in microglia within hours of cortical injury. There are later changes in astrocytes that peak a week or so after the injury. These glial changes may play a role in the synaptic remodeling, but exactly how they do this is unclear. How does the reorganization of the cortical circuitry support behavioral recovery? Increasing intrinsic connectivity could support more behavior, but precisely how it does this remains a question whose answer is far away. Finally, what roles do the lesion-induced changes in behavior play in the synaptic remodeling of the cortex? I turn to this issue in the next section.

THE ROLE OF ACTIVITY IN CORTICAL REMODELING

Rutledge and his colleagues have done a series of provocative experiments that suggest that cortical activity may play a major role in neocortical plasticity. (e.g., Rutledge, 1978; Rutledge, Wright, & Duncan,1974). In their experiments Rutledge and his collaborators first deafferented the neocortex by undercutting the grey matter in the suprasylvian gyrus of cats. This procedure effectively eliminates all inputs and outputs from the underlying white matter but leaves the blood flow and the intrinsic cortical circuitry intact. Using a combination of Golgi and electron microscopic techniques they showed that the pyramidal cells lose 40–50% of their spines after this procedure, that there is a decrease in dendritic and axonal branches, and that there is a loss of synapses. In the second phase of the experiments the authors implanted electrical stimulating electrodes in the undercut tissue. By applying a low-level electrical stimulation over a period of weeks they were then able to produce significant reinnervation of the pyramidal cells (Fig. 5.8). For example, the loss of spines on the apical dendritic terminals was reduced from 40% to 7% of control values, which is a clear example of reinnervation. This recovery of spines reflected a corresponding increase in synapses, which the authors took as evidence of sprouting of new connections. The authors speculated that the source of these connections was either local stellate cells or possibly recurrent collaterals from other pyramidal cells.

The results of the Rutledge experiments are especially intriguing because they suggest activity may be important in altering the structure of an injured brain. It is not known how long after injury this is true, however, nor when the optimal time might be for the activity.

Although brain stimulation is an obvious way to increase neocortical activity, another way is to produce behavior. If the injured cortex is unusually sensitive to activity, then alterations in behavior after cortical injury could have greater consequences than would be expected in the normal brain. Jones and Schallert have addressed this possibility in series of experiments. In their first experiment they made small unilateral sensorimotor cortex lesions in the region of the forepaw representation of rats. This resulted in a postural and motoric asymmetry in which the animals favored the use of the paw opposite the normal hemisphere. This postural asymmetry is large over the first 2 weeks after injury and then slowly reduces as the animal regains some use of the affected limb. Jones and Schallert sacrificed animals at different postoperative times and examined the dendritic structure in the forepaw region of the normal hemisphere, finding an increase in dendritic branching that took several days to develop and that peaked at day 18 before declining (Fig. 5.9). They concluded that the behavior of the animals had effectively stimulated the intact hemisphere, leading to the dendritic growth. There were two important additional details in their experiments, however. First, they found that if they prevented normal rats from using one paw by placing it in a harness, there was no compensatory growth in the hemisphere opposite the paw that the animals were still able to use. This result means that the behavioral asymmetry was effective in changing the brain only when there was also cortical injury. It is difficult to understand why this result was obtained, but it does imply that cortical injury may render the brain more plastic than is normally the case. Second, when they restrained the use of the favored paw after a unilateral lesion, they were able to block the dendritic growth. This result means that the dendritic growth requires both a cortical injury and a behavioral asymmetry (Jones & Schallert, 1992, 1994). The Jones and Schallert results are reminiscent of the Rutledge results, except that the former authors showed that the normal cortex may also be especially sensitive to activity after a cortical injury. This sensitivity is important because it may provide an important mechanism underlying processes of recovery and plasticity.

One of the shortcomings of the Jones and Schallert work is that they did not analyze the dendritic changes in the injured hemisphere. It is of some interest to know whether the lesion produced atrophy in the neurons, because this is what we had found in our studies of rats sacrificed soon after prefrontal lesions. Mike Melnychuk and I therefore replicated the Jones and Schallert study and looked at cells in both hemispheres. In addition, we added another wrinkle to the experiment. We reasoned that if the motor asymmetry was responsible for the changes

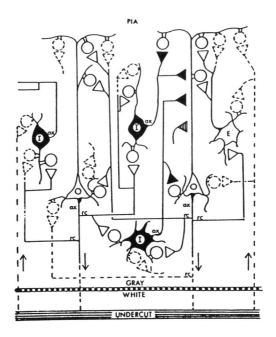

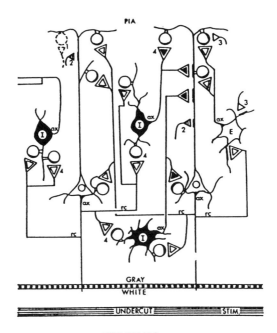

FIGURE 5.8.

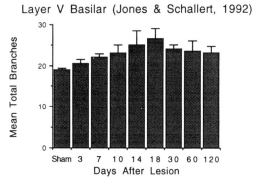

FIG. 5.9. Summary of changes in the dendritic branching of neurons in layer V after a small sensorimotor cortex lesion in the contralateral hemisphere. There is an increase in branching up to a peak around day 18, followed by a pruning of the branching. After Jones and Schallert (1992).

in the normal hemisphere then we should be able to increase the asymmetry and increase the dendritic changes. We therefore gave the animals a forelimb area lesion and then after the animals had recovered for 14 days we gave them a second lesion that included the tissue surrounding the first one. This second lesion reinstated the motor asymmetry (see Chapter 3). We also predicted that if we could reverse or block the motor asymmetry, we should reverse or block the cortical changes. We therefore had another group of rats that received a unilateral lesion, were allowed 14 days to recover, and then were given a lesion in the forelimb region in the opposite hemisphere. Our results were clear. First, there was surprisingly little effect on the dendritic arbor in the injured hemispheres, although there was a 7% drop in spine density in the lesion hemispheres relative to normal control hemispheres. Second, there was an increase in dendritic branching in the normal hemisphere of unilateral operates, and this effect was enhanced in the animals given a second lesion. Analysis of variance on the normal hemispheres showed a significant main effect. Third, a second lesion contralateral to the first one reversed the behavioral asymmetry and abolished the

---

FIG. 5.8. (opposite page) Top: Effects of cortical undercutting. Only two types of neurons are shown, pyramidal cells and generalized stellate cells. Excitatory elements, clear; inhibitory, darkened or hatched. Degenerated structures indicated by dashed lines. The hatched, inhibitory terminal on pyramidal cell dendritic shaft (right center) is a new synaptic element, but presynaptic source is unknown. Arrows depict afferent and efferent axons. Bottom: Effects of chronic electrical stimulation on undercut cortex. 1, Unrecovered spine loss. 2, New excitatory terminals, presynaptic source unknown; note, upper right, one appears as a new, second synapse on a spine. 4, Larger inhibitory and excitatory terminals indicated by double triangles. Longer synaptic membrane contacts indicated by darkened region on dendritic shafts and spines. Abbreviations: ax, axon; rc, recurrent collaterals; I, inhibitory stellate cell; E, excitatory stellate cell. After Rutledge (1978). Adapted by permission of Raven Press, Ltd.

increased branching. This last finding is curious because the animals would seem to have fit the Jones–Schallert criteria: They had an injury and a postural asymmetry. The absence of a behavior-related growth in this group suggests that the behavioral change can only influence a normal hemisphere.

It is clear that neocortical activity influences neocortical plasticity after cerebral injury. This has important clinical implications, because therapies might be expected to be more effective when the cortical activity is most effective in altering connectivity. There is an interesting experimental implication of activity-dependent changes too. When investigators study functional recovery after brain injury they normally use various behavioral paradigms to assess the behavioral changes. However, if activity affects plasticity, then the act of testing animals in behavioral tasks can potentially alter the recovery process! This possibility provides an interesting complication to studies of brain–behavior relationships after cortical injury.

6

Plasticity and Recovery from Cortical Injury During Development

One of the principal conclusions of Chapter 4 was that the functional consequences of cortical injury vary with the developmental stage of the brain at the time of injury. Cortical injury during the end of the mitotic phase or during neuronal migration leads to a very poor functional outcome, whereas similar injury during the period of maximal dendritic differentiation and synapse formation allows a more favorable outcome than at any other time in life. It therefore should come as no surprise that the anatomical sequelae of cortical injury at different ages also vary with developmental stage. Furthermore, it also should not be surprising that the extent of brain plasticity after cortical injury during development is far greater than is observed after similar injury in adulthood. Nonetheless, a major premise of this chapter is that there are clear similarities between some forms of synaptic plasticity after injury in developing and adult animals and that functional recovery is supported by similar mechanisms at different times in life.

BACKGROUND

The possibility that the central nervous system of amphibians was capable of regeneration after injury during development has been known for at least 50 years (e.g., Harrison, 1947; Nicholas, 1957). Curiously, although Hicks showed that rat and mouse fetuses were capable of some of the recovery feats of amphibians (e.g., Hicks, 1954; Hicks, D'Amato, & Glover, 1984), this idea did not really gain acceptance until the 1970s (e.g., Schneider, 1973). It appears that the idea that the mammalian nervous system might be capable of reorganization was treated as a rare curiosity of little consequence for nearly 20 years. This view has vanished, and it is now generally accepted that early cortical injury can produce significant reorganization of both the subcortical and cortico-cortical inputs to the cortex (e.g., Cotman & Nadler, 1978; Goldman & Galkin, 1978; Kolb, Gibb, & van der Kooy, 1994), as well as the outputs of the cortex (e.g., Castro, 1990; Goldman, 1974; Hicks & D'Amato, 1975; Whishaw & Kolb, 1988). It is usually assumed that these aberrant inputs and outputs must somehow be supporting improved functional outcome, but there is surprisingly little study of how the actual synaptic organization is altered in the young animal or how this organization supports behavior. There is also virtually no systematic research devoted to understanding the differences in plasticity after injuries at different times in development. My colleagues and I have focused on this question for the past decade, and most of this chapter is devoted to an examination of our results. I begin by looking at the gross changes in cerebral morphology after injury at different ages and then consider the changes in dendritic morphology in the remaining cortex. Finally, I try to relate the dendritic changes to the changes we have seen in afferent and efferent connectivity of the cortex after early lesions.

GROSS SEQUELAE OF NEOCORTICAL DAMAGE DURING DEVELOPMENT

When we began our studies of neonatal neocortical lesions in rats, Ian Whishaw and I were struck by two unexpected phenomena. First, the adult brains of all animals with cortical lesions in the first 2 weeks of life were visibly smaller than the brains of animals with similar injury in adulthood (e.g., Kolb, Sutherland, & Whishaw, 1983b; Kolb & Whishaw, 1981b). When we quantified both brain weight and brain dimensions we found that both were reduced after damage to the prefrontal, motor, parietal, visual, or temporal cortex (e.g., Kolb et al., 1983b). The loss in brain size is not equivalent at different ages, however, as those animals with the earliest lesions have the smallest brains. For example, rats with large frontal lesions on the day of birth have brains in adulthood that weigh about 80% of the brains of animals with similar lesions in adulthood. Rats with lesions at 10 days of age have brains that weigh about 90% of adult operates (Fig. 6.1). Thus, even the 10-day operates that show marked recovery of function (see Chapter 3) had a much smaller brain than adults with similar lesions but that had a poorer behavioral outcome.[1] This appears to be a case of doing more with less.

---

[1]The possibility that early lesions might lead to the development of smaller brains was first described by Arthur Nonneman (1970). He made small unilateral cortical lesions in rabbits and noticed that the injured hemisphere was markedly smaller than normal. In a series of subsequent experiments with cats, he showed the same phenomenon. Unfortunately, neither his rabbit or cat experiments were ever published.

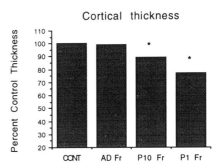

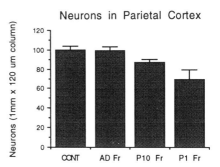

FIG. 6.1.   Top: Summary of the cortical thickness of the brains of adult rats who sustained frontal lesions in adulthood (Ad Fr), on postnatal day 10 (P10 Fr), or on postnatal day 1 (P1 Fr). Bottom: Summary of neuron counts in Golgi-stained tissue of adult rats with lesions in adulthood, P10 or P1. The values represent the mean total number of neurons in layers I–VI in a 1 mm wide × 120 μm thick column. After Kolb and Gibb (1990).

Furthermore, the reduction in brain size in the youngest animals is so profound that these animals sometimes have brains that weigh less than animals with complete decortications in adulthood! We do not know the reasons for the small brains, but we have found that the decrease in brain size is immediate and can be measured 24 hr after the lesion (Kolb, 1987). In addition, the remaining cortex is visibly, and quantifiably, thinner than normal, and this too can be seen 24 hr after the lesion. This thinning of the cortex is worse the earlier the injury, and it is worse after frontal lesions than after posterior lesions. One reason for the decrease in cortical thickness is that there are fewer neurons in the cortex, although we do not know when the neurons disappear, nor do we know why they disappear (Kolb & Gibb, 1990).

The second unexpected observation that Whishaw and I made was that the lesion size varies with the age at injury. In our studies of the effect of cortical injury in rats we normally remove portions of the cortex by gentle aspiration of the grey matter. Thus, at the time of surgery there is a cavity left in the cortical mantle after the surgery. For animals operated in adulthood this cavity usually fills with cerebrospinal fluid and remains about the same size throughout the rest of the animal's life. The only exception occurs when the lesion is small, perhaps less than 2 mm in diameter. In this case the cavity may collapse as the walls in the remaining cortical mantle appear to move together. Similarly, when cortex is removed in the first few days of life there is virtually always a cavity in adulthood unless the removal was very small. In contrast, however, when relatively large amounts of frontal or motor cortex are removed at 7–15 days of age there is often no cavity at all (Fig. 6.2). Indeed, when I first began studying animals with lesions at this age I was so startled by the absence of cavities that I seriously doubted that the animals even had received lesions! If removals at day 7–15 are truly massive and invade the ventricle there is a cavity, but it is still smaller than would be expected from animals with similar lesions earlier or later in life. The absence of lesion cavities appears to be most dramatic with medial prefrontal or motor cortex lesions and does not appear to follow visual or temporal cortex lesions, although I have not systematically looked at the "filling in" phenomenon in different posterior cortical areas. The absence of cavities is perplexing and suggests that either the brain is capable of regrowing the lost tissue or neurons migrate into the cavity from elsewhere. Both hypotheses are reasonable and testable.

One important feature of neocortical development in the rat is that the frontal cortex completes mitosis and migration earlier than the posterior cortex. This may have important implications for cortical plasticity after frontal or posterior lesions. For example, after the frontal cortex is removed at 7 days of age there are still a large number of migrating neurons heading for the posterior cortex, whereas when the visual cortex is damaged there are few neurons still migrating in anterior cortex. This suggests that cells destined for the posterior cortex of frontal operates may contribute to the cavity filling but that in the case of animals with posterior lesions the cells of the frontal cortex are already committed and cannot move to the posterior cortex. This possibility is consistent with the observation that the posterior cortex is abnormally thin in animals with early frontal lesions but the frontal cortex is only marginally thinner in animals with early posterior lesions. Of course, there is the problem of why the cavities of younger frontal operates do not fill in. And there is the problem of how migrating neurons could suddenly abandon their radial glial highways and head for the frontal cortex! Nonetheless, we pursued the possibility of altered migration by labeling neurons *in utero* by injecting the pregnant mothers with BrdU (bromodeoxyuridine) during the time of maximal neuronal mitosis (de Brabander, Gibb, & Kolb, 1993). This compound is incorporated into mitotic neurons during the S-phase of cell division, so that the neurons can be identified later with an immunohistochemical procedure. We then gave rats frontal lesions at 10 days of age, sacrificed them in adulthood, and stained for BrdU.

Fig. 6.3 shows that we found labeled neurons in the "regenerated" frontal cortex, which means that the labeled cells had migrated into the frontal cortex from somewhere else. Notice, too, that the labeled neurons did not migrate to specific layers as in the normal brain but were randomly distributed across the cortex. This experiment does not prove that new neurons are not also present in

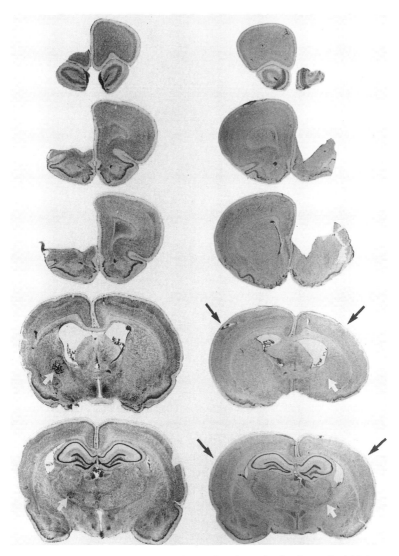

FIG. 6.2.   Photomicrographs illustrating the reduction in cortical thickness ipsilateral to a lesion in a rat with a frontal lesion in infancy (right) versus a similar lesion in an adult rat (left). Compare the cortical thickness at the arrows in the neonatal operate.

the regenerated region, but it does demonstrate that many of the neurons in the filled-in region were born prenatally and thus were already present in the brain at the time of injury.

We have also explored the possibility that frontal lesions at postnatal day 7–10

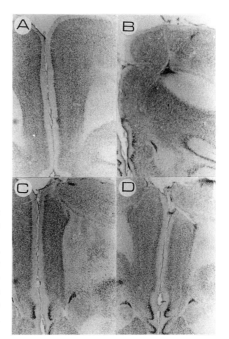

FIG. 6.3. Photomicrographs illustrating normal midline frontal cortex (A) and the "filling-in" of the midline cortex after midline lesions on day 3 (B) or day 10 (C,D). There is a clear separation of the normal tissue to the left and the filled in tissue to the right. After Kolb, Petrie, Cioe, and Gibb (1995).

lead to neurogenesis. Recall that cells along the wall of the anterior horn of the lateral ventricle continue to show mitosis throughout the life of a rat (chapter 4). Although these neurons normally do not migrate away from the ventricle wall, there is now evidence that they do migrate to the olfactory bulb in normal adult brains. Furthermore, the addition of neurotrophic factors, such as epidermal growth factor, into the ventricle stimulates the neurons to migrate (Craig, Morshead, Reynolds, Weiss, & van der Kooy, 1994). In view of these results, perhaps it is not unreasonable to suppose that under some circumstances these cells could migrate into the cortex. Of course, there is the difficulty of migrating in the absence of radial glia, but in the developing brain these glia are still present well after mitosis is complete. Robbin Gibb and I therefore gave rats frontal lesions on postnatal day 10 and injected the animals with large doses of BrdU three times on each of postnatal days 1 and 2. We hoped that by giving large doses we would maximize our likelihood of staining dividing neurons. One difficulty with our experimental design was that we had to be concerned about the development of astrocytes during this time. The BrdU is not specific to neurons, so astrocytes would also be expected to incorporate the compound. In order to control for this problem we counterstained our histological material with an antibody to glial fibrillary acidic protein (GFAP), which would identify the astrocytes, and another antibody to microglia (OX-42), which would identify the microglia for us. The bottom panel of Fig. 6.4 illustrates our results. There were only a few neurons identified in the normal brain, and virtually all of these were located in the midline cortex. In contrast, there were many neurons in the "filled-in" region of the lesion brain, and again there were virtually none lateral to the lesion. These results are truly provocative, for they imply not only that the midline cortex is capable of filling in with newly developed neurons, but they

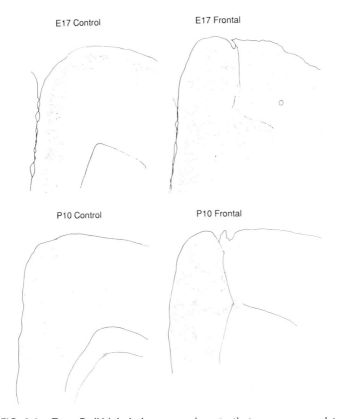

FIG. 6.4.   Top: BrdU-labeled neurons in rats that were exposed to BrdU on embryonic day 17. The control animal has a restricted band of label in layers II/III in the midline cortex as well as more laterally in the sensorimotor cortex. In contrast, the rat with a frontal lesion on post-natal day 10 has labeled cells throughout all layers in the filled-in midline cortex. Bottom: BrdU-labeled neurons in rats that were given six injections of BrdU on postnatal days 10 and 11. There are few labeled neurons in midline cortex of the the control animal and vir-tually none more laterally. There are many labeled neurons in the rat with a frontal lesion on day 10, but the majority of these neurons are localized to the filled-in tissue. Cells were counterstained with anti-bodies to GFAP and microglia (OX-42) in order to exclude glia.

also imply that the midline cortex continues developing neurons long after it is generally believed. This is an exciting result. Our next task is to determine how these neurons are connected and whether there might be any difference in the connectivity of neurons that are born prenatally and migrate into the cavity and those that are born postnatally. Our preliminary Golgi analysis of these neurons suggests that they are very slow in developing relative to the rest of the cortex or the neurons in a normal brain (de Brabander et al., 1993).

To summarize, early cortical lesions in rats lead to the development of a small brain, and if the lesion is at day 7–10 there may be a filling in of the lesion cavity. The small brain is remarkable because animals with day 10 lesions often show behavior that is almost indistinguishable from normal controls. This implies that their brain undergoes a significant reorganization after the injury. In the case of animals with frontal lesions, this may include a rerouting of migrating neurons from more posterior cortex into the region of the cavity. These neurons may play some role in supporting the good functional outcome. Of course, we currently do not know how these neurons are organized or what their afferents or efferents might be. Finally, the fact that infant rats with an injury at day 1 versus day 10 have large differences in both brain size and cavity size is almost certainly important in understanding the different functional outcomes.

DENDRITIC CHANGES AFTER CORTICAL INJURIES DURING DEVELOPMENT

Effects of Frontal Cortex Lesions

We have seen that injury to the cortex of the newborn and 10-day-old rat has different consequences on function as well as brain size and cavity size. We therefore began our dendritic studies by making frontal lesions in one hemisphere of newborn rats and then subsequently made similar lesions in the other hemisphere 9 days later. The animals were allowed to grow into adulthood before being sacrificed, and their brains were prepared for Golgi-Cox staining. It was my expectation that if the neurons of the two hemispheres responded differently to the lesions, we ought to see a clear difference in the dendritic organization of the neurons in the two hemispheres. Indeed, the difference was dramatic (Figs. 6.5 and 6.6).

We had been accustomed to looking at the brains of adult operates in whom the changes in dendritic arborization were quantitative and certainly not obvious, even to the trained eye. In contrast, when we looked at the brains of the day-1/day-10 animals there was a qualitative difference that was immediately apparent: The pyramidal neurons throughout the cortex of the hemispheres with day 10 lesions had far greater dendritic arborizations than those in the day 1 hemispheres. Quantification and comparison to the brains of normal littermates

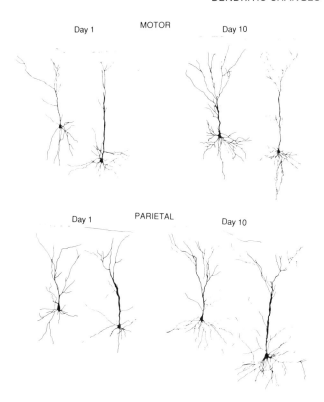

FIG. 6.5.   Representative examples of layer II/III pyramidal neurons in a rat that had a frontal lesion in the left hemisphere on day 1 and in the right hemisphere on day 10. Neurons in both the motor and parietal cortex are visibly more complex in the neurons of the hemisphere with a lesion on day 10. After Kolb, Gibb, and van der Kooy (1994).

revealed that although the rats with day 10 lesions had more branches than normal control animals, the day 1 animals had fewer branches than normal (Kolb & Gibb, 1991b; 1993; Kolb, Gibb, & van der Kooy, 1994). Furthermore, in contrast to the animals with frontal lesions in adulthood, which only showed an increase in dendritic branching in the region proximal to the lesions, the animals with day 10 lesions showed an increase throughout neocortex of the hemisphere. The dramatic contrast between the anatomical changes in animals with day 1 and day 10 frontal lesions complements a similar contrast in the functional outcomes in animals with lesions at these ages (Fig. 6.7, Fig. 6.8). This anatomy–behavior correlation led us to the conclusion that the relationship may be causal. That is, it is possible that increased dendritic growth reflects increased synapse formation and this is necessary for recovery after early cortical injury (Kolb & Gibb, 1990).

The first challenge to this conclusion came from our own experiments in

DAY 10

Apical   Basilai

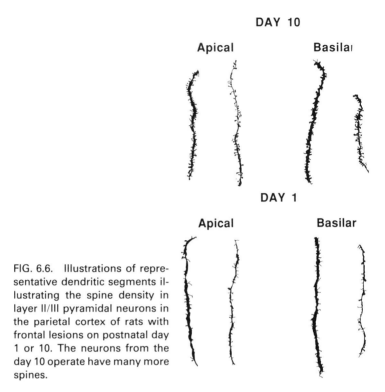

DAY 1

Apical   Basilar

FIG. 6.6. Illustrations of representative dendritic segments illustrating the spine density in layer II/III pyramidal neurons in the parietal cortex of rats with frontal lesions on postnatal day 1 or 10. The neurons from the day 10 operate have many more spines.

which we made frontal lesions on postnatal day 7 and then examined behavior and anatomy in adulthood (Kolb & Sutherland, 1992). We once again found that day 7 lesions allowed significant recovery of function, but, unexpectedly, we found that relative to normal littermate controls there was no increase in dendritic branching in the day 7 operates. This result obviously compromised our hypothesis and led us to examine spine density on the terminal branches of cortical pyramidal cells. The results showed a 15% higher density in the day 7 frontal operates relative to their normal littermates (Kolb & Stewart, in press). Hence, we subsequently reanalyzed the spine density in the day 1 and day 10 operates, and found a decrease in spine density in the day 1 animals and a 15% increase in the day 10 animals. Thus, it appears that both spine density and dendritic length are correlated with recovery. Because increasing both dendritic length and spine density would produce more synaptic space than just increasing spine density, it is therefore not surprising that rats with day 10 lesions show better recovery than those with day 7 lesions. It seems likely that dendritic length can increase independently of spine density, as we saw for the effects of enrichment on the adult cortex (Fig. 2.7).

The second challenge to our dendrite–behavior correlation came from an experiment in which we sought to determine the time course of the developmental changes in dendritic growth (Kolb & Gibb, 1993). In this experiment we took advantage of the finding that normal rats can first learn the Morris water task at about 20 days of age (Rudy, Stadler-Morris, & Albert, 1987). It was our expectation that if we gave infant rats frontal lesions at day 10, they would show functional restitution when they were tested on day 20, and this restitution would be correlated with dendritic growth. Our first surprise came when the day 10 frontal animals did not show any evidence of learning the Morris task when they were trained on days 20–22. Indeed, although the normal animals learned the task, the day 10 animals were indistinguishable from animals with day 1 lesions that were tested at the same time. When we analyzed the dendritic arborization of the pyramidal cells we found a simple explanation: The dendrites of the day 10 animals showed no increase in either branching or spine density relative to normal brains or the brains of day 1 operates. This result has two implications. First, the dendritic compensation to frontal lesions occurs slowly, even in developing animals. Second, in the absence of the dendritic changes there is no functional restitution. This leads to the prediction that functional restitution and dendritic growth should be correlated developmentally. That is, whenever we first find recovery we should also find dendritic growth. We therefore redid our experiment except that half of the animals were trained on day 20–22 and the

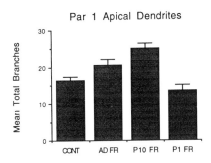

FIG. 6.7. Summary of the performance of rats on the Morris water task and the dendritic morphology of cells in their parietal cortex. Rats with lesions on postnatal day 10 show recovery of spatial learning and their neurons have the most dendritic branching.

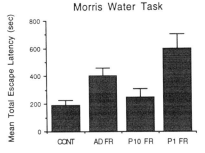

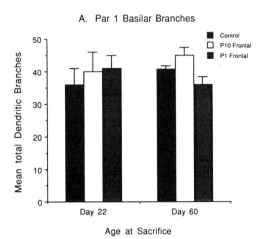

A. Par 1 Basilar Branches

FIG. 6.8. Summary of the dendritic branching and spine density of layer II/III pyramidal neurons in the brains of rats of rats
with lesions on postnatal day 1
or 10. The animals were sacrificed either on postnatal day 22
or 60. On day 22 there were no
differences in dendritic morphology and both frontal groups
were impaired at learning the
Morris water task. On day 60 the
rats with frontal lesions on postnatal day 10 showed an increase
in both dendritic branching and
in spine density. These animals
showed good performance in
the water task at this age. After
Kolb and Gibb (1993).

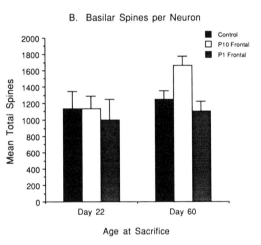

B. Basilar Spines per Neuron

other half were allowed to develop until day 56, at which time they were trained
in the water task. Following behavioral training the pyramidal neurons were
drawn and analyzed. The results were clear. Rats with day 10 lesions learned the
water task as quickly as normal animals on the day 56–58 test, and they showed
increased dendritic branching and spine density. In other words, when the animals showed recovery they showed dendritic growth, whereas if they failed to
show recovery they did not show the requisite dendritic growth. This result is
therefore consistent with the general hypothesis that synaptic organization under-
lies the presence (or absence) of recovery from neocortical injury.

Demonstrations of dendritic changes following neonatal lesions imply
changes in synapse formation, but proof of synaptic change requires an electron
microscopic analysis. Grazyna Gorny has begun this analysis with a study of rats

with day 1 unilateral frontal lesions. Her results to date show a decrease in total synapses and in synapses per neuron in parietal and visual cortex of the damaged hemisphere. Thus, we have evidence of a decrease in synapse numbers when we see a decrease in dendritic branching. What is more important, however, will be a demonstration of an increase in synapse density in brains that show an increase in spine density and dendritic growth.

Effects of Motor Cortex Lesions

Rats with unilateral day 1 motor cortex lesions show substantial recovery of reaching relative to rats with comparable adult lesions (Whishaw & Kolb, 1988). This pattern of recovery is correlated with a difference in the pattern of dendritic changes in the normal hemisphere of the infant and adult operates. Analysis of the dendritic changes in the day 1 rats shows a 16% increase in layer III basilar branches in the parietal cortex in both the damaged and the normal hemisphere, as well as an 8% increase in apical branching in the normal hemisphere (Fig. 6.9). Rats with adult lesions did not show either of these changes. (This contrasts with the effects of bilateral lesions in adult rats, which we discussed in the last chapter.)

The contrasting effect of the adult and neonatal parallels a difference in the effect of the lesions on corticospinal projections. Hicks and D'Amato (e.g.,

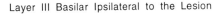

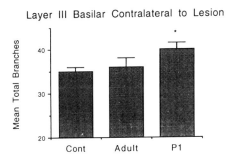

FIG. 6.9. Summary of the dendritic branching of rats with unilateral motor cortex lesions as adults or on postnatal day 1. The neonatal operates showed an increase in dendritic branching in both the normal and injured hemisphere, whereas the adult animals showed no differences from control. After Kolb, Hewson, and Whishaw (1993).

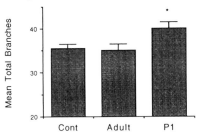

1975) were the first to show that when infant rats sustained unilateral lesions of the corticospinal projection neurons, they were subsequently found to have an anomalous ipsilateral pathway from the intact hemisphere to the spinal cord. Hicks and D'Amato presumed that this pathway was responsible for the improved functional outcome in these animals, relative to adult operates who showed no such connection (Fig. 6.10). It therefore appears that after early motor cortex lesions in rats there is the development of abnormal ipsilateral pathway and an expansion of the cortical connections of the presumed cells of origin of this projection. Together, these changes are correlated with an enhanced recovery of function.

If the anatomical changes in the normal hemisphere are mediating recovery from neonatal motor cortex injury, then bilateral injury to the neonatal motor cortex should preclude recovery. This is indeed the case: Rats with bilateral motor cortex lesions on postnatal 1 are as impaired at motor tasks as rats with bilateral lesions in adulthood. Furthermore, the neonatal bilateral operates show novel behavioral deficits in tasks such as the Morris water task, which are not affected by similar lesions in adulthood. One interpretation of this latter result is that the infant lesions interfere with the operation of the remaining cortex. This interpretation is consistent with the anatomical results. Thus, rats with day 1 bilateral motor cortex lesions show an aberrant corticospinal pathway originating from the parietal cortex (Kolb, Hewson, & Whishaw, 1993). In other words, in the absence of the normal motor cortex projection to the spinal cord there is a new corticospinal projection from the parietal cortex. This projection likely reflects the failure of an exuberant projection in infancy to retract, rather the growth of a new pathway (e.g., Hicks & D'Amato, 1975; O'Leary, 1989). If we examine the dendritic organization of the parietal neurons in the vicinity of this abnormal corticospinal projection, we do not find an increase in dendritic branching but rather we find atrophy. These data suggest that the aberrant pathway is not only not capable of supporting recovery of motor function, but it may actually interfere with other cortical functions.

Whishaw and I tested this idea by making unilateral motor cortex lesions in newborn rats, and then allowing them to recover to adulthood. We assumed that the animals would show motor recovery, which would be supported by changes in the motor cortex of the normal hemisphere, and they would not show deficits in tasks like the Morris water task. We then removed the motor cortex in the intact hemisphere. It was our expectation that this second lesion would abolish the motor recovery but would have no effect upon other behaviors such as the Morris task, because there would be no aberrant motor pathway that could interfere with normal functioning of the remaining cortex. Our expectations were confirmed. The animals with two-stage bilateral lesions performed miserably in a reaching task but performed as well as control animals in the spatial navigation task.

The results of our studies of rats with neonatal motor cortex lesions lead to

A.   Normal

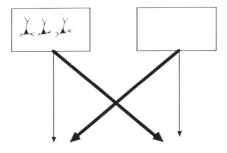

B.   Adult Lesion

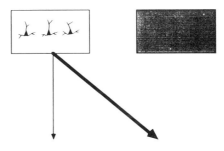

C.   Neonatal Lesion

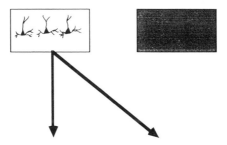

FIG. 6.10.   Schematic illustration of the effects of neonatal motor cortex lesions. (A) In the normal animal there is a large crossed projection
and a small ipsilateral projection. (B) After a unilateral motor cortex
injury in adulthood there is a loss of the crossed projection to the
contralateral paw and of the ipsilateral projection to the same side
paw. There are no changes in dendritic arborization. (C) Rats with
neonatal lesions show an enhanced growth of the ipsilateral pathway
from the normal hemisphere and an increase in the dendritic branching of the neurons presumed to project to the spinal cord.

two conclusions. First, unilateral lesions lead to a remodeling of cortical connectivity and circuitry that may support recovery of function. Second, bilateral lesions lead to a remodeling of cortical connectivity and circuitry that does not support recovery and may actually interfere with other, nonmotor, functions. The finding that the development of abnormal connections may interfere with normal functioning is not without precedent. For example, Schneider (1973) found abnormal orienting responses in hamsters that developed abnormal retino-tectal pathways. Similarly, in our studies of rats with frontal cortex lesions on the day of birth we have found extensive reorganization of cortical connections from the thalamus, amygdala, and brainstem (Kolb, Gibb, & van der Kooy, 1994). As we have already seen, these these connections are associated with a very poor functional outcome. In this case, however, we found only a stunting of dendritic arborization (see earlier discussion).

Effects of Hemidecortication

When Robert Sutherland, Ian Whishaw, and I began to study the functional effects of neonatal hemidecortication we were surprised to find that, in contrast to the effects of frontal lesions, neonatal hemidecortication increased the thickness of the contralateral cortex (Kolb et al., 1983b). This was especially surprising because the brains of hemidecorticated animals would not have any callosal connections, which might be predicted to shrink cortical thickness. We were also surprised by a second finding: Although frontal lesions on the day of birth showed worse outcomes than similar lesions on day 7–10, hemidecortication on the day of birth allowed a better functional outcome than similar injury at 7–10 days of age (Kolb & Tomie, 1988). These two results suggest that there are likely to be substantial differences in the mechanisms underlying recovery in the neonatal frontal and hemidecorticate rat. Analysis of the dendritic changes suggest otherwise, however. In fact, neonatal hemidecortication is associated with a major increase in the dendritic arborization of the pyramidal and stellate cells in the contralateral hemisphere (Kolb, Gibb, & van der Kooy, 1992). This increase is larger in the motor and parietal cortex than in the more posterior cortex, which is consistent with our behavioral observations. That is, there is better restitution of behaviors such as walking and reaching than there is of visually guided behaviors such as maze learning.

The dendritic results from the neonatal hemidecorticates led us to a prediction. I noted in Chapter 3 that when we made small stab wounds in the normal hemisphere of neonatal hemidecorticates we severely compromised recovery. It therefore follows that the stab wound must have interfered with the compensatory dendritic growth in the hemisphere. Our preliminary results support this conclusion, as the stab wound blocked the cortical thickening and reduced the dendritic growth (Kolb, Gibb, & Muirhead, 1995). Thus, once again we see a correlation between increased dendritic growth and functional recovery.

Effects of Visual Cortex and Cingulate Lesions

We have undertaken two sets of experiments in which we failed to find recovery from neonatal cortical lesions. In the first set we made bilateral visual cortex lesions in rats on postnatal days 4, 10, or in adulthood (Kolb, Ladowsky, Gibb, & Gorny, 1994). When the animals were tested in adulthood on the Morris water task and on a visual pattern discrimination problem there was no evidence of visually guided learning in either task by the operated animals. Analysis of the dendritic arborization in the parietal cortex was intriguing, however. Although rats with occipital lesions on day 4 or in adulthood showed no significant changes in dendritic branching, those rats with occipital lesions on day 10 showed a significant increase in pyramidal cell branching relative to normal control animals. Thus, at first look it appears that we have an example of increased branching without recovery. There are two points to be made here. First, we probably should not be surprised to find that there is little recovery of visually guided behavior in animals with neonatal occipital lesions. It is well known that such lesions lead to the complete atrophy of the lateral geniculate nucleus in the thalamus, and because the lateral geniculate nucleus is the major visual afferent to the rat cortex, it would be difficult for the cortex to reorganize to mediate visually guided behavior in the absence of the visual input. Second, although we unfortunately did not directly test somatosensory functions, we had suggestive evidence that the day 10 animals may have had enhanced somatosensory function relative to the animals in the other groups. They had longer vibrissae and were more successful in manicuring their claws. Increases in vibrissal length have been taken as evidence of enhanced tactile sensitivity in cortically blind cats (Rauschecker, Egert, & Han, 1987). In addition, claw cutting is especially sensitive to the loss of sensorimotor cortex (Whishaw, Kolb, Sutherland, & Becker, 1983), so we can speculate that perhaps enhanced function in somatosensory cortex will be associated with better claw cutting.

Our second set of experiments that failed to show recovery looked at the effects of posterior cingulate cortex lesions on postnatal day 1–3. We had previously found that posterior cingulate lesions produced profound deficits in the Morris task and other associated spatial navigation tasks (Sutherland, Whishaw, & Kolb, 1988). Rats with day 3 lesions performed better on the spatial tasks than the adult operates, but even with extensive training they did not reach the performance level of normal control animals (Kolb & Whishaw, 1991). Analysis of dendritic arborization in the pyramidal cells of the remaining cortex showed a significant decrease in cortical thickness and dendritic branching in the neonatal operates. This result was surprising because the animals did show some functional recovery relative to adult animals. Thus, this experiment appeared to show recovery without dendritic growth. One possible explanation for this paradox is that the recovery was not mediated by the neocortex but rather by the hippocampus. It is known that posterior cingulate lesions in adult rats severely disturb the hippocampal electroencephalograph (EEG) because the lesions interfere with the serotoninergic input to the hippocampus that runs through the cingulum bundle (Vanderwolf, Leung, & Stewart, 1985). This disruption of hippocampal EEG is indicative of abnormal hippocampal functioning, which is likely one reason that cingulate lesions produce such devastating effects upon spatial learning. When we analyzed the hippocampal EEG of our animals with neonatal cingulate lesions we were surprised to find it to be indistinguishable from that of normal animals. Because the cingulum bundle was severed by our lesions, it follows that either the serotonergic fibers took an alternate route to the hippocampus or some other serotonergic input to the hippocampus was modified to support normal hippo-campal functioning (Whishaw & Kolb, 1991). In either event, it seems likely that the improved spatial learning in the neonatal operates was dependent on the reorganization of the hippocampus and not of the cortex.

ASTROCYTES AND RECOVERY

As mentioned elsewhere, glia are exquisitely sensitive to cerebral injury. When rats are given even very small cortical lesions there are two distinctive types of glia (microglia and reactive astrocytes) visible throughout the cortical mantle of the ipsilateral hemisphere. It appears that microglia may appear first and their appearance may be triggered by signals elaborated by injured neurons (e.g., Streit, 1993; de Vellis, 1993). This microglial response may be seen even before obvious neuronal death or atrophy (e.g., Morioka, Kalehua, & Streit, 1993), and it precedes reactive astrocyte response by at least 2–3 days. There is some debate over whether the microglial response is ultimately beneficial to recovery (e.g., Giulian, 1993), but it seems likely that the microglia play some role in triggering the astrocyte response to injury, perhaps through the production of cytokines. The astrocyte response is among the most plastic changes seen in the brain. Astrocytes show a marked hypertrophy and a large increase in the extent of filaments made up of glial fibrillary acidic protein (GFAP). Astrocytes have been proposed to have multiple trophic functions in both the developing brain and in response to injury (see Chapter 7). In particular, astrocytes produce various soluble factors that support neuronal growth, at least in vitro (e.g., Giulian, 1993). One important feature of astrocytes in the current context is that although some astrocytes are formed early in development, most are formed after neural mitosis is complete and reach their peak of gliogenesis somewhere around 7–10 days. The correlation between glial development and the age at which there is maximal recovery of function is intriguing. This correlation is especially interest-ing because the worst functional outcome from cortical injury comes after injury just after birth in rats, which is a time at which there are few astrocytes in the cortex. Robbin Gibb and I therefore made frontal or motor cortex lesions on the day of birth, 10 days of age, or in adulthood. We sacrificed animals at different postinjury ages and used immunohistochemical techniques to identify either vimentin- or GFAP-positive astrocytes. (During development astrocytes express vimentin until about 5–10 days of age and begin to express GFAP as the vimentin decreases.) We found that although rats with lesions at 10 days of age showed a large increase in GFAP-positive cells a few days after the injury, rats with day 1 lesions showed no glial response at all. Rats with adult lesions fell in between. Because the astrocytes may produce trophic factors that support neuronal growth, our results suggest that the dramatic differences in dendritic responsivity to cortical injury at different ages may reflect the difference in astrocyte response during development. I return to this idea in the next chapter.

CONCLUSIONS

Our studies of brain plasticity following cortical injury during development lead me to several general conclusions.

1. It is clear that rats with lesions on postnatal day 10 have much smaller brains than normal, but they are capable of doing more functionally than animals with larger brains that have had similar lesions in adulthood. These neonatal animals appear to accomplish this functional recovery by having more synapses per cortical neuron. Thus, it is likely that it is the intrinsic organization of the cortex that is responsible for the functional recovery, rather than the growth of novel cortical afferents or efferents. This is the same mechanism proposed in the last chapter for recovery from cortical injury in adulthood.

2. We have seen a consistent correlation between dendritic growth, spine density, and recovery of function. For example, rats with either day 10 frontal lesions or day 1 hemidecortications show significant sparing of functions, and this is associated with increased dendritic growth. Rats with day 1 frontal lesions have a poor functional outcome and a decrease in dendritic arborization.

3. The development of abnormal cortico-subcortical connections is correlated with recovery when there is an increase in dendritic growth in the pyramidal cells and with an absence of recovery when there is no increase in dendrites or spines. In other words, changing the long afferent or efferent connections of the cortex is not enough in itself to ensure recovery.

4. Unilateral lesions allow more dendritic growth and better functional outcome than bilateral lesions. Even very small perturbations of the hemisphere contralateral to hemidecortication appear to interfere with both recovery and dendritic growth.

5. Behavior does not recover after early lesions until the dendritic changes take place. This does not occur quickly, and appears to take at least 1 month, although the precise time course has not been determined.

6. There is a correlation between the intensity of the astrocytic response to injury and the extent of functional recovery. Rats with frontal lesions on day 10 have an exaggerated astrocyte response, whereas those with day 1 lesions have no astrocyte response. It is proposed that astrocytes may produce some type of trophic factor(s) that may contribute in an important way to both synaptic growth and functional recovery.

7

Factors Influencing Brain Plasticity and Recovery: Hormones, Neuromodulators, Neurotrophins, and Experience

As the brain changes in response to experience, injury, or during development and aging, it is influenced by its environment, both internal and external. The idea that fluctuations of chemicals in the "neuronal soup" might influence brain structure and function was first proposed by Ramon y Cajal at the turn of the century, but it is only now gaining experimental confirmation in studies showing that certain molecules support plasticity whereas others appear to retard it. These molecules include hormones (including thyroid hormones, adrenal hormones, and gonadal steroids), neuromodulators such as noradrenaline, and neurotrophic factors (NTFs) such as nerve growth factor (NGF). The idea that specific experiences can alter the brain goes back at least to Hebb in 1949, and there has been experimental support for this idea since the 1960s. What has not been known, however, is how specific experiences might alter brain structure and to what extent experiential factors interact with the brain's molecular milieu at the time of the experience. This chapter reviews the general role that internal and external factors play on plasticity and functional recovery. Furthermore, in keeping with the theme of the last two chapters, I pay particular attention to the influence of these factors on dendritic reorganization and the correlation between dendritic change and recovery from cortical injury.

GENERAL ROUTES OF ACTION

Neurons have machinery in the cell body to manufacture various proteins that are used to make both chemical messengers, such as transmitters or hormones, as well as structural molecules to build axons, dendrites, spines, or synapses. The instructions to build specific proteins is coded in each cell's genetic material, so that ultimately the capacity to manufacture any given protein resides in the DNA. Practically speaking, however, it is the messenger RNA (mRNA), which is produced by enzymes acting on the DNA, that contains the code for producing a particular protein.

Any process that alters the mRNA will therefore alter the production of proteins by the cell. For example, a specific hormone such as estrogen could function to act to influence the production of specific mRNAs. This could have an important role in controlling the cell's reaction to specific events or circumstances. One mechanism for this type of action is through the production of what are known as *early response genes*. Studies of astrocytes and neurons in culture have shown that the production of early response genes (also known as immediate early genes) is induced by growth factors or neurotransmitters (e.g., de Vellis, 1993). Many of the early response genes code for other transcriptional factors that can modulate, in turn, the expression of secondary genes, whose products may eventually serve to modify synaptic structure (see Fig. 7.1).

Early response genes have been more difficult to study in vivo, but several have been identified, and of particular interest is the finding that environmental events also can trigger the production of early genes. Two of these, known as *c-fos* and *c-jun,* have been studied extensively (e.g., Dragunow, Currie, Faull, Roberston, & Jansen, 1989). These genes are virtually unexpressed in quiescent conditions but can be activated by a wide variety of sensory stimuli. Thus, within an hour or so of a particular experiential event it is possible to identify the protein products of the *c-fos* and *c-jun* genes. The expression of the early genes is therefore a marker of neural plasticity.

Unfortunately, the early enthusiasm over the discovery of *c-fos* and *c-jun* has been dampened by the finding that these early genes are associated with too many aspects of experience to be meaningful to the brain by themselves. Nevertheless, the principle is established that experience can alter the structure of the brain through the genes (Fig. 7.2). In many ways this is a curious conclusion because the question of whether behavior could be ascribed more to genes or environment appears silly in this context. That is, it appears that environment can affect behavior through the genes. The principle that external environment can alter gene expression is also important for understanding how different interactions between hormones, modulators, NTFs, and experience can influence brain plasticity and behavior. That is, not only can both internal and external factors can influence gene expression but so too can the interaction of them.

There is another route of action of different factors on neurons: through the glia. The central nervous system is composed of neurons and glia, the glia outnumbering the neurons by a ratio of up to 10 to 1. Like neurons, glia are not homogeneous. In the central nervous system they can be divided into two general categories: macroglia and microglia. The principal form of macroglia is the astrocyte (Fig. 2.5). Although once considered to play a minor role in neuronal

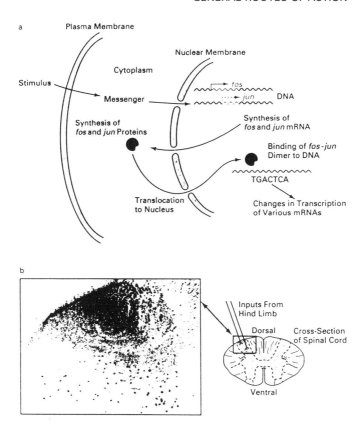

FIG. 7.1. Top: Illustration of the mode of action of stimuli on the genetic material of the neuron. A stimulus activates a proto-oncogene, such as *fos*. Bottom: Hunt, Pini, and Evan (1989) stained sections of the spinal cord of a rat with antibodies to *c-fos*. The animal's hind limb had received noxious stimulation, which activated the proto-oncogenes. After Levitan and Kaczmarek (1991). Adapted by permission of Oxford University Press.

function, the list of putative functions of astrocytes continues to grow and will likely still expand more (Table 7.1). Of particular importance for neural plasticity is the ability of astrocytes to produce, and to respond to, growth factors. Thus, in addition to operating directly on neurons, growth factors can influence glial function, which then can influence neuronal structure and activity. In addition, astrocytes express receptors for neurotransmitters and neuromodulators, which implies that these molecules can directly influence the functions of astrocytes, with a subsequent indirect effect on neurons. In a sense the glia may act something like early genes in the neuron, because they may produce molecules that can influence genetic programs in the neurons. Furthermore, it is known that environmental events can influence astrocytes (e.g., Sirevaag & Greenough,

Genotype ⟶ Epigenesis ⟶ Phenotype

genetic   environment alters   observable
    instructions   genetic instructions   characterisitcs

FIG. 7.2. Summary of the action of the environment on the genome to produce a change in genetic instructions, which produces a change in the phenotype.

1987), although it is not clear how this occurs. Nonetheless, the experiential effects on glia are presumably important in the control of synaptic plasticity. The functions of microglia are less well understood than astrocytes, but it is believed that they are the main mediator of the immunological responses of the brain (e.g., Streit, 1993; Streit, Graeber, & Kreutzberg, 1988). They also may produce signals that stimulate astrocytes to produce trophic factors.

TABLE 7.1
Functions of Astrocytes

Developmental and morphogenic functions
    Axonal guidance
    Promotion of neurite outgrowth
    Guidance of neuronal migration (radial glia)
    Regulation of neuronal cytoarchitecture
    Secretion of extracellular matrix components
Metabolic and trophic functions
    Uptake and metabolism of neurotransmitters
    Urea detoxification
    Metabolism of hormones
    Glycogen storage
    Fatty acids and ketone bodies oxidation
    Production of growth factors and neuropeptides:
        bFGF, BDNF, S100 beta, CNTF, IGF-I, GMF, NGF,
            somatostatin, enkephalin, CCK, angioatensinogen
Regulation of the CNS internal milieu
    Induction of vascular endothelial blood–brain barrier
    Regulation of homeostasis of potassium
    Regulation of extracellular space (astrocyte swelling)
    Regulation of blood supply
Pathological function
    Activation of neurotoxins
    Reactive gliosis, glial scar
    Majority of intracranial tumors

After de Vellis (1993).

ROLE OF HORMONES IN NEURONAL PLASTICITY

The levels of circulating hormones play a critical role both in the determining the structure of the brain and in eliciting certain behaviors. Although it was once believed that the structural effects of hormones were expressed only during development, it is now generally agreed that even adult neurons can respond to hormonal manipulations with dramatic structural changes. Most work on the structural effects of hormones has focused on the sexually dimorphic circuitry of the bird song system and the mammalian hypothalamus, but there is considerable evidence that the cortex is also responsive to hormone manipulations both during development and in adulthood.

Hormonal Effects on the Hippocampal Formation

Discussions of the effect of sex hormones on brain and behavior, especially in humans, is not always considered to be a politically correct topic. This is probably partly due to a feeling that the admission that sex hormones could be responsible for differences in behavior somehow detracts from the "equality of the sexes." To my thinking, this is a strange view, for it denies that biology plays a part in the control of behavior, which seems an indefensible position once we have accepted the "brain hypothesis."

Few people appear to be threatened with the idea that thyroid hormones might affect brain function, presumably because thyroid function is gender neutral. Nonetheless, evidence that thyroid hormones can affect brain structure and function is an important step in understanding the role of sex hormones in brain and behavior because it establishes a clear precedent for hormonal effects. With this in mind, I begin by considering thyroid hormones and brain plasticity. My goal is to demonstrate that hormones can alter brain structure and function, with the idea of showing that gonadal hormones are not so unusual.

There is now an extensive body of literature demonstrating that both hyperthyroidism and hypothyroidism during development can produce significant abnormalities in behavior and cerebral morphology (e.g., Gould, Woolley, & McEwen, 1991). The intriguing thing is that although high or low levels of thyroid hormones alter brain structure in different ways, the behavioral outcomes are similar. Thus, *hypothyroidism* stunts dendritic development and increases neuron death, especially in the hippocampus. This is associated with impaired memory functions. In contrast, *hyperthyroidism* enhances dendritic development and spine density, and decreases neuron death, especially in the hippocampus (see Fig. 7.3). Once again, memory is impaired. Thus, we can see that abnormal levels of thyroid hormone alter both neuronal structure and function in the hippocampus. These deviations from "normal" do not appear to be functionally advantageous, as memory functions are impaired with either excessive growth or

NORMAL

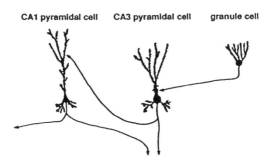

THYROID-HORMONE TREATED

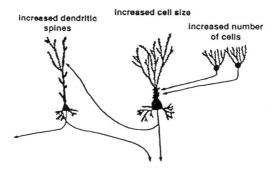

FIG. 7.3. Summary of the effects of an increase in thyroid hormone on the the neurons of the hippocampus. There is a decrease in granule cell death and an increase in dendritic material in CA3 pyramidal cells. After Gould, Woolly, and McEwen (1991). Adapted by permission.

stunting of dendritic growth. The effects of thyroid hormone can be seen in both the developing and the adult brain, although their effects are larger, and likely to be more permanent, in the young brain. The mechanism underlying the action of thyroid hormones on the brain is unclear, but because thyroid hormone stimulates the development of astrocytes, we cannot rule out an indirect effect of thyroid hormone on the hippocampus via the action of astrocytes (Gould et al., 1991).

Having seen that hormones can dramatically alter neuronal structure, we can now turn to the more interesting question of the possible actions of gonadal hormones. The actions of gonadal steroids on the developing hippocampus are less well studied than those of thyroid hormone, but there are several reports of sex differences in the structure of the adult hippocampus. For example, there is evidence that the levels of many neurotransmitters and their receptors are sexually dimorphic (see review by Loy, 1986). Roof has also shown that the dentate gyrus granule cell layer is larger in males compared to females and is enlarged in females treated neonatally with testosterone. This difference was present in prepubescent as well as adult animals, suggesting that it was related to the action of hormones during development (Roof, 1993; Roof & Havens, 1992). The larger size of the dentate gyrus in males suggests that there is more neuropil in males, a result confirmed by Juraska, Fitch, Henderson, and Rivers (1985). The curious thing, however, is that in the Juraska study the sex difference appeared to interact with environmental experience. Thus, when rats were placed in "enriched" environments in the Juraska experiment, there was a marked reversal of the sex difference: Females now had a greater amount of neuropil than males. In a subsequent study on pyramidal neurons in CA3 of the hippocampus, Juraska's group confirmed a sex–experience interaction, but with a slightly different twist (Juraska, Fitch, & Washburne, 1989). The authors noticed that dendrites near the cell body and those at the terminal field (i.e., the end of the dendrites) were differentially affected by sex and experience. Enriched females had more dendritic material near the cell body, whereas enriched males had more in the terminal fields. There were no differences in the cage-reared animals. The Juraska experiments suggest a complex pattern, indeed, with hormone effects being rather specific. A similar conclusion has been made by McEwen and coworkers. These authors have shown that ovarian steroids regulate spine density in hippocampal pyramidal cells in CA1 in two ways in adult female rats. First, ovariectomy dramatically reduced spine density, and therefore the number of synapses. Replacement of the hormones prevented this decrease (Gould, Woolley, Frankfurt, & McEwen, 1990). Second, the authors observed hormonally regulated changes across the estrous cycle as well (Woolley, Gould, Frankfurt, & McEwen, 1990). When estrogen was high the number of synapses rose, whereas when it was low the number declined. This is an amazing result because the estrous cycle of the rat is only 4 days long. Thus, the female rat apparently rebuilds her hippocampal circuitry in 4-day cycles! Even more impressive is the fact that the changes are specific to the pyramidal neurons in CA1. Neurons in the dentate gyrus or in CA3 were not affected by these steroids. Thus, once again it appears that hormonal effects on cortical structures could be very specific. Gonadal hormones appear to target specific parts of specific neuron types in specific cerebral regions. Furthermore, it appears that the hormonal effects interact with environmental stimulation. Viewed in this light one can begin to understand how specific cultural experiences could produce profound, and likely irreversible, effects on the brains of human children.

Hormonal Effects on Neocortical Structure

One of the difficulties in studying hormonal effects on the cortex is that it is not altogether obvious what to look for (dendrites, neuron numbers, transmitters, etc.) or even where to look. As a starting point, Jane Stewart and I began by looking at the effects of neonatal gonadectomy (castration or ovariectomy) on cortical thickness measured at 15 points in each hemisphere (Stewart & Kolb, 1988). Earlier studies had suggested that the cortex was thicker in the right hemisphere than in the left in rats, and an experiment by Diamond even suggested that this was true only in females (Diamond, Dowling, & Johnson, 1981; Kolb, Sutherland, Nonneman, & Whishaw, 1982). In our first study we measured cortical thickness in adult rats from three different strains and failed to find an asymmetry in either intact or neonatally gonadectomized male or female rats. There was, however, a significant increase in cortical thickness in the gonadectomized males but not females (Stewart & Kolb, 1988). These results were puzzling because Ian Whishaw and I had consistently found asymmetries in cortical thickness in our lesion studies. We had two choices: abandon this line of inquiry, or try to figure out what was different about the Stewart and Kolb experiment. We were aware of the phenomenon in science that the largest effect you will ever see is observed the first time you do the experiment, but it was a bit unsettling to completely lose the effect in such a large-scale study. We therefore did some detective work. All of the prior experiments had been done in rats bred, born, and raised in our animal colony in Lethbridge. The Stewart experiment involved animals from a supplier in Montreal. It turned out that while our mother rats were pregnant they were moved from one animal colony room across town to the animal colony at Concordia University. It turns out that prenatal stress is known to lower the levels of testosterone to which male rat fetuses are exposed (Ward & Weisz, 1980), and as a result to prevent complete masculinization and defeminization of behavior and brain (Anderson, Rhees, & Fleming, 1985; Peters, 1986; Ward, 1972). If we assume that being moved is stressful for a pregnant rat, then our results could have been due to the selective effect of stress on the males in utero. We therefore repeated our experiment and found that if pregnant dams were not moved during pregnancy, there was indeed a sex-related difference in cortical thickness (Fig. 7.4). Male rats showed a significant right/left difference in cortical thickness, whereas females or gonadectomized males or females showed no asymmetry. I note, parenthetically, that we were relieved to find that merely being born in Quebec or Alberta was not a critical factor in the experiments! Taken together, our results and those of Diamond and colleagues suggested that testicular hormones could influence cortical morphology. This result was further confirmed by Reid and Juraska (1992a, 1992b), who investigated the cortical thickness and neuron number in the visual cortex of the rat. They found that male rats had thicker cortex and had more neurons in all layers except layer IV. In addition, males also had more glial cells. The authors concluded that the reason for the sex difference in cortical thickness was that males have more neurons and glia. At this point one is led to wonder how females are able to compensate for the lower number of neurons. After all, there is no obvious disadvantage for the females to have fewer neurons. A subsequent

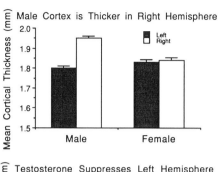

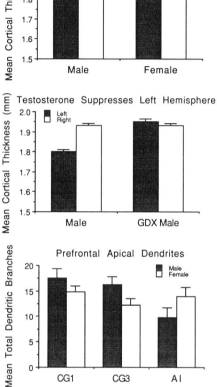

FIG. 7.4. Summary of the effects of testosterone on cortical morphology in the rat. The top panel shows that the cortex of intact males is thicker in the right hemisphere than the left hemisphere and that this difference is not seen in females. The middle panel shows that in the absence of testosterone postnatally (GDX MALE), the asymmetry in the males disappears as the left hemisphere increases in thickness. The lower panel shows that the layer III pyramidal cells have more dendritic material in the intact male than in the intact female in prefrontal areas CG1 and CG3, but the reverse is true in prefrontal area AI. After Kolb and Stewart (1991) and Stewart and Kolb (1988).

paper by Seymoure and Juraska (1992) provided an explanation that is consistent with the idea that the loss of neurons is compensated for by an increase in dendritic material. These authors found that females have more dendritic material in pyramidal neurons than do male rats. In principle, this could mean that they have as many synapses as males, but do so with fewer neurons. Of course, this begs the question of why there are different patterns in the male and female and whether there are functional consequences. It does suggest, however, that there is more than one way to build a brain. This is an important lesson in the context of recovery from brain injury because it leaves open the possibility of rebuilding a damaged brain.

The possibility that there might be a sex-related difference in the dendritic organization of cortical neurons is confirmed by a study in which Jane Stewart and I measured the dendritic material in pyramidal cells in three regions of the prefrontal cortex of rats (Kolb & Stewart, 1991). The prefrontal region of the rat has two major subfields, a medial region, often referred to as medial prefrontal cortex, and a ventral lateral region, known as insular cortex (for a review, see Kolb, 1990). When we measured the dendrites in two medial areas we found that males had more dendritic material than females, whereas when we measured the insular area we found the opposite result (Fig. 7.4). Thus, we see that it is not a case of males or females having more dendritic material but rather that exposure to gonadal hormones influences cortical morphology differently in different cortical regions of males and females. We can speculate that if different regions of cortex have different dendritic organization, then it follows that there must be some difference in behavior as a result. It is interesting in this regard that both the prefrontal subfields have been implicated in species-typical social and sexual behavior, and there is little question that there are significant sex differences in these behaviors, even in rats and cats.

Stewart and I did one additional experiment (Stewart & Kolb, 1994). In the course of studying the role of testosterone on recovery from early frontal lesions we had occasion to ovariectomize or castrate rats in adulthood. We anticipated that these procedures would have little effect on cortical morphology, because it was our belief that such changes would occur during development. To our surprise, however, we found that removing the ovaries of adult female rats provoked a 15% increase in the dendritic material of layer III pyramidal cells (Fig. 7.5). Furthermore, neither females treated with testosterone during infancy nor males showed any change in dendritic pattern after gonadectomy in adulthood. This result leads to interesting questions not only about the role of estrogen in cortical morphology in adulthood, but also leads us to wonder what this result implies regarding the *au current* issue of hormone replacement in postmenopausal women.

Finally, Bryan Fantie and I examined the possibility that circulating hormones in adult animals might influence the development of cortical neurons. We took advantage of our earlier studies showing that transplantation of frontal cortical tissue from newborn rats would allow growth and differentiation of cortical neurons in the transplant (e.g., Fantie & Kolb, 1990; 1993). We had previously shown that when neonatal frontal cortical tissue was transplanted into rats that had received medial frontal lesions 2 weeks earlier, the grafts survived and, in many animals, completely filled the lesion cavity. In order to consider the role of gonadal hormones on graft structure we transplanted male or female tissue into either male or female hosts. After several weeks of recovery we sacrificed the animals and analyzed the neurons in the grafts. The principal finding was grafts grew better in male hosts, regardless of the sex of the donor (Fig. 7.6). We do not know whether female hormones influenced the grafts because we did not study graft growth in rats with prior gonadectomy, although this is an obvious experiment. The conclusion from our study can therefore only be that circulating hormones in the male hosts had a greater influence on neuronal growth than did the circulating hormones in the female hosts. We also do not know if this is a

Apical Dendrites after Adult GDX or OVX

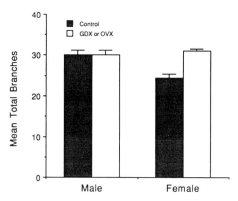

Apical Spine Density after Adult GDX or OVX

FIG. 7.5. Summary of the effects of gonadectomy in adult rats on dendritic branching and spine density in layer III pyramidal cells in parietal cortex. Ovariectomy provokes dendritic growth in the female rat. Gonadectomy provokes an increase in spine density in both male and female rats. Abbreviations: CON, control; GDX, castrated male; OVX, ovariectomized female. After Stewart and Kolb (1994).

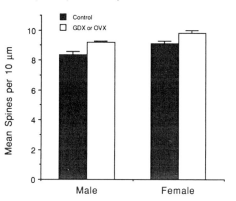

general phenomenon to be observed in the cortex, or if it is specific to the medial prefrontal region. The possibility that it might be a specific response of medial prefrontal tissue would be consistent with our earlier finding of greater dendritic growth in the intact male versus female brain.

In summary, there is considerable evidence that gonadal hormones can alter the structure of cortical neurons. In addition, there is evidence for the provocative idea that experience might influence male and female brains differently. This leads to the interesting possibility that sex hormones might differentially affect cortical functioning in males and females, even in middle age.

Hormonal Effects on Neocortical Function

There is now a large literature indicating that there are significant sex differences in the cognitive behaviors of males and females in many species. For example,

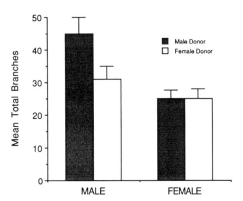

FIG. 7.6. Transplants of male or female donor tissue show an enhanced growth of dendritic material in male versus female hosts. After Kolb and Fantie (1995).

there is converging evidence that males perform many, although not all, spatial tasks more quickly and with fewer errors than females. In contrast, female humans perform better than males on a number of verbal fluency tasks (for reviews, see Kimura, 1992; Kolb & Whishaw, 1995). I restrict my review to two especially germane sets of experiments with laboratory animals.

In the first study, Clark and Goldman-Rakic (1989) studied the role of gonadal hormones in the functional maturation of the orbital frontal cortex of rhesus monkeys.[1] Previous studies had shown that the performance of a task known as *object alternation* was impaired in monkeys with orbital frontal lesions. In this task animals learn that food reward is associated with a particular object such as a toy truck and is not associated with another object such as a cup. Once the animals have learned this task, the rule is switched so that it is the cup that is associated with reward. The rule is switched again once the animals have acquired this discrimination, and so on until the animals have completed six reversals. When normal male and female juvenile monkeys were trained on this task the authors found that the males made about 150 errors to learn the task, whereas females made significantly more—about 210 errors, which is 40% more errors. Treating females with testosterone prenatally and then for 46 days after birth led to performance that was indistinguishable from males (Fig. 7.7). This implies that testosterone (either the endogenous testosterone of normal animals or the exogenous testosterone of the treated females) does something to the brain that allows the animal to solve the task more quickly. Next, the authors examined the effects of orbital frontal lesions at 50 days of age. Males with lesions were severely impaired relative to intact males, making about 250 errors. In contrast, females with lesions were unimpaired relative to intact females. In other words,

---

[1]I have argued elsewhere that the the orbital cortex of the monkey is likely homologous with the insular (or orbital) cortex of the rat (Kolb, 1984). We can presume, therefore, that because there is a sex difference in the organization of the orbital cortex of the male and female rat, this is quite possibly the case in monkeys as well.

it appeared as though the orbital cortex of the male was involved in the task solution in the males, but not in the females. The most interesting group was the hormone-treated and orbital frontal lesioned females: They were indistinguishable from lesioned males. Thus, the testosterone treatment must have provoked the orbital cortex of females to become involved in the task. These results are important for two reasons. First, they show that there is a hormone-related difference in the cognitive functions of neurologically intact animals. Second, they show that there is an interaction between cortical injury and hormonal effects.

The second set of experiments is a series of studies that my colleagues and I have done using rats (e.g., Kolb & Cioe, 1995). In the course of studying the effects of medial frontal lesions in rats we noticed that although intact male and female rats did not usually differ on their performance of different mazes, there were clear sex differences after removal of the medial frontal cortex. Thus, we found that although medial frontal lesions impaired performance of both male and female rats in the Morris water task, the impairments were far larger in females. This difference could be due to many factors. For example, it could be because the remaining regions of the male and female brains are different, and therefore there is a behavioral difference. Or, it could be because the male and female brains react to the injury differently in some way. Finally, it could be that the male and female rats use different strategies to solve the Morris task, and the lesion interferes more with one strategy than another. In order to address this latter possibility, we took advantage of the previous observations of others (e.g., Williams, Barnett, & Meck, 1990) who had found that under some conditions there is a sex difference in intact rats in the solution of a task known as the radial arm maze. This maze consists of an apparatus that looks much like an asterisk when viewed from above. There is a central area and 8–12 arms, which are usually about 1 m long, radiating symmetrically out from the center. Food is located at the end of some of the arms and the animal's task is to find the food.

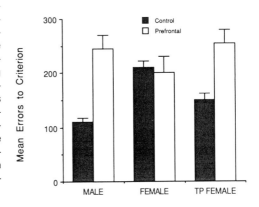

FIG. 7.7. Juvenile male monkeys learn an object alternation task faster than juvenile female monkeys. This difference is blocked by testosterone administration (TP FEM) during early development. Orbital frontal lesions (PFC) produce deficits in both male and TP-treated female monkeys but not in untreated females. Testosterone appears to enhance the maturation of the orbital cortex in males. After Clark and Goldman-Rakic (1989).

Over time the animals learn that food is only in one location and that food is only found in baited arms once each day. In some experiments males learn this task faster than females. In our experiments we have not found a reliable sex difference, although males tend to learn faster. More important, however, is that when we train rats with medial frontal lesions on this task, there is a large sex difference that is similar to that in the water task: Females are more impaired than males. These two experiments are consistent with the general conclusion that frontal lesions are more debilitating in females than in males (Kimura, 1992). In view of this conclusion, the results of our next experiment were unexpected. In this experiment we trained animals on a variation of the Morris task that we called the *landmark task*. In the landmark task the animal must still find a hidden platform but there is a large black square on the wall of the pool near the

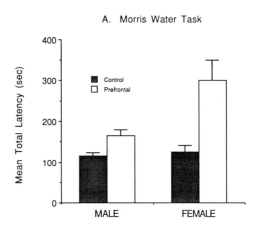

FIG. 7.8. Summary of sex differences induced by medial prefrontal lesions in rats. The top panel shows that after lesions the female rats are significantly worse at performing the Morris water task than the male rats. The bottom panel shows that the reverse is true in the performing landmark task. After Kolb and Cioe (1995).

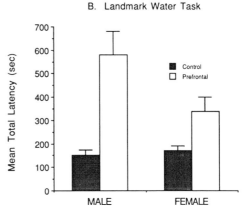

platform. The platform and the cue move on every trial, so the only way to solve the task is to learn the association between a single cue and the platform. This contrasts with the Morris task, in which no single cue will allow solution of the problem. Rather, the animals must use a configuration of at least two or more cues. When we tested intact rats on this task, there was no sex difference. However, when we tested rats with frontal lesions we found that although both sexes were impaired relative to intact controls, males were far worse than females (Fig. 7.8). This result speaks against a simple notion that the frontal cortex is more important to females, but rather suggests that there is some fundamental difference in either cerebral organization or in the way in which male and females approach different problems. In the latter case the effect of the difference in strategy is exacerbated by the frontal lesions.

Taken together, the experiments on animals with frontal lesions suggest that there is a difference in cortical functioning in males and females and that this difference is related to exposure to testosterone during brain development. The next issue is whether the male and female brains react differently to cortical injury.

ROLE OF HORMONES IN RECOVERY
FROM CEREBRAL INJURY

In view of our findings that cortical neurons of the rat are sexually dimorphic and that the effects of frontal lesions are sexually dimorphic, we became suspicious that the male and female rat brains might not show the same plastic response to frontal injury. We had previously found that male rats with frontal lesions showed a chronic increase in dendritic branching in the parietal cortex, and we hypothesized that this increase was somehow related to functional recovery (see chapter 5). We therefore repeated our frontal lesion experiment, but this time we examined both male and female rats. The result was unexpected: Males again showed a postlesion increase in cortical dendritic branching, whereas females did not (Kolb & Whishaw, 1991). This result led to an interesting hypothesis, namely, that the behavioral sex difference observed after frontal lesions could be due to a difference in the way the male and female brains respond to the injury, rather being due to an existing preoperative sex difference. A similar possibility has been raised by others studying the effects of administration of estrogen or progesterone after head trauma or ischemia in male and female rats and gerbils (e.g., Emerson, Headrick, & Vink, 1993; Hall, Pazara, & Linseman, 1991; Roof, Duvdevani, & Stein, 1992). Thus, there is a general consensus emerging that estrogen and progesterone, which are normally produced in large amounts in cycling females, interact with functional recovery. What is not known is whether they influence dendritic changes.

Hormones and Cortical Lesions in Infancy

We next turned our attention to the effect of cortical lesions in infancy. We had previously shown that frontal lesions around day 7 in male rats allowed marked recovery of function, and that this was correlated with an increase in spine density. In view of our failure to find an increase in dendritic growth after frontal lesions in adult female rats, it was reasonable to suppose that the increase in spine density might somehow be related to exposure to testosterone. In order to test this idea we first studied male and female rats with and without frontal lesions. Both sexes showed recovery from the frontal lesion, but, unexpectedly, the changes in the male and female brain were different. Males showed an increase in spine density, which we had seen before, but females did not. Instead, females showed an increase in dendritic branching, which a was change not seen in males. This result has straightforward implications: There is more than one form of cortical plasticity that will support functional recovery. Furthermore, the results suggest that gonadal hormones might be crucial in determining which mechanism is recruited. In order to examine this possibility, we examined male rats that were castrated at birth and female rats that were given testosterone for 3 days after birth. Following this, the animals were either given frontal lesions on day 7 or remained as controls. Again, the results were clear: Both hormonally altered groups of frontal rats failed to show recovery (Fig. 7.9). Inspection of the brains revealed that the changes in spine density and dendrite growth observed in the hormonally intact animals were completely blocked. Thus, it appears that the early hormone manipulations changed the brains in fundamental ways that interfered with the initiation of the plastic changes that normally support recovery. Stated differently, it appears that interference with the gonadal hormonal environment, and thus the course of brain development, reduced the ability of the brain to compensate for the effects of lesions in both male and female animals.

FIG. 7.9. Summary of performance in the Morris water task by rats with medial prefrontal lesions (NEO PFC) on postnatal day 7. Neonatal castration of male rats who subsequently received frontal lesions, or testosterone administration to female rats who subsequently received frontal lesions, blocked recovery of function. After Kolb and Stewart (1995).

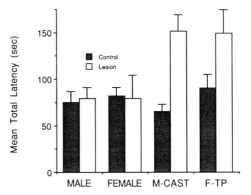

Summary

Taken together, the anatomical and behavioral experiments on laboratory animals lead to the following general conclusions. First, gonadal hormones organize the cortex in both infancy and adulthood. The presence of testosterone alters cortical morphology during development, whereas the absence of estrogen provokes changes in the cortex in adulthood. Second, the effect of hormones is to remodel the cortex, rather than simply stimulating or inhibiting growth. The presence of testosterone influences the number of neurons and glia in the cortex, as well as the dendritic arborization in specific parts of specific regions. The dendritic effects can reflect an increase of synapses in one area of cortex and a decrease in another area in the same brain. In essence, sex hormones build different brains. Third, male and female brains show a differential effect to cortical injury. In general, it appears that the presence of testosterone enhances the dendritic response to injury, and at least in some circumstances this is related to recovery of function. Fourth, stress interacts with the effects of gonadal hormones, possibly through the action of other steroid hormones. Fifth, plastic changes related to experience interact with hormone-related changes in the cortex. That is, the effects of experience depend on whether or not the cortex has been exposed to testosterone. Finally, because the hormonal effects on cerebral organization and plasticity are so profound, it is not surprising that they play a major role in cognitive function in both laboratory animals as well as humans.

CORTICAL INJURY, EXPERIENCE, AND PLASTICITY

The starting point for our studies on cortical injury, experience, and plasticity was the now extensive evidence that experience alters the dendritic organization of the cortex. Housing animals in "enriched environments" increases cortical thickness, increases dendritic branching, and increases the number of synapses in the cortex. Similarly, training animals on specific tasks such as a reaching task selectively increases dendritic arborization in the forelimb representation of the motor cortex (see chapter 2). The logical question that arises is whether such enrichment or training could have the same effects in the injured brain, and if so, whether this experiential effect would enhance functional recovery. Practically speaking, this is an important question. If experience can influence plastic changes in the injured brain, then we are on strong empirical grounds for instituting behavioral therapies after cerebral injury. On the other hand, if we failed to find a beneficial effect of therapies, then we would want to reevaluate the use of rehabilitation procedures after cerebral injury.

The idea that various types of experience or training might influence recovery from cortical injury is not new. Indeed, the use of postoperative rehabilitation both for motor and cognitive dysfunctions is based on an assumption that such treatments might be beneficial. The most extensively used paradigm has been the "enriched environment." Animals are housed in complex environments that contain "toys" and other rats, and the recovery is compared to animals living alone in standard laboratory cages. Although there many reports of beneficial effects of such treatments, there have also been many reports that such experience is of little benefit (see review by Walsh & Greenough, 1976; Will & Kelche, 1992). The complexity of the issue, and perhaps some insight on how to approach it, can be illustrated in an experiment by Whishaw and his colleagues (Whishaw, Sutherland, Kolb, & Becker, 1986). Rats were hemidecorticate in either infancy or adulthood and either were then placed in large tubs filled with objects, plastic pipes, branches, and so on, or were housed in standard laboratory cages. After 90 days the animals were trained in Morris water task. Rats with neonatal hemidecortications showed no benefit of the enrichment, whereas rats with adult hemidecortications benefited significantly from the experience.[2] Thus, we see in the same experiment that hemidecorticate rats both did and did not benefit from the treatment. The critical predictor was whether the hemidecorticate animal already showed evidence of recovery. Neonatal hemidecorticates already showed recovery relative to the adult operates, and enrichment did not enhance this recovery. This result suggests that there might be limits to the plasticity of the brain, and that enrichment will be most beneficial under conditions in which there is normally little recovery of function. A practical implication of this conclusion is that it would appear that people who show the worst outcome from cerebral injury might show the greatest gains from rehabilitation. If this is true, then they also ought to show the most change in synaptic organization. The nature of these changes and the issue of what constrains changes in animals with relatively good "spontaneous" recovery have formed the basis of a series of studies over the past decade.

We began our experiments by giving adult rats frontal lesions and then either placing them in an enriched environment or leaving them in standard laboratory cages for 3 months (Kolb & Gibb, 1991a). Behavior was measured periodically throughout the 3-month treatment. Our first finding was that the enrichment had a selective effect on behavioral recovery. There was no significant effect in acquisition of the Morris task, but the performance of various motor tasks did show a small, but significant, effect of the experience in the brain-damaged animals. When we sacrificed the rats and examined the dendritic changes, there were two principal findings. First, isolated rats with frontal lesions showed an increase in dendritic branching in the sensorimotor cortex, which was proximal to the injury, but not in the occipital cortex, which was further removed. We hypothesized that these changes were important in the recovery that we observed

---

[2]Of course, we cannot rule out the possibility that all of the infant rats had a type of enrichment. That is, until weaning all of the infant operates had an opportunity to live in a family, play, and so forth. This may act as a form of enrichment for the young hemidecorticate.

over time in the isolated animals. Second, after enrichment, the frontal rats showed no additional increase in the dendritic arborization of the parietal neurons but did show an increase in the occipital cortex. In other words, the parietal cortex changed after the lesion but showed no additional change after enrichment. In contrast, the occipital cortex changed after the enrichment, but showed no change in response to the lesion. The absence of an enrichment effect in the parietal neurons again suggests that there is a limit to the extent that a region of cortex will change. Evidently it can change in response to the injury or in response to experience, but not to both. Of course, we do not know whether the changes in synapses after the lesion in the brain-damaged rats were the same in the isolated and enriched conditions. It is possible that the enrichment does affect the parietal neurons but our dendritic analysis was too crude to detect it. In fact, our next experiment suggests that this may be the case.

Our next experiment moved to the analysis of rats with neonatal lesions. We had previously shown that animals with frontal lesions at 10 days of age showed extensive recovery of function, whereas rats with lesions at 5 days of age showed no recovery, and those with lesions on the day of birth were functionally devastated (see Chapter 4). In view of Whishaw's hemidecorticate experiment discussed earlier, it was our expectation that enrichment would be of limited value in the day 10 operates but would be more beneficial in the animals showing little recovery. This was indeed the case. Rats with lesions on day 1 or day 5 showed dramatic functional improvement after 3 months of enriched rearing, whereas rats with day 10 lesions showed no beneficial effect (e.g., Kolb & Elliott, 1987). In fact, the enriched rats with lesions on postnatal day 5 were functionally equivalent to rats with lesions on postnatal day 10. This functional recovery was correlated with a remarkable 16% increase in cortical thickness in the early operates, which was nearly threefold greater than the 6% increase in unoperated rats. Evidently the brain of the perinatally brain-injured rat is capable of significant plasticity, but it apparently does not occur without environmental stimulation. This result implies that behavioral therapies may indeed play an important role in treatment of cortical injuries that are normally associated with a poor behavioral outcome. This conclusion is further supported by an experiment in which we tried a different form of enrichment.

Field had reported that premature babies grow more quickly and are released from hospital sooner if they are stimulated by stroking with a brush for 15 min three times a day (Field et al., 1986; Schanberg & Field, 1987). We reasoned that if tactile stimulation in premature babies could affect brain growth, then a similar treatment in infant brain-damaged rats might facilitate recovery and increase plastic changes in the cortex. After all, newborn rats are embryologically equivalent to premature humans. Rats were given frontal lesions on days 3–5 after birth and were stroked for 15 min three times daily until weaning at 21 days. The results were dramatic. The stimulated frontal lesioned rats grew faster than unstimulated frontal lesioned rats, and they were significantly better at the Morris water task and the Whishaw reaching task when tested in adulthood. Furthermore, the brains of the stroked rats were heavier and there was an increase in dendritic arborization in cortical pyramidal cells relative to the unstroked rats. Immunohistochemical analyses also revealed a marked increase in cortical acetylcholinesterase (AChE) activity after just 2 weeks of stimulation. This AChE increase was still present 3 months later in adulthood. These results imply that human infants with perinatal injury may benefit from extensive tactile experience during infancy. In addition, the fact that we obtained similar results with both stroking in infants and rearing in enriched environments in older rats suggests that there is more than one way to stimulate cortical plasticity after early injury. We are not yet in a position to determine which type of treatment may prove to be more beneficial.

One question that arises from our experiments is whether animals with good recovery from brain injury can benefit from experience, or if there is a limitation on the plastic changes that prevents further modification of cortical circuitry. Our experiments with adult rats suggested that regions that showed changes in response to cortical lesion might not be responsive to environmental effects, so it is possible that a similar phenomenon is operating in the developing brain as well. Rats with lesions at 7–10 days of age show remarkable recovery of function, even when they are raised in standard laboratory caging. They are still not normal, however, so in principle it would be useful to attempt to potentiate their recovery further. The observed recovery is associated with extensive growth of dendrites and spines, which we have presumed to be critical in supporting recovery (see Chapter 6), and the absence of additional recovery after enrichment suggests that the treatment is ineffective in changing the brain further. However, when we investigated the dendritic organization of enriched rats with day 7 frontal lesions we made a curious discovery that suggests a rather different interpretation. Rats were given lesions on postnatal day 7 and were placed in enriched environments or isolated cages for 3 months after weaning. They were then tested on a variety of tasks, including the Morris water task and Whishaw reaching task (Kolb, Buday, Gorny, & Gibb, 1992). As in our previous experiments, there was virtually no effect of experience on the behavior of the operated rats. However, when we analyzed the dendritic arborization in cortical neurons we discovered that there had indeed been an effect of experience on the brain of these animals. As expected, normal control rats showed an increase in dendritic branching and a decrease in spine density in enriched versus isolated conditions (see Fig. 2.7). We had interpreted these effects in the normal brain as an illustration of a mechanism by which the brain is prepared for further plastic changes, such as in learning specific problems. Further, as we had found previously, rats with frontal lesions on postnatal day 7 showed no change in dendritic branching, but had an increase in spine density relative to control rats (Fig. 6.6). It was our hypothesis that the increased spine density was supporting the functional recovery. However, when we examined the brains of frontal rats with enriched rearing, we were surprised to see that there was an effect of enrichment on the dendritic branches, with about a 15% increase in dendritic branching, which was equivalent to unoperated control rats (15%) who were also given the enriched housing. More importantly, however, as in unoperated rats there was also a decrease in spine density. In fact, this decrease completely reversed the lesion effect! This result provides an interesting conundrum. If the changes in spine density were supporting recovery of function, then how is it that a reversal of the spine changes with the enriched experience can still support recovery? One solution to this problem is that the enriched experience has actually remodeled the cortical circuitry in a different way. After all, there was an increase in dendritic material with enrichment, and this alone could be expected to enhance recovery. Thus, it appears that although the enriched experience did not provide much additional behavioral benefit on the tasks we used, it did remodel the cortex. In other words, perhaps the enriched experience has had a generalized effect on cortical structure in animals that normally exhibit recovery. We can speculate that had we done a more extensive behavioral assessment we might have found functional effects of the treatment in the brain-injured animals. We can speculate further that perhaps children who show good recovery from brain injury might benefit from intense behavioral experiences in more general ways, such as improved performance in school.

I have emphasized the role of experience in facilitating synaptic plasticity. There is another rather different perspective that one could take, however. Consider the following example. If a person has a stroke that renders it more difficult to move the digits in one hand, they might very well reduce their use of the impaired hand and increase their use of the unaffected hand. Over time, they may come to depend almost completely on the normal limb, with the end result being that they lose much of the residual function that they still had in the affected limb. Indeed, this is not an uncommon scenario in stroke patients. What might happen if the patient were forced to continue using the impaired hand? Might therapy actually prevent the additional functional loss? In this case the therapy would be acting to prevent additional loss rather than stimulating recovery of lost behaviors. An experiment by Randy Nudo (Nudo & Grenda, 1992) is instructive. Nudo stimulated the motor cortex of squirrel monkeys and mapped the location of digits, wrist, and forearm as illustrated in Fig. 7.10. The animals were then given a vascular lesion of part of the digit and wrist representation. Four months later Nudo reinvestigated the cortical representation of the digit, wrist, and forearm in the same hemisphere and found that he could no longer elicit movements of any of the hand areas with electrical stimulation. Thus, the loss in cortical representation of movement was far greater than would be predicted from the lesion alone. In order to determine if it were possible to prevent secondary loss of function, Nudo forced other monkeys to use their affected limb

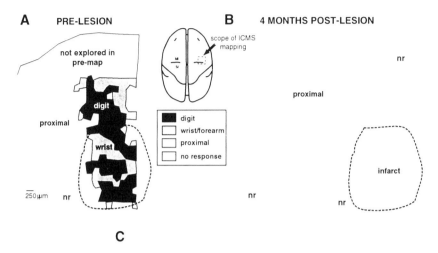

FIG. 7.10. (A) Summary of the pattern of movements evoked by stimulation of the motor cortex of a squirrel monkey. The dotted area indicates the region in which the vasculature was cauterized, leading to an infarct. (B) No movements could be elicited in the cortex 4 months after the lesion, even though much of the forelimb representation was spared in the lesion. This experiment shows the importance of forced use of the impaired limb after a cortical infarct. Figure courtesy of Randy Nudo.

after surgery. When he remapped the cortex in these animals they still had an extensive region from which he could elicit movement of the digits, hand, and wrist. In other words, the training had prevented the loss of function.

Nudo's result is important because it forces us to focus on alternative role of experience. Not only can experience provoke plastic changes, but it can also prevent plastic changes involved in atrophy. Thus, behavioral therapy may have different roles after different types of cerebral injuries.

Summary and Lingering Questions

There is little doubt that experience can have profound effects on both functional recovery and synaptic plasticity after cerebral injury. There is also little doubt that the effects of experience are most dramatic in those cases in which outcome is worst, both in infancy and in adulthood. Nonetheless, it does appear that experience may still have effects on the brain even in those cases in which there appears to be little functional change. We can speculate that one effect of experience is to provoke dendritic growth and connectivity, such as in animals with perinatal lesions, whereas another effect is to remodel the existing connections (see Fig. 7.11). This remodeling may take the form of "pruning" back unneces-

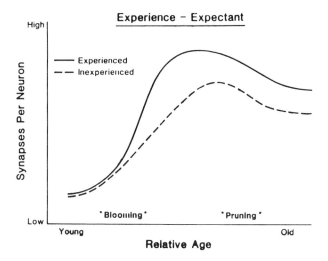

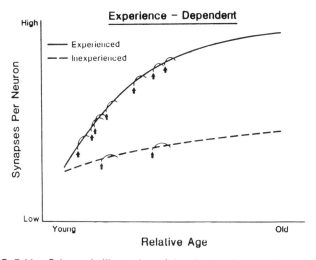

FIG. 7.11.   Schematic illustration of the changes in synaptic numbers in the cortex during aging. The top panel illustrates the effect of general experience on the development of cortical synapses. The cortex is especially sensitive to experience during the developmental blooming of cortical synapses. Greenough refers to these changes as experience expectant. This reflects the innate sensitivity of developing neurons to experience. The bottom panel illustrates the effects of specific experiences on cortical synapses. There are small, localized changes that occur on the background of the general experiential changes. Greenough refers to these changes as experience dependent. This reflects that these small changes occur in response to specific experiences. After Greenough, Black, and Wallace (1987).

sary connections, much as a rose bush is pruned back to enhance future growth. This idea has been proposed by Greenough, Black, and Wallace (1987) to account for the synaptic reduction that occurs normally during development of the cortex.

There are two important questions that have not yet been adequately examined in brain-damaged animals. First, since there are sex differences in the structure of the cortex and in the changes of the cortex of after injury, might there also be sex differences in the effect of experience on the injured brain? Juraska (e.g., 1990) showed that there are sex-related differences in the effect of experience on the cortex, so it seems likely that there may be differences in the way experience alters in injured brain. Indeed, we might also wonder whether different types of postinjury experiences might be more beneficial to one or the other sex. Second, one of the difficulties in examining the recovery from cortical injury is that the mere act of measuring functional recovery could act itself as a experience that could alter the brain! This problem has not been systematically investigated, but work by Pat Goldman-Rakic and colleagues is intriguing. They have shown that if monkeys are given prefrontal lesions in infancy and then tested on cognitive tasks as juveniles, their performance on the same tasks in adulthood is far better than the performance of similar monkeys with no such experience (e.g., Goldman, 1974; Goldman & Mendelson, 1977). These studies did not attempt to measure changes in the brain, but it is reasonable to assume that the early training must have provoked some changes in cerebral organization that later influenced behavior. Future studies will have to determine the necessary and sufficient conditions for inducing such behavioral changes, as well as determining what neural changes are responsible for the functional improvement.

NEUROTROPHIC FACTORS AND BRAIN PLASTICITY

When the brain is damaged there is a series of molecular events unleashed that have a strict temporal sequence (Fig. 7.12). One approach to studying functional recovery and brain plasticity is to try to manipulate these events to initiate or to enhance processes that will lead to recovery. Because the brain produces trophic factors that appear to stimulate neuropil growth in vitro, it is reasonable to wonder if the introduction of trophic factors might enhance recovery. It has been nearly 50 years since nerve growth factor (NGF) was first shown to be essential for the development of the peripheral nervous system, but it is only recently that NGF has been recognized as a likely neurotrophic factor active in certain neurons in the adult central nervous system.

The modes of action of neurotrophic factors have been the subject of some debate. The classic view was that the trophic compound is synthesized by neurons or glia and was taken up by axon terminals. It was then retrogradely transported from the axon terminal to the cell soma and acted much like a "life

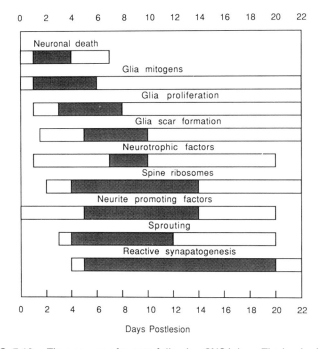

FIG. 7.12.   Time course of events following CNS injury. The beginning of the bars indicates the time postlesion when the event is initiated. The intensity of the shading parallels the intensity of the phenomenon indicated by the bar. After Nieto-Sampedro and Cotman (1985).

tonic" for the neuron. Indeed, this does seem to be the most likely route of NGF action. However, it now appears that many neurons depend on a different type of trophic action for their survival (Korsching, 1993). It is therefore proposed that there are also *anterogradely transported trophic factors*, which would be synthesized in a cell body, transported to the axon terminals, and then released to be taken up by the postsynaptic neuron. Basic fibroblast growth factor (bFGF) may work in this manner. In addition, there may be a release of trophins from the neuron soma, which has a local action on surrounding neurons. Granule cells in the cerebellum seem to depend on the presence of Purkinje cells for their survival, suggesting that a trophic factor may be released by the Purkinje cells. Various factors including acidic FGF (aFGF), brain-derived neurotrophic factor (BDNF), and neurotrophin-3 (NT-3) are plausible candidates for this action (Korsching, 1993). Glial cells are known to synthesize neurotrophic factors, and may be influenced, in turn, by such factors. For example, FGF enhances NGF release by astrocytes. Finally, it appears that some neurons not only produce neurotrophic factors, but also have receptors for their own factors. For example, hippocampal pyramidal neurons not only synthesize BDNF, but they also have the BDNF receptor, trk-B. This autocrine action of neurotrophic factors may serve to maintain neurons until an appropriate target contact is established.

In sum, there are a variety of neurotrophic factors that are proposed to influence cellular development and function in the central nervous system in a number of ways. To date, there are few studies showing that neurotrophic factors can influence plasticity in the injured brain, but the potential of such actions is clearly important. Two factors (NGF, FGF) have been shown to have actions in the injured brain, so I consider each separately.

Nerve Growth Factor

Nerve growth factor is made by cerebral neurons and by astroctyes in the adult brain. It is believed to be released by cell bodies and dendrites and to be taken up by cholinergic axon terminals. Once taken up by the terminals, the NGF is retrogradely transported to, and selectively accumulated in, the cell bodies. The accumulation of NGF is believed to cause an increase in the synthesis of acetylcholine, and appears to prevent the death of cholinergic neurons. In a sense, NGF acts like a "life tonic" for cholinergic neurons. When cholinergic axons are cut, there is an interruption in the retrograde delivery of NGF, and this appears to be critical in the death or atrophy of the neurons (for a review, see Hagg, Louis, & Varon, 1993). Intraventricular injection of NGF appears to prevent this degeneration, and therefore represents a potential treatment for preventing neuron death or atrophy after injury or perhaps even in aging (e.g., Gage, Armstrong, Williams, & Varon, 1988; Hefti, 1986; Kromer, 1987). In addition, when neurons are axotomized they may die or atrophy, but the remaining healthy neurons can undergo a sprouting reaction in which the axon terminals grow and form new synapses (e.g., Garofalo, Ribeiro-da-Silva, & Cuello, 1992). Nerve growth factor may influence this sprouting either by its direct actions on neurons or indirectly either by influencing neuronal activity or by acting on glia.

There has been little direct evidence that NGF can influence recovery from neocortical injury, but NGF has been shown to facilitate functional recovery after injury to the entorhinal cortex or the striatum (Pallage, Knusel, Hefti, & Will, 1993; Stein & Will, 1983). It is not immediately obvious how changes in cholinergic neurons would allow recovery of lost behaviors after a cortical injury, unless increased cortical activity somehow can alter the postsynaptic neurons that could, in turn, mediate recovery processes. For example, although corticospinal neurons are not cholinergic and are not known to be directly responsive to NGF, NGF infusion improves their ability to transport other molecules, suggesting that NGF could influence the functioning of these neurons.

In order to examine the possible role of NGF in functional recovery and cortical plasticity, my colleagues and I gave rats unilateral cortical strokes that involved the territory of the middle cerebral artery (Kolb, Ribeiro-da-Silva, & Cuello, 1995). The region of damage included much, but not all, of the motor and somatosensory cortex of the left hemisphere. Half of the operated animals received intraventricular infusions of NGF. The animals were allowed to recover for 2 months and then were tested in the Morris water task and Whishaw reaching task and were trained to run across a narrow beam to obtain food reward. The brains were then analyzed for dendritic changes in both the injured and intact hemispheres. The NGF treatment led to improved performance on all of the behavioral tasks. For example, on the reaching task the stroke animals reached very poorly, with median accuracy of less than 20%. Indeed, many of these animals learned to reach only with extended training. In contrast, NGF-treated stroke rats performed at about 40% accuracy (Fig. 7.13). The anatomical results were exciting. Cortical strokes led to an atrophy of both dendritic branches as well as a reduction in spine density in the normal hemisphere, with little change in the intact hemisphere. Treatment with NGF not only prevented this atrophy, but actually stimulated a significant increase in both dendritic branching and spine density (Fig. 7.14). These changes were surprisingly generalized, as we found them in layer III and layer V pyramidal neurons in both the remaining motor cortex and in the anterior cingulate cortex. Thus, as in our previous experiments, an improvement in behavioral outcome is correlated with dendritic growth and increased spine density. Our real surprise came when we analyzed the brains of normal rats that were also given NGF. Relative to untreated normal

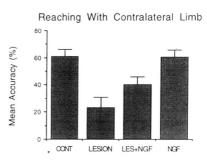

FIG. 7.13. Summary of the effects of unilateral cortical stroke (LESION) and nerve growth factor (NGF) on the performance of the Whishaw reaching task (top) and walking across a narrow beam (bottom). The stroke severely impaired performance on both tasks and the NGF partially reversed the functional impairments. After Kolb, Ribeiro-da-Silva, and Cuello (1995).

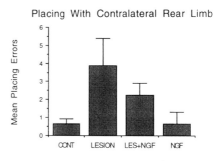

Area Fr 2, Layer V, Basilar

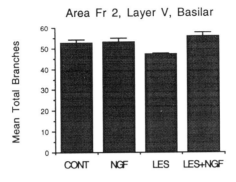

Area Fr 2, Layer V, Terminal Basilar Spines

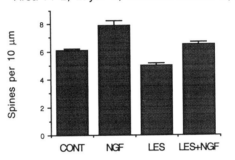

Area Fr 2, Layer V, Oblique Basilar Spines

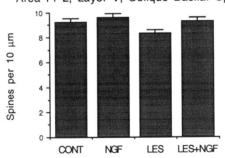

FIG. 7.14. Summary of the effects of cortical stroke (LES) and nerve growth factor (NGF) on dendritic morphology in the cortex of normal (CON) and NGF-treated normal rats as well as in the injured hemisphere of the stroke and NGF-treated stroke rats. The cortical lesion led to atrophy of dendritic branching and spine density in the cortical pyramidal cells. The NGF provoked growth in the dendrites of normal brains and blocked the atrophy in the injured brain. After Kolb, Ribeiro-da-Silva, and Cuello (1995).

brains, the brains of the NGF-treated animals showed a dramatic increase in dendritic growth and spine density in layer V pyramidal cells (Fig. 7.15). The effects of NGF were not as generalized in the normal brain, however, as we found no changes in layer III pyramidal cells. It appears that NGF not only facilitates recovery from cortical injury but it is also able to remodel the normal brain. Our behavioral analyses were not designed to detect behavioral enhancement in normal animals, but we cannot exclude this possibility. It seems more likely, however, that the effects of NGF in the normal brain are more like those seen in the brain exposed to enriched rearing. What is unknown at present is whether NGF treatment might interact with specific training in order to produce a further change in synaptic organization.

One question that remains in our NGF studies is how a trophic factor, whose action is on cholinergic neurons, is able to stimulate growth in pyramidal cells, which are glutamatergic. One possibility is that enhanced cholinergic activity leads to enhanced activity in other neurons, which in turn leads to their growth. Acetylcholine is responsible for activating one form of cortical electroencephalographic (EEG) activity, although it is not known if fluctuations in cholinergic levels above some critical level can actually alter the details of the EEG activity (e.g., Vanderwolf, Leung, & Stewart, 1985). Another possibility is

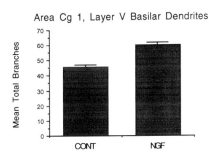

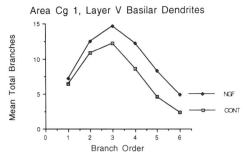

FIG. 7.15. Summary of the effects of nerve growth factor on the layer V pyramidal cells in the prefrontal area CG1. There was a 35% increase in dendritic material in the NGF treated brains. After Kolb, Ribeiro-da-Silva, and Cuello (1995).

that increased activity in cells such a pyramidal cells can lead to an increase in NGF production. It is known, for example, that hippocampal seizures, which are characterized by massive increases in pyramidal cell firing, can stimulate a rapid increase in mRNA for NGF, which appears in hippocampal granule cells and neocortical neurons (Gall & Isackson, 1989). A further possibility is that NGF has actions on astrocytes, which in turn are able to influence neuronal morphology.

Fibroblast Growth Factors

Like NGF, fibroblast growth factor (FGF) has a trophic action in the adult brain and is able to reduce cell death after axotomy (Cotman, Cummings & Pike, 1993). Unlike NGF, however, the actions of FGF are not limited to cholinergic neurons, but rather FGF appears to have a fairly widespread effect, making it the most general growth factor known. There are two forms of fibroblast growth factor, acidic FGF (aFGF) and basic FGF (bFGF). Both forms appear to have trophic effects, although there is more evidence with respect of bFGF.

One interesting characteristic of FGF is that it shows a marked increase in the brain after injury. This increase is correlated with an increase in astrocyte size and number, and Cotman et al. (1993) proposed that the astrocyte actually produces the FGF, which would account for the apparent correlation between regeneration and the presence of astrocytes (Fig. 7.16). The regenerative capacity of FGF may be due to some direct action on neurons, but it has been proposed that FGF stimulates the production of NGF, which could then influence cholinergic neurons at least. To date there have not been behavioral studies with FGF, but these experiments are underway in several laboratories. The wide-

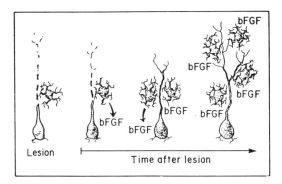

FIG. 7.16.   Basic fibroblast growth factor (bFGF) levels and astrocyte numbers increase after brain injury. These changes are hypothesized to stimulate neuronal regeneration. After Cotman, Cummings, and Pike (1993).

spread actions of FGF on dendrite growth suggest that FGF may be at least as beneficial as NGF.

In summary, it appears that neurotrophic factors may provide a tonic for stimulating brain plasticity and recovery of function after cerebral injury. In addition, there are other trophic compounds, especially BDNF and NT-3, that have somewhat different actions than NGF and FGF, and these too hold some promise of facilitating brain plasticity and recovery (e.g., Maisonpierre et al., 1990). One of the difficulties with administering either NGF or FGF is that they do not pass the blood–brain barrier and therefore must be placed directly into the brain. This restriction is clearly important if one is to use these factors as treatments for people with brain injury. One solution to this problem is to use NGF- or FGF-stimulating compounds that do cross the blood–brain barrier. There are now numerous studies showing that NGF can be upregulated with various compounds (e.g., Carswell, 1993), although there are not yet any reports that these compounds can facilitate recovery.

NEUROMODULATION OF BRAIN PLASTICITY

The brain has several diffusely projecting fiber systems that appear to regulate neural activity by releasing "modulatory" transmitters in the forebrain. These modulatory systems include the noradrenergic and serotonergic inputs from the brainstem and the cholinergic input from the basal forebrain. Neuromodulatory systems have been implicated in the facilitation of virtually all types of learning, ranging from habituation and imprinting to complex cognitive learning (e.g., Dudai, 1989). The prevalent view on the role of neuromodulators is that they facilitate or inhibit cerebral circuits. For example, one common view is that neuromodulators act to "arouse" the cortex such that incoming inputs are attended to. Another possibility is that neuromodulators could act on glial cells. For example, astrocytes have noradrenaline (NA) receptors, so NA could stimulate astrocytes to produce trophic factors. Perhaps the most extensively studied modulator is noradrenaline (NA), which acts to increase plasticity in a variety of conditions. The importance of noradrenaline is usually demonstrated in experiments in which the noradrenergic cells in the brainstem, the ascending pathway from these cells, or the cerebral terminals of these cells are damaged and plasticity is blocked or at least attenuated. One of the most interesting examples comes from the work of Kaverne and colleagues (e.g., Brennan, Kaba, & Kaverne, 1990). Kaverne has taken advantage of the observation that mice have an olfactory recognition system in which the identity of a male mouse is learned by the female during mating. This can be demonstrated rather simply. Mating normally results in nearly 100% of female mice becoming pregnant, and the pregnancy is sustained whether or not the male is present afterward. However, if the female encounters a strange male or his urine, pregnancy fails. Kaverne has

shown that this memory of the odor of the first male lasts several weeks, imply-
ing a relatively permanent synaptic change. One key feature of this learning is
that it is contingent on noradrenergic activation at mating. If this activation is
blocked, there is no learning. Thus, encountering the odor of a strange male does
not produce a pregnancy block if the female's olfactory bulb is not exposed to
NA at mating. A similar facilitatory role of noradrenaline has been demonstrated
in other types of neural plasticity as well. For example, blockade of noradrenaline prevents cortical changes in response to visual stimulation in kittens
(e.g., Kasamatsu, Pettigrew, & Ary, 1979), and in some experiments NA has
been claimed to block enrichment effects in rats (e.g., Murtha, Pappas, & Raman, 1990). The apparently general role of NA in various types of experience-
dependent plasticity suggests that NA could also play a role in recovery from
cortical injury. My colleagues and I took advantage of our observations that

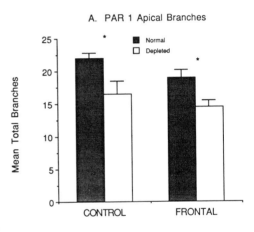

FIG. 7.17. (A) Neonatal depletion of noradrenaline leads to a
stunted development of dendrites in pyramidal neurons in
parietal cortex of both control
rats and rats with frontal lesions
on postnatal day 7. (B) The neurons of the depleted rats show a
compensatory increase in spine
density in the control brains. In
the lesioned brains there is an
increase in spine density in the
untreated lesion rats but no further increase in the depleted
brains. The depleted rats with
frontal lesions do not show recovery of function. After Kolb
and Sutherland (1992).

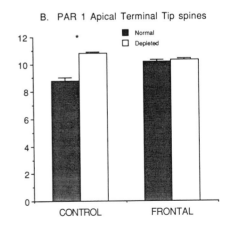

frontal lesions around 7–10 days of age allow substantial sparing of function, which is correlated with dendritic changes. Rats were depleted of cortical noradrenaline on the day of birth by special treatment with a neurotoxin, 6-hydroxydopamine. They were then given frontal lesions on day 7 and were allowed to grow into adulthood before being studied on various behavioral tasks, such as the Morris water task (Kolb & Sutherland, 1992; Sutherland, Kolb, Whishaw, & Becker, 1982). Frontal rats with NA depletion were behaviorally devastated, performing as poorly on the Morris task as animals with similar lesions on the day of birth. When we examined the cortex, we found that the noradrenaline depletion had reduced dendritic arborization by 30% in both normal and frontal lesioned rats (Fig. 7.17). This is an enormous reduction and was especially surprising because the unoperated animals were indistinguishable from normal rats with no depletion. This implied that there might be some type of compensatory change in the brains of the depleted controls. Indeed, when we looked at the spine density we found such a change: There was an 11% increase in spine density in pyramidal neurons in the depleted control rats. Once again, we found a correlation between functional recovery and dendritic change. But what about the frontal rats whose recovery was blocked by the NA depletion? Recall that rats with day 7 frontal lesions show an increase in spine density of about 10%, and we have suggested that this plays a key role in their functional recovery. However, when we examined the neurons of the NA-depleted frontal rats we found no additional increase in spine density. It appeared that the brain was unable to compensate for both the frontal lesion and the loss of dendrites. We cannot tell if the neurons of these rats compensated for the loss of noradrenaline and failed to compensate for the frontal lesion, but this is most parsimonious with the other evidence that NA plays a role in cortical plasticity in response to experience.

FURTHER CONSIDERATIONS

In the healthy brain there are several factors that can enhance neural plasticity. These include hormones, trophic factors, neuromodulators, and experience. When the brain is damaged, multiple molecular events are stimulated that may recruit some or all of these factors to help in the repair of the damaged brain. What we have not considered is the interaction of these factors, and how they might influence the processes of recovery. One assumption we could make is that a combination of different factors would be beneficial, and we could hope that this might be the case. There are two interesting problems in this assumption, however. We have seen that there are likely to be limits to the extent of plasticity that the brain may show. Thus, there may simply be no way for the brain to take advantage of the additive properties of the different factors. There is another, somewhat disturbing, possibility as well. We have assumed that plastic changes in the injured brain are good things and they will support recovery. Suppose,

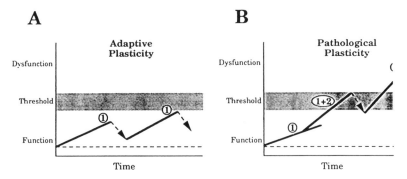

FIG. 7.18. Although normally compensatory in function, plasticity mechanisms may interact in an aberrant manner and lead to pathology. Minor disturbances are accommodated by the plastic changes in the healthy brain (A), but the compounding of different disturbances may lead to pathological plasticity (B). After Cotman, Cummings, and Pike (1993).

however, that too much change was not beneficial. That is, what if too much change interfered with the functioning of the normal brain? This idea has been proposed by Cotman et al. (1993) in their consideration of the causes of Alzheimer's disease (Fig. 7.18). They propose that as the brain ages it becomes subject to multiple adaptive mechanisms, injuries, and compensations. Most of these are beneficial but the cumulative effects of these changes may not be, and thus lead to an enhanced risk of pathology and degeneration. According to their reasoning, disorders like Alzheimer's disease may not be caused by a single aberrant mechanism, but rather by a series of changes, each of which causes risks and benefits. In this scenario, there is a need to identify the primary aberrant mechanisms and to slow these plastic changes in order to block to the progression of dementia. This is a sobering idea that must be acknowledged as we search for ways of enhancing recovery from cerebral injury.

8 Epilogue

One of the most intriguing and perplexing questions in neuroscience concerns the manner in which the brain, and especially the neocortex, can modify its structure and ultimately its function throughout one's lifetime. As the preceding chapters in this book have suggested, the cortex can be dramatically changed during its development and aging, by experience, and by injury. Furthermore, change at all these times is profoundly influenced by hormones, neurotrophins, and neuro-modulators. It would be a daunting task to try to summarize all that I have covered in the preceding chapters. However, in this chapter I attempt to extract some basic principles regarding the nature of brain plasticity and behavior.

1. One of the most interesting properties of the brain is its plasticity. This feature allows us to benefit from experience and to live a relatively long life with a brain that is largely unable to replace lost neurons.

2. I have assumed that the principle way in which the brain modifies itself is through change at the synapse. This synaptic change may be reflected in alterations in the axon terminals, dendritic arborization, and spine density, or by changes in ultrastructure of existing synapses. These changes allow either the production of new synapses, the loss of old synapses, or the modification of existing synapses. I have focused on morphological studies in which synaptic change and behavioral change are correlated. Of course, synaptic and behavioral change remains a correlation, and the critical experiments to establish causation are yet to be done.

3. It is possible to visualize with light and electron microscopes the morphological changes in the cerebral neurons and synapses that are associated with behavioral change. Although I did not discuss it explicitly, it is also possible

to identify some physiological changes in neural activity that accompany plasticity. A challenge for the future will be to demonstrate how changes in cerebral morphology are translated into physiological activity that is "meaningful" to the organism.

4. The plastic changes observed after brain injury are very similar in kind to those observed when animals learn from experience and those that occur during development and aging. This similarity suggests that there may be basic mechanisms of synaptic change in the mammalian brain that are used in many forms of plasticity. This is an encouraging conclusion, for it allows hope that we will be able to improve recovery from cerebral injury by taking advantage of the innate mechanisms that the brain uses for other forms of plasticity.

5. There is more than one way for plastic changes in the brain to accomplish the same function. For example, males and females have brains that, in some cerebral regions, are fundamentally different. Experience may have different morphological effects on the brain of males and females, and even a single sex may have different morphological changes to the same experience at different ages.

6. There are limits to amount that a brain can change. We still do not know what determines the limits, or in most cases, what the limits are. It seems likely that some major limitations are those imposed by the brain's compensation for the loss of neurons during aging.

7. In spite of the limits to brain plasticity, the brain is far more plastic than was once believed. It is clear that the brain is capable of modifying its structure until well into old age. There is also tantalizing evidence that the mammalian brain is also capable of mitosis well into adulthood. There is even suggestive evidence that neurons that grow after birth may be functional.

8. Not all brain plasticity is necessarily functionally beneficial and, in some cases, it may be dysfunctional. This may be especially important in the aging brain where it could play a role in the appearance of dementia.

9. The demonstration of recovery of function after brain injury is not as simple as it might seem. People and laboratory animals with brain injury use many "tricks" to compensate from brain injury. Recovery of lost function is rare in adults, although it does happen. Recovery is more common after early brain injury, but only at certain times in embryonic development. Recovery does not occur if the brain is damaged before mitosis is complete and before migration is well under way, if not complete. Recovery does follow injury during the blooming of cortical connectivity in development.

10. Evidence of a correlation between brain plasticity and recovery of function has important clinical implications. The task will be to determine ways of turning on the plastic processes that underlay plasticity, while at the same time maintaining control of their extent so that they can be turned off too.

11. Experience can alter the brain in a relatively diffuse way or with rather

selective changes. The development of techniques to induce the global changes may be of profound importance in establishing therapies for the brain-injured human. The task may be to provoke general dendritic growth that will subsequently allow for more rapid synapse formation in response to specific experiences. The use of "enriched" environments provides an animal model of a global dendritic growth. The training of animals to do specific behavioral tasks provides a model of selective dendritic growth. The challenge is to translate this basic animal research into practical clinical solutions. For example, what is the optimal "enriched" environment after brain injury? Is there a single such environment or does it vary with age and/or sex?

I began with the story of Donna, but a similar story can be told about each of us. Her brain changed during her development, as she learned to talk, as she went to school and took up dancing, as she had her children, as she returned to dancing, as she recovered from her brain injury, and as she aged. Were it possible to study her brain as she passed through life, we would have been able to see changes in her neurons, including their cell bodies, axons, dendrites, and synapses, as well as changes in her glia and blood vessels. One of the remarkable things about all these changes is that throughout them all, she remained the same Donna. I have emphasized the ways in which the brain changes over a lifetime, but I would be remiss if I did not finish by noting that in spite of its plasticity, the brain manages to show amazing constancy in its functions. This simple observation leaves us with a major question. If we accept the brain hypothesis, then how is it that billions or trillions of synapses can change throughout our lifetime yet we remain essentially the same? I leave this for the reader to contemplate.

REFERENCES

Anderson, D. K., Rhees, R. W., & Fleming, D. E. (1985). Effects of prenatal stress on differentiation of the sexually dimorphic nucleus of the preoptic area (SDN-POA) of the rat brain. *Brain Research, 332,* 113–118.

Banich, M. T., Cohen-Levine, S., Kim, H., & Huttenlocher, P. (1990). The effects of developmental factors on IQ in hemiplegic children. *Neuropsychologia, 28,* 35–47.

Becker, L. E., Armstrong, F., Chan, F., & Wood, M. M. (1984). Dendritic development in human occipital cortical neurons. *Developmental Brain Research, 13,* 117–124.

Berry, M. J. (1974). Development of the cerebral neocortex of the rat. In G. Gottlieb (Ed.), *Aspects of neurogenesis* (pp. 7–67). New York: Academic.

Black, J. E., Sirevaag, A. M., & Greenough, W. T. (1987). Complex experience promotes capillary formation in young rat visual cortex. *Neuroscience Letters, 83,* 351–355.

Blue, M. E., & Parnavelas, J. G. (1983a). The formation and maturation of synapses in the visual cortex of the rat. I. Qualitative analysis. *Journal of Neurocytology, 12,* 599–616.

Blue, M. E., & Parnavelas, J. G. (1983b). The formation and maturation of synapses in the visual cortex of the rat. II. Quantitative analysis. *Journal of Neurocytology, 12,* 697–712.

Brennan, P. Kaba, H., & Kaverne, E. B. (1990). Olfactory recognition: A simple memory system. *Science, 250,* 1223–1226.

Buell, S. J., & Coleman, P. D. (1981). Quantitative evidence for selective dendritic growth in normal human aging but not in senile dementia. *Brain Research, 214,* 23–41.

Carswell, S. (1993). The potential for treating neurodegenerative disorders with NGF-inducing compounds. *Experimental Neurology, 124,* 36–42.

Castro, A. J. (1990). Plasticity in the motor system. In B. Kolb & R. Tees (Eds.), *The cerebral cortex of the rat* (pp. 563–588). Cambridge, MA: MIT.

Clark, A. S., & Goldman-Rakic, P. S. (1989). Gonadal hormones influence the emergence of cortical function in nonhuman primates. *Behavioral Neuroscience, 103,* 1287–1295.

Coleman, P. D., & Buell, S. J. (1985). Regulation of dendritic extent in developing and aging brain. In C. W. Cotman (Ed.), *Synaptic plasticity* (pp. 311–334). New York: Guilford.

Coleman, P. D., & Flood, D. G. (1987). Neuron numbers and dendritic extent in normal aging and Alzheimer's disease. *Neurobiology of Aging, 8,* 521–545.

Corkin, S. (1989). Penetrating head injury in young adulthood exacerbates cognitive decline in later years. *Journal of Neuroscience, 9,* 3876–3883.

Cotman, C. W., & Lynch, G. S. (1976). Reactive synaptogenesis in the adult nervous system: The effects of partial deafferentation on new synapse formation. In S. Barondes (Ed.), *Neuronal recognition* (pp. 69–108). New York: Plenum.

Cotman, C. W., & Nadler, J. V. (1978). Reactive synaptogenesis in the hippocampus. In C. W. Cotman (Ed.), *Neuronal plasticity* (pp. 227–271). New York: Raven.

Cotman, C. W., Cummings, B. J., & Pike, C. J. (1993). Molecular cascades in adaptive versus pathological plasticity. In A. Gorio (Ed.), *Neuroregeneration* (pp. 217–240). New York: Raven.

Cowan, W. M. (1979). The development of the brain. *Scientific American, 241,* 112–133.

Craig, C. G., Morshead, C., Reynolds, B., Weiss, S., & van der Kooy, D. (1994). *Growth factor induced proliferation and migration of adult CNS subependymal stem cells in vivo.* Manuscript submitted for review.

Craig, C. G., Morshead, C., Roach, A., & van der Kooy, D. (1994). Evidence for a relatively quiescent stem cell in the subependyma of the adult mammalian forebrain. *Journal of Cellular Biochemistry, 18* (Supplement), 176.

Damasio, A. R., Lima, A., & Damasio, H. (1975). Nervous function after right hemispherectomy. *Neurology, 25,* 89–93.

de Brabander, J., Gibb, R., & Kolb, B. (1993). Neonatal medial prefrontal lesions alter dendritic branching and cell migration of adjacent tissue. *Society for Neuroscience Abstracts, 19,* 165.

de Vellis, J. (1993). Supporting cells central and peripheral. In A. Gorio (Ed.), *Neuroregeneration* (pp. 61–75). New York: Raven.

Diamond, M. C., Lindner, B., & Raymond, A. (1967). Extensive cortical depth measurements and neuron size increases in the cortex of environmentally enriched rats. *Journal of Comparative Neurology, 131,* 357–364.

Diamond, M. C., Dowling, G. A., & Johnson, R. E. (1981). Morphologic cerebral cortical asymmetry in male and female rats. *Experimental Neurology, 71,* 261–268.

Douglas, R. J., Martin, K. A. C., & Whitteridge, D. (1989). A canonical microcircuit for neocortex. *Neural Computation, 1,* 480–488.

Dragunow, M., Currie, R. W., Faull, R. L. M., Robertson, H. A., & Jansen, K. (1989). Immediate early genes, kindling and long-term potentiation. *Neuroscience and Biobehavioral Reviews, 13,* 301–313.

Dudai, Y. (1989). *The neurobiology of memory.* New York: Oxford University Press.

Ellingson, R. J., & McBeath, J. (1967). Evoked potentials and serial EEGs following total left hemispherectomy in a 47-year-old. *Electroencephalography and Clinical Neurophysiology, 22,* 190–195.

Emerson, C. S., Headrick, J. P., & Vink, R. (1993). Estrogen improves biochemical and neurologic outcome following traumatic brain injury in male rats, but not in females. *Brain Research, 608,* 95–100.

Fantie, B., & Kolb, B. (1988). Performance of complex arm- and facial-movement sequences after closed head injury. *Canadian Psychology, 29,* 235.

Fantie, B., & Kolb, B. (1989). Tasks traditionally used to assess callosal function reveal performance deficits associated with mild closed head injury. *Society for Neuroscience Abstracts, 15,* 132.

Fantie, B., & Kolb, B. (1990). An examination of prefrontal lesion size and the effects of cortical grafts on performance of the Morris water task by rats. *Psychobiology, 18,* 74–80.

Fantie, B., & Kolb, B. (1993). Functional consequences of transplantation of frontal neocortex vary with age of donor tissue and behavioral task. *Restorative Neurology and Neuroscience, 5,* 141–149.

Field, T., Schanberg, S. M., Scafidi, F., Bauer, C. R., Vega-Lahr, N., Garcia, R., Nystrom, J., &

Kuhn, C. M. (1986). Tactile/kinesthetic stimulation effects on preterm neonates. *Pediatrics, 77,* 654–658.

Finger, S., Hart, T., & Jones, E. (1982). Recovery time and sensorimotor cortex lesion effects. *Physiology and Behavior, 29,* 73–78.

Finger, S., & Stein, D. G. (1982). *Brain damage and recovery: Research and clinical perspectives.* New York: Academic Press.

Flood, D. G. (1993). Critical issues in the analysis of dendritic extent in aging humans, primates, and rodents. *Neurobiology of Aging, 14,* 649–654.

Gage, F. H., Armstrong, D. M., Williams, L. R., & Varon, S. (1988). Morphological response of axotomized septal neurons to nerve growth factor. *Journal of Comparative Neurology, 269,* 147–155.

Gall, C. M., & Isackson, P. J. (1989). Limbic seizures increase neuronal production of messenger RNA for nerve growth factor. *Science, 245,* 758–760.

Garofalo, L., Ribeiro-da-Silva, A., & Cuello, C. A. (1992). Nerve growth factor-induced synaptogenesis and hypertrophy of cortical cholinergic terminals. *Proceedings of the National Academy of Sciences, USA, 89,* 2639–2643.

Gentile, A. M., Green, S., Nieburgs, A., Schmelzer, W., & Stein, D. G. (1978). Disruption and recovery of locomotor and manipulatory behavior following cortical lesions in rats. *Behavioral Biology, 22,* 417–455.

Gilbert, C. D., Hirsch, J. A., & Wiesel, T. N. (1990). Lateral interactions in visual cortex. *Cold Spring Harbor Symposia on Quantitative Biology, LV,* 663–677.

Giulian, D. (1993). Reactive glia as rivals in regulating neuronal survival. *Glia, 7,* 102–110.

Globus, A., Rosenzweig, M. R., Bennett, E. L., & Diamond, M. C. (1973). Effects of differential experience on dendritic spine counts in rat cerebral cortex. *Journal of Comparative and Physiological Psychology, 82,* 175–181.

Goldman, P. S. (1974). An alternative to developmental plasticity: Heterology of CNS structures in infants and adults. In D. G. Stein, J. J. Rosen, & N. Butters (Eds.), *Plasticity and recovery of function in the central nervous system* (pp. 149–174). New York: Academic.

Goldman, P. S., & Galkin, T. W. (1978). Prenatal removal of frontal association cortex in the fetal rhesus monkey: Anatomical and functional consequences in postnatal life. *Brain Research, 152,* 451–485.

Goldman, P., & Mendelson, M. J. (1977). Salutary effects of early experience on deficits caused by lesions of frontal association cortex in developing rhesus monkeys. *Experimental Neurology, 57,* 588–602.

Goldman-Rakic, P. S., Isseroff, A., Schwartz, M. L., & Bugbee, N. M. (1983). The neurobiology of cognitive development. In P. H. Mussen (Ed.), *Handbook of child psychology: Biology and infancy development* (pp. 311–344). New York: Wiley.

Gould, E., Woolley, C. S., Frankfurt, M., & McEwen, B. S. (1990). Gonadal steroids regulate dendritic spine density in hippocampal pyramidal cells in adulthood. *Journal of Neuroscience, 10,* 1286–1291.

Gould, E., Woolley, C. S., & McEwen, B. S. (1991). The hippocampal formation: Morphological changes induced by thyroid, gonadal, and adrenal hormones. *Psychoneuroendocrinology, 16,* 67–84.

Greenough, W. T., Black, J. E., & Wallace, C. S. (1987). Experience and brain development. *Child Development, 58,* 539–559.

Greenough, W. T., Juraska, J. M., & Volkmar, R. F. (1979). Maze training effects on dendritic branching in occipital cortex of adult rats. *Behavioral and Neural Biology, 26,* 287–297.

Greenough, W. T., Larson, J. R., & Withers, G. S. (1985). Effects of unilateral and bilateral training in a reaching task on dendritic branching of neurons in the rat motor-sensory forelimb cortex. *Behavioral and Neural Biology, 44,* 301–314.

Greenough, W. T., West, R. W., & de Voogd, T. J. (1978). Sub-synaptic plate perforations: Changes with age and experience in the rat. *Science, 202,* 1096–1098.

Gronwall, D. (1989). Cumulative and persisting effects of concussion on attention and concussion. In H. S. Levin, H. M. Eisenberg, & A. L. Benton (Eds.), *Mild head injury* (pp. 153–162). New York: Oxford University Press.

Hagg, T., Louis, J.-C., & Varon, S. (1993). Neurotrophic factors and CNS regeneration. In A. Gorio (Ed.), *Neuroregeneration* (pp. 265–287). New York: Raven.

Hall, E. D., Pazara, K. E., & Linseman, K. L. (1991). Sex differences in postischemic neuronal necrosis in gerbils. *Journal of Cerebral Blood Flow and Metabolism, 11,* 292–298.

Harlow, H. F., Akert, K., & Schiltz, K. A. (1964). The effects of bilateral prefrontal lesions on learned behavior of neonatal, infant and preadolescent monkeys. In J. M. Warren & K. Akert (Eds.), *The frontal granular cortex and behavior* (pp. 126–148). New York: McGraw-Hill.

Harrison, R. G. (1947). Wound healing and reconstitution of the central nervous system of the amphibian embryo after removal of parts of the neural plate. *Journal of Experimental Zoology, 106,* 27–84.

Hebb, D. O. (1947). The effects of early experience on problem solving at maturity. *American Psychologist, 2,* 737–745.

Hebb, D. O. (1949). *The organization of behaviour.* New York: McGraw-Hill.

Hebb, D. O. (1980). *Essay on mind.* Hillsdale, NJ: Lawrence Erlbaum Associates.

Hefti, F. (1986). Nerve growth factor promotes survival of septal cholinergic neurons after fimbrial transection. *Journal of Neuroscience, 6,* 2155–2162.

Hicks, S. P. (1954). Mechanisms of radiation anencephaly, anopthalamia, and pituitary anomalies. Repair in the mammalian embryo. *Archives of Pathology, 54,* 363–378.

Hicks, S. P., & D'Amato, C. J. (1968). Cell migrations to the isocortex of the rat. *Anatomical Record, 160,* 619–634.

Hicks, S. P., & D'Amato, C. J. (1970). Motor-sensory and visual behavior after hemispherectomy in newborn and mature rats. *Experimental Neurology, 29,* 416–438.

Hicks, S. P, & D'Amato, C. J. (1975). Motor-sensory cortex corticospinal system and developing locomotion and placing in rats. *American Journal of Anatomy, 143,* 1–42.

Hicks, S. P., D'Amato, C. J., & Glover, R. A. (1984). Recovery or malformation after fetal radiation and other injuries. In C. R. Almli & S. Finger (Eds.), *Early brain damage* (pp. 127–147). New York: Academic.

Hoff, S. F. (1986). Lesion-induced transneuronal plasticity in the adult rat hippocampus. *Neuroscience, 19,* 1227–1233.

Horner, C. H. (1993). Plasticity of the dendritic spine. *Progress in Neurobiology, 41,* 281–321.

Hunt, S. P., Pini, A., & Evan, G. (1987). Induction of c-fos-like protein in spinal cord following sensory stimulation. *Nature, 328,* 632–634.

Huttenlocher, P. R. (1984). Synapse elimination and plasticity in developing human cerebral cortex. *American Journal of Mental Deficiency, 88,* 488–496.

Huttenlocher, P. R. (1990). Morphometric study of human cerebral cortex development. *Neuropsychologia, 28,* 517–527.

Hyman, B. T., Kromer, B. A., & van Hoesen, G. W. (1987). Reinnervation of the hippocampal perforant pathway zone in Alzheimer's disease. *Annals of Neurology, 21,* 259–267.

Jones, T. A., & Schallert, T. (1992). Overgrowth and pruning of dendrites in adult rats recovering from neocortical damage. *Brain Research, 581,* 156–160.

Jones, T. A., & Schallert, T. (1994). Use-dependent growth of pyramidal neurons after neocortical damage. *Journal of Neuroscience, 14,* 2140–2152.

Jones, W. H., & Thomas, D. B. (1962). Changes in the dendritic organization of neurons in the cerebral cortex following deafferentation. *Journal of Anatomy, 96,* 375–381.

Juraska, J. M. (1990). The structure of the cerebral cortex: Effects of gender and the environment. In B. Kolb, & R. Tees (Eds.), *The cerebral cortex of the rat* (pp. 483–506). Cambridge, MA: MIT Press.

Juraska, J. M., Fitch, J., Henderson, C., & Rivers, N. (1985). Sex differences in the dendritic branching of dentate granule cells following differential experience. *Brain Research, 333,* 73–80.

Juraska, J. M., & Kopcik, J. R. (1988). Sex and envrionmental influences on the size and ultrastructure of the rat corpus callosum. *Brain Research, 450,* 1–8.

Juraska, J. M., Fitch, J. M., & Washburne, D. L. (1989). The dendritic morphology of pyramidal neurons in the rat hippocampal CA3 area. II. Effects of gender and experience. *Brain Research, 79,* 115–121.

Kasamatsu, T., Pettigrew, J. D., & Ary, M. (1979). Restoration of visual cortical plasticity by local microperfusion of norepinephrine. *Journal of Comparative Neurology, 185,* 163–182.

Kennard, M. (1938). Reorganization of motor function in the cerebral cortex of monkeys deprived of motor and premotor areas in infancy. *Journal of Neurophysiology, 1,* 477–496.

Kennard, M. (1940). Relation of age to motor impairment in man and in subhuman primates. *Archives of Neurology and Psychiatry, 44,* 377–397.

Kennedy, H., & Dehay, C. (1993). Cortical specification of mice and men. *Cerebral Cortex, 3,* 171–186.

Kertesz, A. (1979). *Aphasia and associated disorders.* New York: Grune and Stratton.

Kimura, D. (1992). Sex differences in the brain. *Scientific American, 267(3),* 118–125.

Kimura, D., & Archibald, Y. (1974). Motor functions of the left hemisphere. *Brain, 97,* 337–350.

Kolb, B. (1984). Functions of the frontal cortex of the rat: A comparative review. *Brain Research Reviews, 8,* 65–98.

Kolb, B. (1987). Recovery from early cortical damage in rats. I. Differential behavioral and anatomical effects of frontal lesions at different ages of neural maturation. *Behavioural Brain Research, 25,* 205–220.

Kolb, B. (1990a). Animal models for human PFC-related disorders. *Progress in Brain Research, 85,* 501–520.

Kolb, B. (1990b). Recovery from occipital stroke: A self-report and an inquiry into visual processes. *Canadian Journal of Psychology, 44,* 130–147.

Kolb, B. (1990c). Sparing and recovery of function. In B. Kolb & R. Tees (Eds.), *The cerebral cortex of the rat* (pp. 537–561). Cambridge, MA: MIT Press.

Kolb, B., Buday, M., Gorny, G., & Gibb, R. (1992). Sex and environment affect behavioral recovery and dendritic growth after neonatal frontal lesions in rats. *Society for Neuroscience Abstracts, 18,* 869.

Kolb, B., & Cioe, J. (1995). *Sex-related differences in cortical function after prefrontal lesions in rats.* Submitted for review.

Kolb, B., & Elliott, W. (1987). Recovery from early cortical damage in rats. II. Effects of experience on anatomy and behavior following frontal lesions at 1 or 5 days of age. *Behavioural Brain Research, 26,* 47–56.

Kolb, B., & Fantie, B. (1989). Development of the child's brain. In C. R. Reynolds (Ed.), *Handbook of child clinical neuropsychology* (pp. 17–39). New York: Plenum.

Kolb, B., & Fantie, B. (1995). *Frontal cortical transplants grow more complex dendritic arbors in male than in female hosts.* Manuscript in preparation.

Kolb, B., & Gibb, R. (1990). Anatomical correlates of behavioural change after neonatal prefrontal lesions in rats. *Progress in Brain Research, 85,* 241–256.

Kolb, B., & Gibb, R. (1991a). Environmental enrichment and cortical injury: Behavioral and anatomical consequences of frontal cortex lesions. *Cerebral Cortex, 1,* 189–198.

Kolb, B., & Gibb, R. (1991b). Sparing of function after neonatal frontal lesions correlates with increased cortical dendritic branching: A possible mechanism for the Kennard effect. *Behavioural Brain Research, 43,* 51–56.

Kolb, B., & Gibb, R. (1993). Possible anatomical basis of recovery of spatial learning after neonatal prefrontal lesions in rats. *Behavioral Neuroscience, 107,* 799–811.

Kolb, B., Gibb, R., & Muirhead, D. (1995). *Recovery from neonatal hemidecortication is blocked by perturbation of the intact hemisphere.* Manuscript submitted for review.

Kolb, B., Gibb, R., & van der Kooy D. (1992). Cortical and striatal structure and connectivity are altered by neonatal hemidecortication in rats. *Journal of Comparative Neurology, 322,* 311–324.

Kolb, B., Gibb, R., & van der Kooy, D. (1994). Neonatal frontal cortical lesions in rats alter cortical structure and connectivity. *Brain Research, 645,* 85–97.

Kolb, B., Gorny, G., & Gibb, R. (1995). *Experience differentially effects dendrites and spines in rat cortex.* Manuscript in preparation.

Kolb, B., Hewson, J., & Whishaw, I. Q. (1993). Neonatal motor cortex lesions alter corticospinal projections and dendritic organization in the absence of behavioural sparing. *Society for Neuroscience Abstracts, 19,* 165.

Kolb, B., & Holmes, C. (1983). Neonatal motor cortex lesions in the rat: Absence of sparing of motor behaviors and impaired spatial learning concurrent with abnormal cerebral morphogenesis. *Behavioral Neuroscience, 97,* 697–709.

Kolb, B., Holmes, C., & Whishaw, I. Q. (1987). Recovery from early cortical damage in rats. III. Neonatal removal of posterior parietal cortex has greater behavioral and anatomical effects than similar removals in adulthood. *Behavioural Brain Research, 26,* 119–137.

Kolb, B., Ladowsky, R., Gibb, R., & Gorny, G. (1994). *Does dendritic growth underlay recovery from neonatal occipital lesions in rats?* Manuscript submitted for review.

Kolb, B., MacIntosh, A., Sutherland, R. J., & Whishaw, I. Q. (1984). Evidence for anatomical but not functional asymmetry in the hemidecorticate rat. *Behavioral Neuroscience, 96,* 44–58.

Kolb, B., & Milner, B. (1981a). Observations on spontaneous facial expression after focal cerebral excisions and after intracarotid injection of sodium Amytal. *Neuropsychologia, 19,* 505–514.

Kolb, B., & Milner, B. (1981b). Performance of complex arm and facial movements after focal brain lesions. *Neuropsychologia, 19,* 491–504.

Kolb, B., & Muirhead, D. (1995). *Prenatal lesions of prefrontal cortex allow sparing of function in the presence of gross morphological abnormalities.* Manuscript in preparation.

Kolb, B., & Nonneman, A. J. (1976). Functional development of the prefrontal cortex continues into adolescence. *Science, 193,* 335–336.

Kolb, B., & Nonneman, A. J. (1978). Sparing of function in rats with early prefrontal cortex lesions. *Brain Research, 151,* 135–148.

Kolb, B., Petrie, B., Cioe, J., & Gibb, R. (1995). *Recovery from early cortical damage in rats. VII. Comparison of the behavioural and anatomical effects of medial prefrontal lesions at different ages of neural maturation.* Manuscript submitted for review.

Kolb, B., Ribeiro-da-Silva, A., & Cuello, C. (1995). *Nerve growth factor enhances recovery of function and provokes dendritic growth after cerebral stroke.* Manuscript submitted for review.

Kolb, B., & Stewart, J. (1991). Sex-related differences in dendritic branching of cells in the prefrontal cortex of rats. *Journal of Neuroendocrinology, 3,* 95–99.

Kolb, B., & Stewart, J. (in press). Changes in neonatal gonadal hormonal environment prevent behavioral sparing and alter cortical morphogenesis after early frontal cortex lesions in male and female rats. *Behavioral Neuroscience.*

Kolb, B., & Sutherland, R. J. (1992). Noradrenaline depletion blocks behavioral sparing and alters cortical morphogenesis after neonatal frontal cortex damage in rats. *Journal of Neuroscience, 12,* 2221–2330.

Kolb, B., Sutherland, R. J., Nonneman, A. J., & Whishaw, I. Q. (1982). Asymmetry in the cerebral cortex of the rat, mouse, rabbit and cat: The right hemisphere is larger. *Experimental Neurology, 78,* 348–359.

Kolb, B., Sutherland, R. J., & Whishaw, I. Q. (1983a). A comparison of the contributions of the frontal and parietal association cortex to spatial localization in rats. *Behavioral Neuroscience, 97,* 13–27.

Kolb, B., Sutherland, R. J., & Whishaw, I. Q. (1983b). Abnormalities in cortical and subcortical morphology after neonatal neocortical lesions in rats. *Experimental Neurology, 79*, 223–244.

Kolb, B., Sutherland, R. J., & Whishaw, I. Q. (1983c). Neonatal hemidecortication or frontal cortex ablation produce similar behavioral sparing but opposite effects upon morphogenesis of remaining cortex. *Behavioral Neuroscience, 97*, 154–158.

Kolb, B., & Taylor, L. (1981). Affective behavior in patients with localized cortical excisions: An analysis of lesion site and side. *Science, 214*, 89–91.

Kolb, B., & Taylor, L. (1988). Facial expression and the neocortex. *Society for Neuroscience Abstracts, 14*, 219.

Kolb, B., & Tomie, J. (1988). Recovery from early cortical damage in rats. IV. Effects of hemidecortication at 1, 5, or 10 days of age. *Behavioural Brain Research, 28*, 259–274.

Kolb, B., Tomie, J., & Ouellette, A. (1995). *Bilateral and unilateral motor experience have equivalent effects on cortical neurons.* In preparation.

Kolb, B., & Whishaw, I. Q. (1981a). Decortication of rats in infancy or adulthood produced comparable functional losses on learned and species typical behaviors. *Journal of Comparative and Physiological Psychology, 95*, 468–483.

Kolb, B., & Whishaw, I. Q. (1981b). Neonatal frontal lesions in the rat: Sparing of learned but not species-typical behavior in the presence of reduced brain weight and cortical thickness. *Journal of Comparative and Physiological Psychology, 95*, 863–879.

Kolb, B., & Whishaw, I. Q. (1983a). Dissociation of the contributions of the prefrontal, motor, and parietal cortex to the control of movement in the rat: An experimental review. *Canadian Journal of Psychology, 37*, 211–232.

Kolb, B., & Whishaw, I. Q. (1983b). Problems and principles underlying interspecies comparisons. In T. E. Robinson (Ed.), *Behavioral approaches to brain research* (pp. 237–263). New York: Oxford.

Kolb, B., & Whishaw, I. Q. (1985a). Neonatal frontal lesions in hamsters impair species-typical behaviors and reduce brain weight and cortical thickness. *Behavioral Neuroscience, 99*, 691–704.

Kolb, B., & Whishaw, I. Q. (1985b). Earlier is not always better: Behavioural dysfunction and abnormal cerebral morphogenesis following neonatal cortical lesions in the rat. *Behavioural Brain Research, 17*, 25–43.

Kolb, B., & Whishaw, I. Q. (1990). *Fundamentals of human neuropsychology* (3rd ed.). New York: W. H. Freeman.

Kolb, B., & Whishaw, I. Q. (1991). Mechanisms underlying behavioral sparing after neonatal electroencephalographic activity. *Brain Dysfunction, 4*, 75–92.

Kolb, B., & Whishaw, I. Q. (1995). *Fundamentals of human neuropsychology* (4th ed.). New York: W. H. Freeman.

Konorski, J. (1948). *Conditioned reflexes and neuron organization.* Cambridge: Cambridge University Press.

Korsching, S. (1993). The neurotrophic factor concept: A reexamination. *Journal of Neuroscience, 13*, 2739–2748.

Kromer, L. F. (1987). Nerve growth factor treatment after brain injury prevents neuronal death. *Science, 235*, 214–216.

Lenneberg, E. (1967). *Biological foundations of language.* New York: John Wiley.

Levitan, I. B., & Kaczmarek, L. K. (1991). *The neuron.* New York: Oxford University Press.

Levin, H. S., Benton, A. L., & Grossman, R. G. (1982). *Neurobehavioral consequences of closed head injury.* New York: Oxford University Press.

Levin, H. S., Eisenberg, H. M., & Benton, A. L. (Eds.). (1989). *Mild head injury.* New York: Oxford.

Levin, H. S., Grossman, R. G., Rose, J. E., & Teasdale, G. (1979). Long-term neuropsychological outcome of closed head injury. *Journal of Neurosurgery, 50*, 412–422.

Loesche, J., & Steward, O. (1977). Behavioral correlates of denervation and reinnervation of the hippocampal formation of the rat: Recovery of alternation performance following unilateral entorhinal cortex lesions. *Brain Research Bulletin, 2,* 31–39.

Loy, R. (1986). Sexual dimorphism in the septohippocampal system. In R. Isaacson, & K. Pribram (Eds.), *The hippocampus* (Vol. 3, pp. 301–321). New York: Plenum.

Lynch, G. S., & Cotman, C. W. (1975). The hippocampus as a model for studying anatomical plasticity in the adult brain. In R. L. Isaacson, & K. H. Pribram (Eds.), *The hippocampus* (Vol. 1, pp. 123–154). New York: Plenum.

Maisonpierre, P. C., Belluscio, L., Squinto, S., Ip., N. Y., Furth M. E., Lindsay, R. M., & Yancopoulos, G. D. (1990). Neurotrophin-3: A neurotrophic factor related to NGF and BDNF. *Science, 247,* 1446–1451.

Marin-Padilla, M. (1970a). Prenatal and early postnatal ontogenesis of the human motor cortex: A Golgi study. I. The sequential development of the cortical layers. *Brain Research, 23,* 167–183.

Marin-Padilla, M. (1970b). Prenatal and early postnatal ontogenesis of the human motor cortex: A Golgi study. II. The basket-pyramidal cell system. *Brain Research, 23,* 185–191.

Mathews, D. A., Cotman, C. W., & Lynch, G. (1976). An electron microscopic study of lesion-induced synaptogenesis in the dentate gyrus of the adult rat. II. Reappearance of morphologically normal synaptic contacts. *Brain Research, 115,* 23–41.

Milner, B. (1964). Some effects of frontal lobectomy in man. In J. M. Warren, & K. Akert (Eds.), *The frontal granular cortex and behavior* (pp. 313–334). New York: McGraw-Hill.

Milner, B. (1975). Psychological aspects of focal epilepsy and its neurosurgical management. *Advances in Neurology, 8,* 299–321.

Mohr, J. P., Weiss, G. H., Caveness, W. F, Dillon, J. D., Kistler, J. P., Meirowsky, A. M., & Rish, B. L. (1980). Language and motor disorders after penetrating head injury in Viet Nam. *Neurology, 30,* 1273–1279.

Morioka, T., Kalehua, A. N., & Streit, W. J. (1993). Characterization of microglial reaction after middle cerebral artery occlusions in rat brain. *Journal of Comparative Neurology, 327,* 123–132.

Morris, R. G. M. (1980). Spatial localization does not require the presence of local cues. *Learning and Motivation, 12,* 239–261.

Morrison, J. H., & Hof, P. R. (1992). The organization of the cerebral cortex: From molecules to circuits. *Discussions in Neuroscience, IX,* 1–80.

Morshead, C. M., Reynolds, B. A., Craig, C. G., McBurney, M. W., Staines, W. A., Morassutti, D., Weiss, S., & van der Kooy, D. (1994). Neural stem cells in the adult mammalian forebrain: A relatively quiescent subpopulation of subependymal cells. *Neuron, 13,* 1071–1082.

Murtha, S., Pappas, B. A., & Raman, S. (1990). Neonatal and adult forebrain norepinephrine depletion and the behavioral and cortical thickening effects of enriched/impoverished environment. *Behavioral Brain Research, 39,* 249–261.

Nicholas, J. S. (1957). Results of inversion of neural plate material. *Proceedings of the National Academy of Science, USA, 43,* 253–283.

Nicoll, A., & Blakemore, C. (1993). Patterns of local connectivity in the neocortex. *Neural Computation, 5,* 665–680.

Nieto-Sampedro, M., & Cotman, C. W. (1985). Growth factor induction and temporal order in central nervous system repair. In C. W. Cotman (Ed.), *Synaptic plasticity* (pp. 407–456). New York: Guilford.

Nonneman, A. J. (1970). *Anatomical and behavioral consequences of early brain damage in the rabbit.* Unpublished doctoral dissertation, University of Florida, Gainesville, FL.

Nonneman, A. J., Corwin, J. V., Sahley C. L., & Vicedomini, J. P. (1984). Functional development of the prefrontal system. In S. Finger & C. R. Almli (Eds.), *Early brain damage* (Vol. 2, pp. 139–153). New York: Academic.

Nonneman, A. J., & Kolb, B. (1979). Functional recovery after serial ablation of prefrontal cortex in the rat. *Physiology and Behavior, 22,* 895–901.

Nudo, R., & Grenda, R. (1992). Reorganization of distal forelimb representations in primary motor cortex of adult squirrel monkeys following focal ischemic infarct. *Society for Neuroscience Abstracts, 18,* 216.

Ogden, J. A. (1988). Language and memory functions after long recovery periods in left-hemispherectomized subjects. *Neuropsychologia, 26,* 645–659.

O'Leary, D. (1989). Do cortical areas emerge from a protocortex? *Trends in Neuroscience, 12,* 400–406.

Pallage, V., Knusel, B., Hefti, F., & Will, B. (1993). Functional consequences of a single nerve growth factor administration following septal damage in rats. *European Journal of Neuroscience, 5,* 669–679.

Pascual-Leone, A., Cammarota, A., Wassermann, E. M., Brasil-Neto, J. P., Cohen, L. G., & Hallett, M. (1993). Modulation of motor cortical outputs to the reading hand of braille readers. *Annals of Neurology, 34,* 33–37.

Passingham, R. E., Perry, V. H., & Wilkinson, F. (1983). The long-term effects of removal of sensorimotor cortex in infant and adult rhesus monkeys. *Brain, 106,* 675–705.

Patrissi, G., & Stein, D. G. (1975). Temporal factors in recovery of function after brain damage. *Experimental Neurology, 47,* 470–480.

Peters, A., & Sethares, C. (1991). Organization of pyramidal neurons in area 17 of monkey visual cortex. *Journal of Comparative Neurology, 306,* 1–23.

Pinel, J. P. J., & Treit, D. (1983). The conditioned burying paradigm and behavioral neuroscience. In T. E. Robinson (Ed.), *Behavioral approaches to brain research* (pp. 212–234). New York: Oxford.

Purves, D., & Voyvodic, J. T. (1987). Imaging mammalian nerve cells and their connections over time in living animals. *Trends in Neurosciences, 10,* 398–404.

Pylyshyn, Z. W. (1980). Computation and cognition: Issues in the foundations of cognitive science. *Behavioral and Brain Sciences, 3,* 11–69.

Rakic, P. (1972). Mode of cell migration to the superficial layers of fetal monky neocortex. *Journal of Comparative Neurology, 145,* 61–84.

Rakic, P. (1988). Specification of cerebral cortical areas. *Science, 241,* 170–176.

Ramirez, J. J., Labbe, R., & Stein, D. G. (1988). Recovery from perseverative behavior after entorhinal cortex lesions in rats. *Brain Research, 459,* 153–156.

Ramon y Cajal, S. (1928). *Degeneration and regeneration of the nervous system.* London: Oxford University Press.

Rasmussen, T., & Milner, B. (1977). The role of early left-brain injury in determining lateralization of cerebral speech functions. *Annals of the New York Academy of Sciences, 299,* 355–369.

Rauschecker, J., Egert, U, & Han, S. (1987). Compensatory whisker growth in visually deprived cats. *Neuroscience, 22,* S222.

Reid, S. N. M., & Juraska, J. M. (1992a). Sex differences in the gross size of the rat neocortex. *Journal of Comparative Neurology, 321,* 442–447.

Reid, S. N. M., & Juraska, J. M. (1992b). Sex differences in neuron number in the binocular area of the rat visual cortex. *Journal of Comparative Neurology, 321,* 448–455.

Reynolds, B., & Weiss, S. (1992). Generation of neurons and astrocytes from isolated cells of the adult mammalian central nervous system. *Science, 255,* 1707–1710.

Riva, D., & Cazzaniga, L. (1986). Late effects of unilateral brain lesions sustained before and after age one. *Neuropsychologia, 24,* 423–428.

Rockel, A. J., Hiorns, R. W., & Powell, T. P. S. (1980). The basic uniformity in structure of the neocortex. *Brain, 103,* 221–244.

Roof, R. L. (1993). The dentate gyrus is sexually dimorphic in prepubescent rats: Testosterone plays a significant role. *Brain Research, 610,* 148–151.

Roof, R L., Duvdevani, R., & Stein, D. G. (1992). Progesterone treatment attenuates brain edema following contusion injury to male and female rats. *Restorative Neurology and Neuroscience, 4,* 425–427.

Roof, R. L., & Havens, M. D. (1992). Testosterone improves maze performance and induces the development of a male hippocampus in females. *Brain Research, 572,* 310–313.

Rudy, J. W., Stadler-Morris, S., & Albert, P. (1987). Ontogeny of spatial navigation behaviors in the rat: Dissociation of "proximal" and "distal" cue-based behaviors. *Behavioral Neuroscience, 101,* 221–244.

Rutledge, L. T. (1978). Effects of cortical denervation and stimulation on axons, dendrites, and synapses. In C. W. Cotman (Ed.), *Neuronal plasticity* (pp. 273–289). New York: Raven.

Rutledge, L. T., Wright, C., & Duncan, J. A. (1974). Morphological changes in pyramidal cells of mammalian neocortex associated with increased use. *Experimental Neurology, 44,* 209–228.

Schadé, J. P., & van Groenigen, W. B. (1961). Structural organization of the human cerebral cortex. *Acta Anatomica (Basel), 47,* 74–111.

Schallert, T. (1983). Sensorimotor impairment and recovery of function in brain-damaged rats: Reappearance of symptoms during old age. *Behavioral Neuroscience, 97,* 159–164.

Schallert, T., Hernandez, T. D., & Barth, T. M. (1986). Recovery of function after brain damage: Severe and chronic disruption by diazepam. *Brain Research, 379,* 104–111.

Schallert, T., & Whishaw, I. Q. (1984). Bilateral cutaneous stimulation of the somatosensory system in hemidecorticate rats. *Behavioral Neuroscience, 98,* 518–540.

Schallert, T., & Whishaw, I. Q. (1985). Neonatal hemidecortication and bilateral cutaneous stimulation in rats. *Developmental Psychobiology, 18,* 501–514.

Schanberg, S. M., & Field, T. M. (1987). Sensory deprivation stress and supplemental stimulation in the rat pup and preterm human neonate. *Child Development, 58,* 1431–1447.

Schneider, J. (1973). Early lesions of superior colliculus: Factors affecting the formation of abnormal retinal projections. *Brain, Behavior, and Evolution, 8,* 73–109.

Seymoure, R., & Juraska, J. M. (1992). Sex differences in cortical thickness and the dendritic tree in the monocular and binocular subfields of the rat visual cortex at weaning age. *Developmental Brain Research, 69,* 185–189.

Sirevaag, A. M., & Greenough, W. T. (1987). Differential rearing effects on rat visual cortex synapses. III. Neuronal and glial nuclei, boutons, dendrites, and capillaries. *Brain Research, 424,* 320–332.

Skinner, B. F. (1938). *The behavior of organisms.* New York: Appleton-Century-Crofts.

Smith, A. (1966). Speech and other functions after left (dominant) hemispherectomy. *Journal of Neurology, Neurosurgery, and Psychiatry, 29,* 467–471.

Smith, A. (1969). Nondominant hemispherectomy. *Neurology, 19,* 442–445.

Smith, A. (1984). Early and long-term recovery from brain damage in children and adults: Evolution of concepts of localization, plasticity and recovery. In C. R. Almli, & S. Finger (Eds.), *Early brain damage: Research orientations and clinical observations* (pp. 299–324). New York: Academic.

Stein, D. G., & Will, B. E. (1983). Nerve growth factor produces a temporary facilitation of recovery from entorhinal cortex lesions. *Brain Research, 261,* 127–131.

Stephen, H., Bauchot, R., & Andy, J. (1970). Data on the size of the brain and of various parts in insectivores and primates. In C. R. Noback, & W. Montagna (Eds.), *The primate brain* (pp. 289–297). New York: Appleton.

Steward, O. (1989). *Principles of cellular, molecular, and developmental neuroscience.* New York: Springer-Verlag.

Steward, O. (1991). Synapse replacement on cortical neurons following denervation. In A. Peters, & E. G. Jones (Eds.), *Cerebral cortex* (Vol. 9 pp. 81–132). New York: Plenum.

Steward, O., Loesche, J., & Horton, W. C. (1977). Behavioral correlates of denervation and reinnervation of the hippocampal formation of the rat: Open field activity and cue utilization following bilateral entorhinal cortex lesions. *Brain Research Bulletin, 2,* 41–48.

Stewart, J., & Kolb, B. (1988). The effects of neonatal gonadectomy and prenatal stress on cortical thickness and asymmetry in rats. *Behavioral and Neural Biology, 49,* 344–360.

Stewart, J., & Kolb, B. (1994). Dendritic branching in cortical pyramidal cells in response to ovariectomy in adult female rats: Suppression by neonatal exposure to testosterone. *Brain Research, 654,* 149–154.

Streit, W. J. (1993). Microglial-neuronal interactions. *Journal of Chemical Neuroanatomy, 6,* 261–266.

Streit, W. J., Graeber, M. B., & Kreutzberg, G. W. (1988). Functional plasticity of microglia: A review. *Glia, 1,* 301–307.

Sutherland, R. J., Kolb, B., Whishaw, I. Q., & Becker, J. (1982). Cortical noradrenaline depletion eliminates sparing of spatial learning after neonatal frontal cortex damage in the rat. *Neuroscience Letters, 32,* 125–130.

Sutherland, R. J., Whishaw, I. Q., & Kolb, B. (1983). A behavioral analysis of spatial localization following electrolytic, kainate- or colchicine-induced damage to the hippocampal formation in the rat. *Behavioral Brain Research, 7,* 133–153.

Sutherland, R. J., Whishaw, I. Q., & Kolb, B. (1988). Contributions of cingulate cortex to two forms of spatial memory. *Journal of Neuroscience, 8,* 1863–1872.

Szentagothai, J. (1975). The "module-concept" in cerebral cortex architecture. *Brain Research, 95,* 475–496.

Tallal, P., Stark, R. E., & Mellits, E. D. (1985a). The relationship between auditory temporal analysis and receptive language development: Evidence from studies of developmental language disorder. *Neuropsychologia, 23,* 527–534.

Tallal, P., Stark, R. E., & Mellits, E. D. (1985b). Identification of language-impaired children on the basis of rapid perception and production skills. *Brain and Language, 25,* 314–322.

Tanaka, K. (1993). Neuronal mechanisms of object recognition. *Science, 262,* 685–688.

Teuber, H. -L. (1975). Recovery of function after brain injury in man. In *Outcome of severe damage to the nervous system* (Ciba Foundation Symposium 34). Amsterdam: Elsevier North-Holland.

Tieman, S. B., & Hirsch, H. V. B. (1982). Exposure to lines of only one orientation modifies dendritic morphology of cells in the visual cortex of the cat. *Journal of Comparative Neurology, 211,* 353–362.

Tjossem, H. H., Goodlett, C. R., & West, J. R. (1987). Sprouting responsiveness in the dentate gyrus is reduced by ethanol administered following but not preceding an entorhinal lesion. *Experimental Neurology, 97,* 441–453.

Tomie, J., & Whishaw, I. Q. (1990). New paradigms for tactile discrimination studies with the rat: Methods for simple, conditional, and congfigural discriminations. *Physiology and Behavior, 48,* 225–231.

Turner, A. M., & Greenough, W. T. (1983). Synapses per neuron and synaptic dimensions in occipital cortex of rats reared in complex, social, or isolation housing. *Acta Sterologica, 2* (Suppl. 1), 239–244.

Turner, A. M., & Greenough, W. T. (1985). Differential rearing effects on rat visual cortex synapses. I. Synaptic and neuronal density and synapses per neuron. *Brain Research, 329,* 195–203.

Uylings, H. B. M., van Eden, C. G., Parnavelas, J. G., & Kalsbeek, A. (1990). The prenatal and postnatal development of rat cerebral cortex. In B. Kolb & R. Tees (Eds.), *The cerebral cortex of the rat* (pp. 35–76). Cambridge, MA: MIT.

Vanderwolf, C. H., Leung, L- W. S., & Stewart, D. J. (1985). Two afferent pathways mediating hippocampal rhythmical slow activity. In G. Buzsaki, & C. H. Vanderwolf (Eds.), *Electrical activity of the archicortex* (pp. 47–66). Budapest: Akademiai Kiado.

Vargha-Khadem, F., & Polkey, C. E. (1992). A review of cognitive outcome after hemidecortication in humans. In F. D. Rose, & D. A. Johnson (Eds.), *Recovery from brain damage* (pp. 137–168). New York: Plenum.

Vargha-Khadem, F., Watters, G., & O'Gorman, A. M. (1985). Development of speech and language following bilateral frontal lesions. *Brain and Language, 37,* 167–183.

Vicedomini, J. P., Corwin, J. V., & Nonneman, A. J. (1982). Role of residual anterior neocortex in recovery from neonatal prefrontal lesions in the rat. *Physiology and Behavior, 28,* 797–806.

Villablanca, J. R., Burgess, J. W., & Sonnier, B. J. (1984). Neonatal cerebral hemispherectomy: A model for postlesion reorganization of the brain. In S. Finger, & C. R. Almli (Eds.), *Recovery from brain damage* (pp. 179–210). New York: Academic.

Villablanca, J. R., Hovda, D. A., Jackson, G. F., & Infante, C. (1993). Neurological and behavioral effects of a unilateral frontal cortical lesion in fetal kittens: II. Visual system tests, and proposing "an optimal developmental period" for lesion effects. *Behavioural Brain Research, 57,* 79–92.

Volkmar, R. F., & Greenough, W. T. (1972). Rearing complexity affects branching of dendrites in visual cortex of the rat. *Science, 176,* 1445–1447.

Wallace, C. S., Kilman, V. L., Withers, G. S., & Greenough, W. T. (1992). Increases in dendritic length in occipital cortex after 4 days of differential housing in weanling rats. *Behavioral and Neural Biology, 58,* 64–68.

Walsh, R., & Greenough, W. T. (1976). *Environments as therapy for brain damage.* New York: Plenum.

Ward, I. L. (1972). Prenatal stress feminizes and demasculinizes the behavior of males. *Science, 175,* 82–84.

Ward, I. L., & Weisz, J. (1980). Maternal stress alters plasma testosterone in fetal males. *Science, 207,* 328–329.

Warren, J. M. (1972). Evolution, behavior and the prefrontal cortex. *Acta Neurobiologiae Experimentalis, 32,* 581–594.

West, R. W., & Greenough, W. T. (1972). Effect of environmental complexity on cortical synapses of rats. *Behavioral Biology, 7,* 279–284.

Whishaw, I. Q. (1989). Dissociating performance and learning deficits in spatial navigation tasks in rats subjected to cholinergic muscarinic blockade. *Brain Research Bulletin, 23,* 347–358.

Whishaw, I. Q., Dringenberg, H. C., & Pellis, S. M. (1990). Spontaneous forelimb grasping in free feeding by rats: Motor cortex aids limb and digit positioning. *Behavioural Brain Research, 48,* 113–125.

Whishaw, I. Q., & Kolb, B. (1983). "Stick out your tongue": Tongue protrusion in neocortex and hypothalamic damaged rats. *Physiology and Behavior, 30,* 471–480.

Whishaw, I. Q., & Kolb, B. (1984). Behavioral and anatomical studies of rats with complete or partial decortication in infancy: Functional sparing, crowding or loss and cerebral growth or shrinkage. In S. Finger, & C. R. Almli (Eds.), *Recovery from brain damage* (pp. 117–138). New York: Academic.

Whishaw, I. Q., & Kolb, B. (1988). Sparing of skilled forelimb reaching and corticospinal projections after neonatal motor cortex removal or hemidecortication in the rat: Support for the Kennard Doctrine. *Brain Research, 451,* 97–114

Whishaw, I. Q., & Kolb, B. (1989). Tongue protrusion mediated by spared anterior ventrolateral neocortex in neonatally decorticate rats: Behavioral support for the neurogenetic hypothesis. *Behavioural Brain Research, 32,* 101–113.

Whishaw, I. Q., & Kolb, B. (1991). Two types of hippocampal activity in the neonatal decorticate rat. *Brain Research Bulletin, 26,* 425–427

Whishaw, I. Q., Kolb, B., & Sutherland, R. J. (1983). The behavior of the laboratory rat. In T. E. Robinson (Ed.), *Behavioral contributions to brain research* (pp. 141–211). New York: Oxford.

Whishaw, I. Q., Kolb, B., Sutherland, R. J., & Becker, J. (1983). Cortical control of claw cutting in the rat. *Behavioral Neuroscience, 97,* 370–380.

Whishaw, I. Q., O'Connor, R. B., & Dunnett, S. B. (1986). The contributions of the motor cortex, nigrostriatal dopamine and caudate-putamen to skilled forelimb use in the rat. *Brain, 109,* 805–843.

Whishaw, I. Q., & Pellis, S. M. (1990). The structure of skilled forelimb reaching in the rat: A proximally driven movement with a single distal rotatory component. *Behavioural Brain Research, 41,* 49–59.

Whishaw, I. Q., Pellis, S. M., Gorny, B. P., Kolb, B., & Tetzlaff, W. (1993). Proximal and distal impairments in rat forelimb use in reaching follow pyramidal tract lesions. *Behavioural Brain Research, 56,* 59–76.

Whishaw, I. Q., Pellis, S. M., Gorny, B. P., & Pellis, V. C. (1991). The impairments in reaching and the movements of compensation in rats with motor cortex lesions: An endpoint, videorecording, and movement notation analysis. *Behavioural Brain Research, 42,* 77–91.

Whishaw, I. Q., Sutherland, R. J., Kolb, B., & Becker, J. (1986). Effects of neonatal forebrain noradrenaline depletion on recovery from brain damage: Performance on a spatial navigation task as a function of age of surgery and postsurgical housing. *Behavioral and Neural Biology, 6,* 285–307.

Will, B., & Kelche, C. (1992). Environmental approaches to recovery of function from brain damage: A review of animal studies (1981 to 1991). In F. D. Rose, & D. A. Johnson (Eds.), *Recovery from brain damage: Reflections and directions* (pp. 79–104). New York: Plenum.

Williams, C. L., Barnett, A. M., & Meck, W. H. (1990). Organization effects of early gonadal secretions on sexual differentiation in spatial memory. *Behavioral Neuroscience, 104,* 84–97.

Woods, B. T. (1980). The restricted effects of right-hemisphere lesions after age one; Wechsler test data. *Neuropsychologia, 18,* 65–70.

Woods, B. T., & Teuber, H.-L. (1973). Early onset of complementary specialization of cerebral hemispheres in man. *Transactions of the American Neurological Association, 98,* 113–117.

Woolley, C. S., Gould, E., Frankfurt, M., & McEwen, B. S. (1990). Naturally occurring fluctuation in dendritic spine density on adult hippocampal pyramidal neurons. *Journal of Neuroscience, 10,* 4035–4039.

Zangwill, O. L. (1975). Excision of Broca's area without persistent aphasia. In K. J. Zulch, O. Creutzfeldt, and G. C. Galbraith (Eds.), *Cerebral localization* (pp. 179–196). Berlin: Springer-Verlag.

Author Index

Subject Index